MORALITY AND HUMAN NATURE

ROBERT J. MCSHEA

Morality and Human Nature

A New Route to Ethical Theory

TEMPLE UNIVERSITY PRESS
PHILADELPHIA

Temple University Press, Philadelphia 19122
Copyright © 1990 by Temple University. All rights reserved
Published 1990
Printed in the United States of America

The paper used in this publication meets the minimum
requirements of American National Standard for Information
Sciences—Permanence of Paper for Printed Library Materials,
ANSI Z39.48–1984 ∞

Library of Congress Cataloging-in-Publication Data
McShea, Robert J.
    Morality and human nature: a new route to ethical theory / Robert
J. McShea.
      p. cm.
    Includes bibliographical references.
    ISBN 0–87722–735–7 (alk. paper)
    1. Ethics. 2. Man. 3. Philosophical anthropology. I. Title.
BJ1031.M354   1990
171'.2—dc20   90–32382
                                                                         CIP

CONTENTS

PREFACE / vii
INTRODUCTION / 3
Part I
1. Alternatives / 21
2. Skepticism / 31
3. The Unique Individual / 41
4. God, Nature, Reason / 49
5. An Historical Interlude / 65
6. Reductionist Human Nature Theory / 73
7. What Is Culturalism? / 89
8. Problems of Culturalism / 99
9. Culturalism as Historicism / 127

Part II
10. Traditional Human Nature Value Theory / 151
11. Biological Human Nature / 167
12. The Human Animal / 189
13. Value Judgments / 201
14. Moral Communication / 213
15. Obligation / 223
16. Illustrations and Complications / 241
17. Conclusions / 265

NOTES / 271
INDEX / 289

PREFACE

This book proposes a view of human nature within which conflicting value judgments, arising within and between different cultures, are rendered discussable and in principle capable of resolution. "How shall I live?" and "what is to be done?" are shown to be real questions to which there can be reasonable and defensible answers. The book does not offer such answers, only the means by which we might arrive at them. In the present climate of opinion, this claim may seem arrogant or, worse, quaint. Nevertheless, although far from confident that my mode of presentation is the best possible, I believe that the book will be clear to most and persuasive to many readers.

Not to all. Experience has shown me that my own expository limitations and the complexities and ambiguities inherent in value theory are not the greatest bar to the understanding of human nature theory. The book is "controversial," a code word for the intrusion of systematically irrelevant but passionately held prejudices into a field of inquiry—as evolution became "controversial" when creationists began to attack it. In the present case, "prejudices" mean culturalist prejudices. For some culturalists, the phrase "human nature" arouses a host of negative associations. I appeal to them to rise above reflexive name-calling and imputations of guilt by association.

An understanding of the argument herein depends upon the reader's grasp in some depth of the significant fact that humans are a part of nature, part of the animal world of species, that we are most profoundly understood in the light of our common species nature. Before the Industrial Revolution, our ancestors lived in a milieu that included many wild and domesticated animals and so easily gained an intuitive sense of the fact and the implications of species being. What they had without effort we must arrive at by deliberate study. I have had to introduce, perhaps too briefly, some elementary biology and ethology (the study of other species in their natural environment). I claim no expertise in these subjects nor do I hold a brief for any school of thought within them. My effort to make clearer the concept of species being has led some to classify me as a reductionist and even as a sociobiologist. I am neither, and in fact offer what I hope are conclusive arguments against both.

I have taught political philosophy for twenty-five years. I know how long it takes to understand even a few of the major writers and how vehemently specialists disagree on what those writers are saying. The reader ought not become involved in such disputes and so, despite the many writers cited, I want to emphasize that I treat here of ideas, not of those to whom I fallibly attribute them.

I extend a half-apology to the culturalists—but not to the historicists, anti-foundationalists, intimationalists, and deconstructionists—for the vigor of my attack on them. I am no less a culturalist than they, up to but short of the point where culturalism is made the ultimate mode of explanation for human action and valuing.

Finally, some acknowledgments. First to Aristotle, Spinoza, and Hume for teaching me this way of looking at things. Then to my wife, Naomi, and children, Sarah and Daniel, who conspired, affectionately but firmly, to coax and badger me into completing this book.

MORALITY AND HUMAN NATURE

INTRODUCTION

Two intellectual problems, interrelated and of critical importance to the management of the most important practical problems, haunt and perplex us today.

The first problem is formally described as the question of the status of value judgments. To the extent to which each of us has shaken off the spell of cultural values, the question of how we shall live hangs on the solution of this question. In the course of our lives we make countless decisions, most of them trivial, some of them very important to us, about what we and our community shall do. We make those decisions on the basis of an opinion that some things are better or worse than some other things. Can we account for what we mean by "better"? In what sense can a value judgment be true? In the absence of fraud, coercion, or indoctrination, is it possible for numbers of us to come to agreement on what is socially or politically desirable and to conduct our mutual affairs with a sense of common interest and purpose?

During most of human history, such questions would have been regarded as not very interesting. Most people, most of the time, have thought they knew very well what is worthwhile; their problem has been in attaining it. Even now, educated, skeptical, intelligent, and sensitive persons such as those who read books like this find little difficulty in making the ordinary practical value decisions that come before them. Their problem arises when they must make decisions that they see as fateful for themselves and when they attempt to communicate with others who do not share their value jargon. They discover, then, that they have no substantial or credible basis for making value decisions in their own affairs, no common vocabulary or method for discussing value priorities with others.

Especially since about the turn of the century, the conclusions of major philosophers, the ruling paradigms of the social sciences, and the cultural assumptions we find in literature and in ordinary language have combined to urge us to the conclusion that there is no basis for value judgments, that there is no sense to the question "how shall I live?" How, then, do we in fact live? We are guided by the remnants of the moral indoctrination of our childhood, by the fear of immediately painful consequences, by the hope of achieving conventional goals, by the attitudes and life style of our immediate circle, by random intuitions of value that happen to strike us. Our awareness of the chaotic and mutually contradictory character of these guides undermines our capacity for decisive or long-range actions. Many of us take refuge in irony, as did Pilate when he asked "what is justice?" and "waited not for an answer." If we mean that irony to imply a superior view not to be revealed to the vulgar, we are simply lying. Our value irony at best expresses a wry despair and at worst implies some sordid or even terrible thing we will do or have done. When value irony prevails, those who might struggle to realize communal ideals turn to contemplation and the private life; people who might combine to resist terrible things are immobilized.

Specifically, what do current notions about the basis of value authorize us to say, or do, against the child abuser, the racist, the terrorist, the oppressor and the exploiter, the liar and the cheat? In that calmly detached and tolerant mood that we recommend to ourselves and to each other, we are struck dumb. Of course we can say that we do not like what they do, that we have excellent logical and empirical refutations of their carelessly formulated justificatory rhetoric, that if we are stronger than they we will make their practices costly to them. But we are uneasily aware that our likes and dislikes, the accident of our superior force, are not arguments at all. As for our arsenal of logic and facts, it is mostly irrelevant. Racists are not merely ignorant of the scientific information about racial differences; they hate and want to injure some easily identifiable group. Their hatred and our revulsion to that hatred are feelings: How can we argue about them? Child abusers are not necessarily ignorant or irrational. They simply do what they feel like doing, as do we in condemning them. When they turn on us to demand our reasons for objecting to their practices, we open our mouths eagerly to explain, then stand gaping in frustration, for we have reasoned ourselves out of every good reason for objecting. We shut our mouths firmly and hit them, hard, to make them understand the error of their ways. The unexamined life has always been in style. Only recently has it become mandatory for enlightened people.

How did we arrive at so painful and absurd a position? One explanation is intellectual: we have come to understand that values, norms, morality, are but the expression of individual feelings or of the interests of classes or cultures, that all human action is directed toward some single egoistic end, as survival or pleasure, that the gap between facts and values is unbridgeable and so values are not quite real. Most of us believe that one or more of these truths are self-evident and believe further that holding them makes us free. Of course, no matter how self-evident, they cannot all be true, for they are not compatible. It cannot be denied that each of them frees us in some way, although for what, and in what sense, remains to be seen.

The belief that we have now arrived at intellectual truth about the status of values—in the same sense in which we think we have arrived at truth about the relative movements of the sun and the earth or about the square of the hypotenuse—is naive. However gratifying it might be to us to know that our present value uncertainties are the reward of our more refined and critical intelligence, it is much more likely that we are the beneficiaries, or victims, of an impersonal social process. Generally held beliefs about particular values, and about their basis or lack of basis, are cultural products. (This leaves open the question of the possible validity of those values or of their asserted bases.)

Another explanation of our present absurd value position is historical. Cultural values in a stable society are roughly functional for it. But no society is completely stable, and as it changes, its values change. When the change is slow enough, it is possible for its members gradually to shift their attitudes and institutions and so maintain a general sense of value continuity and of value legitimacy. In recent times, social change has been so rapid that it was impossible for changes in conventional morality to keep pace. It was impossible because, while purely intellectual judgments can be quickly arrived at and lightly displaced, loyalty to concrete value formulations builds slowly and once achieved resists dissolution. The result, for our society, is that conventional values have become increasingly non-functional. The further result of this is that the life experience of many people leads them to believe not only that conventional morality is generally false but that by its very nature it is obstructive and oppressive. The folk hero of our time has been the iconoclast, the bold defier of convention. The iconoclast wins; a determined skeptic is the most probable victor in all intellectual contests; conventional morality, however fearsomely powerful in appearance, is a paper tiger, is defenseless against a simple "why?" There is no use in complaining about this collapse of the power of convention. Whether we believe in social and historical forces or not, we see a certain inevitability in the contemporary dissolution of conventional values and the present skepticism about value bases. However much we may sometimes envy the calm certitudes, the confident value orientation, of our ancestors, we cannot but also see them as victims of illusion. Meanwhile, the continuing fluidity of our society, its pluralism and intercultural penetrations, render impossible the emergence of a new set of authoritative conventions.

Nevertheless, for whatever intellectual or historical reasons, here we are, confronted with local varieties of the same crucial personal and social decisions that humans have always faced. Here we are, haunted by the awareness of terrible secrets—that all value talk is mere confusion of speech or of mind, that there is no principled defense against the universal rule of force and fraud, and that, finally, nothing makes any difference. As the secrets become open secrets, the general recognition of their truth itself produces the climate for the brazen practice of force and fraud at every level of human interaction. Even our hopes for a better society and a just polity are eroded. The assault on "bourgeois morality," for example, has been quite successful, but it was carried out at such a fundamental level that socialist and other values are swept along with it into the ash heap of history.

The present state of value theory implies a total separation of value theory and value practice. The consequence of this division is the steady decline in the level of moral practice. It is evident that we need to rejoin theory and practice, to produce a theory to which we can appeal in practical decision making. Not any theory will do, of course, for we cannot believe by an act of will. We need a way of basing values that will bear up under the analysis of logicians and the testing of empiricists and that is supported not only by our psychological needs but also by our most responsible vision of the realities of the world. We cannot expect such a theory to tell us precisely what to do in every circumstance, but neither can we accept a theory that does not tell us how to conduct a value discussion with some hope of eventual agreement.

In this attempt to find a reasonable basis for value judgments, we are commonly caught between two fears. One is that there is no such basis and so we are condemned to consent to live subject to the will of the cleverer or stronger. The other fear is that there is such a basis and that we will be condemned to live under a moral absolutism. The second fear has prevailed throughout most of this century; the first is now coming to prevail. Both fears are legitimate. The reader is assured that the conclusions supported here do not in turn support a moral absolutism. What is sought is a reasonable method by which to think and talk about the value choices we must make and want to make well. No such method can attain reasonableness unless it acknowledges the uncertainties that must attend conclusions on matters so complex and so riddled with ambiguities. On this understanding, attempts such as this to find a method for the validation of value judgments are entitled to our good wishes, however skeptical the mood in which we extend them.

The other intellectual problem, closely related to the first, is that of the method or approach appropriate to thinking about society and politics. Some of us believe that the fundamental unit of explanation and analysis is the species-normal human, that social and political events and institutions are to be understood as the result of the interplay of the diversely informed but uniform passions of large numbers of individuals. When adherents of this approach advocate political causes, they do so on the basis of values that they see as grounded in the genetic structure of human feelings, in human nature. It is fair to call them psychologists, even biologists. Others of us believe that humans have no interesting enduring nature, that human consciousness and motivation are the shifting product of shifting social and historical conditions, that the elemental units in the study of society are irreducible social or historical laws. It follows for these others that social and political change is to be evaluated, not in terms of enduring and therefore genetic human passions, but as in conformity or not with the present culture or times. The study of human affairs consists in the discovery and application of sociological or historical laws.

We rightly resist being forced into either/or choices, but in this case we have no alternative. We must decide whether the ultimate mode of value explanation is to have a psychological or a sociological basis; we cannot fudge the choice. No hybrid approach is conceivable; while we refuse to decide, we are operating on one set of data with two discordant models of reality, a recipe for futility. Both approaches are solidly entrenched in our scientific and ordinary talk; it is not suggested here that we embrace one and destroy the other. Rather, maintaining both, we simply must decide which is the ultimately acceptable vocabulary, which shall include the other as a useful supplement.

To those outside the social sciences, this controversy may seem like the war in Swift's *Gulliver's Travels* between the Little Endians and the Big Endians, a war about which end of a boiled egg ought to be opened first. The analogy is reinforced by the consideration that, just as it makes no real difference which end of the egg is broken first, so no concrete proposal for social or political change depends upon whether we follow the human nature or the culturalist model. Those within the social sciences know, however, that the contending parties think otherwise, that each has evolved a vocabulary that is incomprehensible or hateful to the other. Less attention is given here to this problem than to that of the basis of value, mostly because the solution of the latter pretty well determines the solution of the former.

The resistances to a search for a positive value theory are many and strong. Some believe that it is superfluous—we already know all we need to know. We have clear instructions from God, conscience, or self-evident standards of decency. Some find the undertaking quixotic, impossible. We know that values are the product of unique individual psyches and so indiscussable; they are solely the consequence of cultural conditioning or ideological commitment and so not binding on those who understand this. Some philosophers tell us that no connection can be established between facts or concepts and values, and so value judgments are not discussable except as verbal behavior: an unbridgeable chasm between fact and values, between what is and what ought to be, divides value talk from discourse about real things.

The arguments in this book take account of and surmount these resistances. The claim may seem excessive and immodest. The reader must decide whether it is excessive, but I can explain why it is not immodest.

Machiavelli opens his major theoretical work, *The Discourses*, with the offer of a "new route" to a true understanding of, and effective action in, social and political affairs. Once he has thus gained our attention, he admits that the new route is not new at all; it is the route discovered and used by the Classical world and subsequently either forgotten or thought to be no longer usable. A similarly qualified revelation is promised here. I offer a new route to the understanding of value and value judgments, and with it some hints about a method for arriving at a universal basis for the understanding of society and politics. This route will seem new to most readers, for there is no serious discussion of it in the ethical literature of the past two hundred years. The route is not new at all, nor are there any important ideas here that I can claim for my own. The theory, awkwardly called the non-reductionist human nature theory, or the traditional theory, is the one that has been held by every major secular moral and political thinker, with the single exception of Hobbes, from Plato to Rousseau, inclusive, and by no one since then. Because such agreement by so many weighty philosophers will not easily be conceded and will not be demonstrated here (although I shall argue briefly for it), and even if demonstrated would not lend much support to the theory (we are not now very reverential toward authority), I make the argument as though it were my own, in contemporary language, using contemporary standards of evidence and reasonableness.

A practical difficulty in presenting the argument arises out of the fact that there are two radically different potential groups of readers. One is the class of educated and concerned people who know little or nothing of academic ethical theory, but who yearn for release from the burden of the belief that the values with which they order their lives are merely arbitrary or accidental. Such readers can only be reached through the language that they themselves use. The other class is that of the academic philosophers. Here the problem is quite different. Formal ethical theory is today a charred battleground littered with the dead hulks of smashed value hypotheses. Above the level of that wasteland hardly the slightest tendril of a suggestion as to how we might live is permitted to emerge. Pyrrhonistic criticism dominates the field.

I write for both groups of readers at once, with the hope that what I say will not fall into the space between them. When I must choose, I choose to speak to the concerned educated public, to those who care, not for ingenious puzzles, but for some way of looking at values that will be useful to them, some way that meets reasonable standards of credibility and coherence. Yet although I have minimized the use of technical language and reference to current controversies, the student of ethical philosophy will discern my effort to meet the minds of the professionals in that field.

In the course of its development, every coherent area of study evolves those standards of demonstration that its actual practitioners consider appropriate to it. It is a sign of the condition of the study of value that it has produced no such standards. Some of the academic writers apply to value theory the sort of rigorous logical and linguistic analysis under which no existing science could survive. Most of the others practice moral casuistry, the derivation of subjectively preferred conclusions from arbitrarily chosen strands of our cultural value assumptions. Of these latter, no more need here be said; we ought to examine the pretensions of the logicians.

Most of those who practice logical and linguistic analysis make one or both of two mistakes. The first mistake is that, although they have every right to subject all kinds of language, including value language, to critical study, they err in their assumption that their conclusions have some practical reference to the topic they analyze. The study of, say, biology or physics is neither helped nor hindered, is not affected in any way, by their critiques. There is no known instance of an established science taking its cue from the philosophers of science; the line of influence is in quite the other direction. Similarly, the study of value, if it ever becomes a coherent field of study, need pay no attention to those logicians who presently pretend to dictate to it. Their second and most serious mistake, however, is a philosophical error. They seem not to understand what has been a commonplace at least since Aristotle, that there is a critical distinction between knowledge of what is and knowledge of what to do, between physics and engineering, between theory and practice. The object of the study of value is not the formulation of true propositions about objects or forces out in space and time, nor is it the analysis of concepts and of their relations. Its object is the determination of what to do; it is not theoretical but practical. Logicians and philosophers of science have investigative tools that are not suitable to the study of value judgments, and so they turn to what they can indeed handle, the study of behavior and of propositions. They illustrate a common folly of our time, the distortion of fields of study to fit the capacities of fashionable technologies and techniques.

Thinking about value ought to begin with the right questions. The central question may be phrased in many ways: "What is to be done?," "What sort of life do I want to lead?," or "How shall a man live?" We cannot deal with those who might say: "It makes no difference what is done; it doesn't matter, even to you, how you live." We are on the right track when we continually recur to our original question, a practical question. In answering that question we need all the facts and logical rigor we can summon to our aid. We are not entitled here, where we are most serious, to have easy recourse to pleasing but nebulous language, to cultural cliches or nostalgia, to pleas for blind faith or the acceptance of arbitrary definitions or postulates. Ethics is neither science nor logic, but it ought not be unscientific or illogical. It is not a "soft" subject, where subjective yearnings and passing fancies can pass for reality. It calls for hard thinking, openness to new ideas, and a determination to find true answers. This book does not offer any true answers: I do not pretend to know better than the reader how life should be lived. It offers a method for finding true answers, a foundation for these answers. As foundations tend to be, it is rather plain; it aims at usefulness and solidity rather than elegance. Those who prefer the higher flights of fancy and of idealism, a deeper profundity, are neither attacked nor disowned. Rather they are invited to use the set of notions that follow for their starting place. Without such a foundation the best insights flash past us like shooting stars, leaving no trace. Unless they can find a basis in our overall understanding, they perish like good seed on stony ground. Of a foundational theory we may require considerable solidity, but not proof. Proof is not to be had in value theory and so we cannot simply dismiss a value theory as "not proven." In the life of action we must act on the basis of the most probable hypothesis. I argue here for the most probable hypothesis.

To the question of how we shall live we must bring our total selves, every bit of knowledge, every developed intellectual and intuitive capacity we have. If we refuse to attempt to answer the question, we allow it to be answered for us by trivial or alien forces. The penalty for making, or having made for oneself, seriously wrong decisions is literally worse than death, for death comes equally to all and may even come as a friend, but a life in which our strongest and most enduring feelings are defeated is the greatest human defeat possible. Is it likely that this most important of all questions will be solved by clever linguistic or logical analysis, by a study of historical or social laws, or by "nothing but" pronouncements from the latest school of blinkered reductionists?

The general outline of the argument is as follows: What is to be shown is that there is a method, derived from the non-reductive human nature theory, by which we can come to agreement on prescriptive value judgments. The method will be sufficiently justified if it can be shown to be better than any alternative. This might seem impossible, for the possible alternatives are sometimes thought to be all but infinite in number. Fortunately, this is not so. There are only a few conceivable general theories about the basis of value judgments and each of them consists of a rather simple assertion. A classification is not essential to the conclusions, but it is independently interesting and can be useful even to those who disagree with the conclusions. It is inclusive of all possible coherent views and yet distinguishes sharply among them. One of its interesting uses is that it enables us to expose pseudo-theories as radically incomplete or incoherent.

The first part of the book, after the classification, is purely controversial. Each one of the possible views on the basis of value judgments is examined and all but one are shown to be inadequate.

How much attention is given to each view depends upon its prevalence among the educated public. Culturalism and historicism, the most widespread and strongly held of the alternatives to the human nature position, are given three chapters. Because longstanding conventional and ideological loyalties easily survive intellectual refutation, I make a point of discussing the emotional and intuitive foundations on which some of the rejected views rest.

Part II explains and argues for the non-reductionist human nature view. We are, as Spinoza put it, "a part of nature, not a kingdom within it." Our common membership in a distinct and determinate biological species makes all humans, within a relatively narrow range, very much alike in physical form and functioning and in intellectual capacity. It also determines not only that we can experience a large number of more or less subtly distinguishable emotions but also that those emotions will be aroused in specific ways by experiences and situations that have been common and important during the very long history of our species. We have evolved to have particular emotions in certain sorts of situations. The vast development of our intellectual and imaginative powers in the past few hundred thousand years, along with our genetic need for life in a culture, has complicated but not essentially altered the fundamental character and function of our species' emotional profile.

The species-typical feelings are, for humans and for the higher animals, the only possible motivating force. Our feelings are the only basis on which we can make value judgments. Every slightest voluntary motion, every desire or aversion, every obligation or preference, is the expression of one or more emotions. There is no external standard, no inner resource, that can either instruct or resist our feelings; every capacity we have at our command is in their service. We are the sum of our feelings. It follows that there is no conceivable good for us but the maximum satisfaction of our strongest and most enduring feelings. There is no basis on which we can mount a moral criticism of someone who pursues that satisfaction effectively and with the most singleminded intensity.

"Do what you want" is a true but misleading conclusion of the non-reductive human nature theory of value and of morality. The conclusion is misleading because it slides over some important complications that occur to us as soon as we think about it. The first complication lies in the "do what." It is often not at all clear what we should do to satisfy a feeling. What we think of first may actually defeat that feeling. We learn caution very early in life, learn to consider a great many circumstantial facts that are relevant to the satisfaction of our feelings. The second complication has to do with "want." We have many feelings, and in the process of considering the circumstantial context of the proposed satisfaction of one of them, the other feelings become aroused. Our emotions are very commonly in clamorous contention. We cannot do what we want until we know what we want. How do we discover what we want?

Each genetic feeling has an independent basis in us. The feelings are not reducible one to another. Since there is nothing that is not a feeling to which we can appeal when our feelings conflict, they must work out their conflicts among themselves. Introspection shows us how they do it. The strongest present feeling, or the strongest coalition of feelings, simply overpowers the rest and we move on to that action that our knowledge of the circumstances tells us is appropriate to the satisfaction of the single feeling or of the coalition.

The complications are not ended. We live in three dimensions of time, the actual present and the imaginatively portrayed past and future. We react with feeling to all three. A strong feeling aroused by a present circumstance may be overmastered by a stronger feeling aroused by an imagined past or future circumstance. We do well, from the standpoint of the satisfaction of strong and enduring passions that may at the moment be latent in us, to delay action urged upon us by present feelings, to search out consequences of and alternatives to that action, to restudy our overall situation and rethink what it is that we really do want, all things considered.

Our lives are short, too short for one of us to learn, on one's own account, much about the world or about oneself. Fortunately, all or almost all humans have much the same emotional profile and live in much the same universe and so we can learn a great deal from others. Further, like all other species, we embody in our nature a genetic strand of altruism and, like some other species, are social, have feelings that favor not only our children and other close relatives but also neighbors, friends, and our community. Tricked by our own symbolic systems, we easily come to care even for small (baby) nations, our "fatherland" or "motherland," the "brotherhood" of humanity, and the "global village." Communication of feelings, and therefore of values, is easy for humans. Agreement about values, outside of a few zero-sum situations, would be easier than it is now if our intelligence were a better servant of our important feelings.

All this might be thought to be a mere description of how humans come to make value judgments. The great problem for contemporary value theory is how to get from description to prescription, from fact to value, how to get from an is to an ought. It is in fact impossible to reason, either in the empirical or in the logical sense, from the fact that something exists to the judgment that something ought to be. What is puzzling is how this truth ever came to be thought relevant to the question of the prescriptivity, the obligatory character, of value judgments. Percepts and concepts have to do with knowing; feelings have to do with doing. Our only motivation to doing is feeling. We are intelligent creatures capable of complex adjustments to a very densely complex environment, capable through imagination of living each moment in the light of a view of our whole life. When we feel that we have responsibly taken into account our whole life and all relevant circumstances, the value judgment to which our whole feeling structure leads us is experienced by us as peremptory, as prescriptive. That peremptoriness is all that obligation can mean.

Although it is presented unsentimentally and in a rather academic prose, the theory is not reductionist. It can contain the most elevated moral insights of any of the human cultures and without loss. It is not a theory of how we ought to act but a schematic view of what it is to be human, of the meaning and use of values in human life. It explains how we can explain ourselves to each other and come to value agreement and also how some values are, for us, necessarily true and others necessarily false.

Social theory and the social sciences do not need a value theory, any more than does physics. But like physics they need a model of their universe, the human universe, that they describe. The relevance of the non-reductive human nature view to social theory and social science is a subordinate theme in what follows.

It is remarkable how almost all aspects and levels of our intellectual, scientific, and aesthetic culture have concurred to bring us to the conclusion that value judgments are subjective or trivial. Rarely do we find so striking an example of the power of culture over the human mind, for the conclusion is as much in contradiction with our elemental intuitions about real life as would be the assertion that A does not equal A, that two and two are five. It is literally impossible for humans to believe that nothing matters, or ought to matter, even to themselves.

In retrospect, it is easy to trace the route we took to the divorce of value theory and moral practices. We somehow never seemed to see, in our vigorous attack on the old repressive social values, that the standards of value we used in that attack were simply a newer set of social values, equally vulnerable to the line of criticism we used on the old ones. We wanted the right things: the liberty of science and art to speak openly and honestly, the liberty to stretch our minds freely in an open universe now seen to be endlessly pluralistic, the embodiment of pure potentiality. Even our science is thought to be not really true, not even probable, merely a set of choices from among an infinite range of alternative models of reality. In that openness we found yet further freedom. The ruthless criticism of everything existing has been exhilarating. But now we are somewhat less exhilarated; we do not feel very free; the general opinion is that the world is getting to be a worse place in which to live. We remember now that we are not only eagerly questioning intellects, we are also organisms, feeling organisms that cannot carry on their vital processes in the cold vacuum of empty space. We need a way of looking at things that puts no limits on the questioning intellect but that also accommodates and justifies our emotional need for a realm of commitment and meaning of which the intellect itself denies it can have any knowledge. Important human needs are in question here. If we do not find our way, we invite others to find a different way, a way that may not include room for the questioning intellect.

We are the victims of two bankrupt paradigms. One defines the meaningful as what may be observed by the passionless eye of the fact- and relation-oriented intellect. The other defines culture and history as real and humans, their product, as unreal. What is presented here is not an argument within the current models of reality, but a newly revived paradigm, a route to the understanding, not of nature, but of our situation within nature. This new way is naturalistic; it meets the standards of a skeptical mind; it is a method that starts from one natural fact, human emotion, rather than from another, human thought. It is truly for us a new route, but argument and evidence for it will be of no avail if the reader is content with the old routes. Only despair with the present state of value thought can motivate us to make the effort to see things in a new way. I ask the reader, not to believe, but to see.

Part I

CHAPTER I

Alternatives

A common notion about value theory is that it either is gaseously diffuse or consists of an infinity of pedantic quibbles masquerading as precision, that there is no starting place. In fact, there are a number of intelligible starting places and if we are to have any confidence in the conclusions we reach we must first achieve an overview of all of them. In this chapter I attempt to furnish such an overview in the form of a classification of all possible bases for value thinking, a classification that makes it possible to assess and compare the different theories and to arrive at an opinion as to their relative credibility.

Value Judgments

Some preliminary remarks about value judgments are necessary. Such judgments assert that something is better or worse, desirable or not, that some action ought or ought not be taken. They are made in the context of concrete factual situations, but they say nothing about those situations in themselves. Facts and values are distinct. Facts constitute knowledge; values motivate action. The philosophy of science, or more generally the theory of knowledge, is concerned with the conditions under which we can agree on factual judgments; value theory is concerned with the conditions under which we can agree on value judgments. Action requires that we find a common vocabulary for fact and value.

Not all statements that include value terms are of interest here. Simple reports of an individual state of feeling, as "I hate oysters!," will not be discussed; they are too narrowly autobiographical. A more important exclusion is that of instrumental value judgments of the sort called for by the question: "What is the best way to get to Hoboken?" If the only considerations that are to be allowed to count in the reply are out-of-pocket costs and time, then the question is a request for factual information. Even such questions as whether it is better to go to Hoboken at all, to marry, to wage war, can be so posed that they require only facts for an answer. A computer can be programmed to give a more or less sophisticated reply to the question "To be or not to be?" All it needs is a set of clear directions as to what shall be counted and how much. The kind of value judgments we shall discuss are those that would have to be considered by the person who is to program that computer. An instrumental value cannot function alone as a motivation for action. It must depend upon at least one ultimate value. There are many ultimate values. None of them is unconditionally prescriptive, nor are they necessarily few or very important. Dessert and salvation are not equally valuable, but they are equally ultimate values. Consciously or not, in every action we take we appeal to ultimate values.

Classification

The word "basis" suggests a convenient spatial metaphor for the classification of possible bases for value judgments. (See figure.) The minimum basis must be an individual human, considered to be unique of his or her kind. Nothing smaller, say a constituent cell of such a person, and nothing less conscious, as a stone or a zebra, will serve. If we look for a broader basis than this, we find no stopping place until we come to a group or society of humans

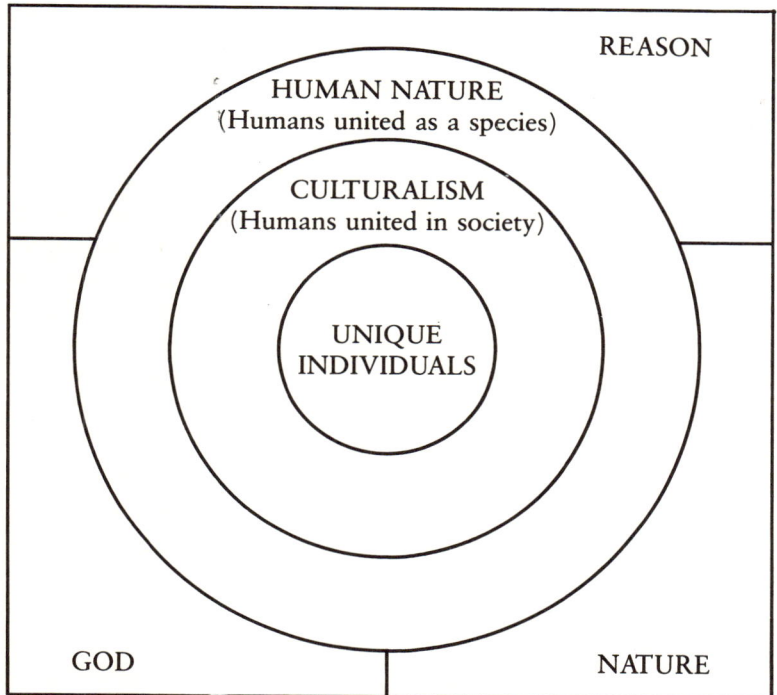

made similar to each other by membership in a common culture. Beyond this location lies the whole human species, a group of beings made similar to each other by their possession of similar genes. All other locations must transcend humanity, as do God, Reason, and Nature. The denial that there is a basis, value skepticism, sometimes called value nihilism, is not itself a basis or place, yet we must consider that notion along with the rest.

I will sketch the outlines of the basic positions here and devote at least a chapter to each of them later:

1. A value skeptic does not deny that value judgments are made, simply that they can be valid, prescriptive, or substantively discussable. The skeptic maintains that no course of action can

truly be said to be better than any other: pain is not undesirable, pleasure is not desirable, life is not better than death. Perhaps only disingenuous disputants attempt to defend this position at length, but we must take it seriously, for we find it tacitly assumed in much casual value talk.

2. The minimum basis for a positive value judgment is a single valuing person. Something can be said to be better or worse, good or bad, to the extent to which I believe it to be so, and when I do believe it so, it actually is better or worse, for me, although not necessarily for anyone else. Such value solipsism is like value skepticism in that it does not allow for intersubjective value discussion, different in that it holds that values are, for the person who holds them, true and prescriptive.

3. "Culturalism" is the word I adopt to signify the view that culture, or the history of cultures, supplies not only the source but also the validation of value judgments. Burke, Hegel, Marx, Durkheim, Parsons, and many cultural anthropologists and sociologists may occupy this position. The usefulness of the category does not, however, depend on the accuracy with which we place particular writers in it. We are classifying ideas, not people. The position that all value judgments are the product of culture, but that none are validated by culture, is not culturalism but skepticism.

4. The human species is a biological category that includes humans of all times and cultures. The "human nature" position asserts that the values of humans can be validated, for humans, by their species nature and that the commonality of that nature makes value discussion possible among us. It seems to me that every major secular ethical writer before Burke—notably Plato, Aristotle, Spinoza, Hume, and Rousseau, as well as Hobbes and Bentham—was a human nature thinker. Hobbes, and all human nature thinkers since Rousseau—such as James Mill and B. F. Skinner—have been of a special variety that I describe as "single-

factor reductionist." There is less risk in identifying human nature, as opposed to culturalist, thinkers, but it is well to repeat that we are considering ideas, not persons.

5. Finally we must entertain the possibility that the human species, its cultures, or its unique individuals are insufficient foundations for the solidity and authority we demand for a value basis. The humanly transcendent bases that have been suggested, and I can think of no others, are God, Reason, and Nature. "History" belongs in the category of "culturalism," but even if we think of it as a force or basis outside of humanity, it would yet not constitute a fourth transcendent category. Augustine's "History" represents the power of God; Hegel's that of Reason; Marx's and Spengler's that of Nature.

Value theories have been offered that seem at first glance not to fit into any of the above pigeonholes. Some have suggested that we have an immediate intuition into "the good."[1] If they mean that one can have such an immediate intuition that is unique to oneself, or that all or most humans have identical intuitions, or that the intuition comes from God, Nature, or Reason, we know at once, in each case, how to classify their position. If they mean something else, they have not told us what it is and so their position must remain mysterious.

More complex and obscure is the theory of the "ideal observer."[2] It has been supposed that we can know what to do, what is right, by an imaginative consultation with some entity, humanlike or not, that observes our value problem disinterestedly. Yet if that entity has no passions, it can take no interest in our problem, will not care what we do, cannot help us. If it has passions, but not human passions, we ought not listen to it, for its purposes will be foreign to ours. If we do not know what its passions are, then we might as well resort to the toss of a coin, for its verdict will be, for us, arbitrary. If its passions are human, then when we appeal to it we appeal to our idea of how a balanced, knowledgeable, wise person would evaluate our case. This is human nature theory.

"Value relativism" cannot be considered a theory at all until we learn what it is to which values are supposed to be relative. When we learn what that is thought to be, we will find that it is included in one of the four positive categories outlined.

I urge the reader to reflect on this classification, to test and to criticize it. The conclusions to be arrived at do not depend upon acceptance of the categories, but our ability to think coherently about value theory may. I do not know of any alternative categorial system that makes a similarly serious attempt to structure our value thinking. Western and Oriental, British and Continental, Classical and Modern, Gemeinschaft and Gesellschaft, deontological and teleological, religious and secular, utilitarian and intuitive—such divisions of value theory correspond to the superficial labeling of organisms prior to Linnaeus; they do not locate the intelligible cleavages in the subject. Productive thinking waits upon appropriate structuring of what is to be thought about. The present anarchy in value thinking is largely the consequence of superficial classification.

Several claims are made. The first is that the classification is complete. Every possible coherent theory falls into at least one of the categories. Some unexpected associations appear. Despite the radical differences between the actual value judgments at which each arrives, Spinoza and B. F. Skinner, for example, are both human nature thinkers, although of different varieties; a point made for or against the general human nature thesis will apply equally to both writers. A corollary to the claim of completeness is the assertion that any supposed moral theory that cannot find a place in the classification must be discarded as literally baseless, as not a value theory at all.

The second claim is for the exclusivity of the categories. In the final analysis, no coherent value theory can be based on more than one of them. It is common for theories to claim support from more than one, if not from all. The tactic is understandable; a theory reaches out for all the support it can get. One basis is all a theory needs or can have, however, and when it claims more than one, we must consider each claimed basis as supportive of a distinct theory, one to be considered on its own merits. Indeed, a theory that seeks multiple bases is ill advised. The possible bases are ultimately incompatible with each other; an ethical theory that attempts to stand on two or more of them is in trouble. We know, especially from the history of religious value theory, that when Reason, God, Nature, and the unique individual conscience are appealed to as though they must concur, endless paradoxes follow. The easygoing assumption that all or several bases can contribute faithfully to a single method for the determination of correct value judgments can be maintained only on the further assumption that they so concur only for "men of good will." It always turns out that "good will" is the sole real basis, and a worthless one at that. One of the tragedies of human political life is the impossibility of institutionalizing means for identifying "men of good will."

The classification is useful. Like any good classification it displays the deep structure of the material it organizes. It delves beneath the level of surface differences and resemblances, puts the whole study in a new light. As a good biological classification usefully shows that bats and whales are mammals, not birds and fishes, so that classification makes it possible to conduct an orderly comparative study of the different kinds of value theory. It frees us from the bafflement produced by the powerfully persuasive rhetoric, the subtleties and endless qualifications, that characterize the major developed value theories, frees us to the sober study of the relatively simple ideas and intuitions that underlie them. We can expect that such a study will reveal that some value bases are better than others, that some do not hold up at all under analysis.

I hope to show that only the non-reductionist human nature theory can serve as a sufficient basis for intersubjective and prescriptive value judgments. It does not follow from this that the others are to be regarded as worthless. In fact, every one of the bases to be considered has roots in true intuitions and in experience. All but the one are false only when they claim to embody the truth about the ultimate foundation and justification of value. All the positions, including the skeptical, have been held by highly moral and intelligent people. There is no implication here that having a wrong opinion as to the basis of one's value choices has anything to do with the validity of those choices. If some values seem more at home in the context of a particular theory, the reason is to be found in the accident of historical association, in our lazy subjection to the facile packaging of ideas, or to the devotional language of sectarians.

Once it is clear that no value basis favors any particular value judgment, one might hope that the author and his readers might go their abstract way, reasoning coolly on what seems a purely intellectual matter, that the partisans of particular values would turn away from the discussion in boredom. Unfortunately, this is not to be expected. Religious and ideological zealots will not admit of alternative routes to their conclusions; we must agree not only with those conclusions but also with their method for arriving at them; otherwise we are but heathen. Nothing can be said to those who will not listen. Others, less dogmatic, or not dogmatic at all, are urged only to unchain their critical faculties, intellectual curiosity, and moral passion to roam freely through the sequence of arguments and speculations that follows.

CHAPTER 2

Skepticism

One of the possible answers to the question "on what basis are value judgments discussable?" is that there is no such basis. I call this reply "skepticism." Hume defined and condemned the position:

> Those who have denied the reality of moral distinctions may be ranked among the disingenuous disputants, nor is it conceivable that any human creature could seriously believe that all characters and actions were alike entitled to the affection and regard of everyone.[1]

The value skeptic asserts that all value distinctions are false or meaningless. To the fundamental moral question—how shall a man live?—the skeptic replies that it makes no difference how one lives, briefly or at length, happily or in pain—none of this ought to be of interest, *not even to the person involved.*[2]

When skepticism is defined in this way, few or no skeptics are to be found. Those who define it in some other way will be discussed later; for now, we may point out that many self-styled skeptics are, in fact, individual or cultural relativists, quite another thing. Someone who asserts that "there is nothing either good or bad, but thinking makes it so" is not a skeptic. That person believes that the basis of value judgments is thinking, "thinking so," although we are not told whose thinking is to count. Similarly, those who believe that value judgments are "merely" or "nothing but" expressions of personal feeling, cultural prejudice, historical development, genetic predisposition, and the like are not thereby skeptics. Their intent is to undermine or destroy the authority of some common value judgments by showing that their origin is of a sort that lacks the prestige or compelling character we commonly require of a moral basis.

Hume himself, although he expected to construct a science of morality upon the ruin of metaphysical systems, saw no need to refute the value skeptics. He assumed their position to be obviously dishonest. His confidence seems justified. If I maintain that nothing is humanly preferable to anything else, I should act as thought what I say is true or admit that I speak only for effect. In the first case, I ought to take no action to avoid pain or death, should show no elation, sadness, or interest on any occasion. To do any of these things is to imply that some state of affairs is preferable, at least to me—and that preference would be a value judgment. The consistent skeptic cannot perform even the most trifling purposeful action, or even attempt to carry on a coherent train of thought, for all these imply value.

Value skepticism must be the most difficult of skepticisms to maintain. Someone who holds that matter is an illusion cannot be criticized for walking confidently upon the surface of the earth, for metaphysical skepticism has no necessary consequences for voluntary actions. An illusory earth is support enough for an illusory body. Somewhat closer to the position of the value skeptic is someone who argues that, since "secondary qualities" as sound, color, odor, do not exist in the physical world but only in our subjective perception, we ought to deny their reality. Even such a skeptic can consistently stop at a traffic light, knowing that the subjective experience of color is common among humans and so can be an element in human communication. Value skeptics are in quite another position. Values are about doing rather than knowing. Value skeptics seem hopelessly muddled about this when they say that no action is to be preferred to any other and then act, as they must, as though some actions are preferable to others.

It might be thought that any further treatment of the skeptical position is a waste of time. Not so; skepticism relies not on reasoned argument but on some basic intuitions that are had by all, or almost all, of us. Unless we can account for these intuitions, skeptics can claim to have had a direct perception of the unreality of value judgments. Against such immediate perceptions, argument is in vain. We must also show that the perceptions do not have the meaning commonly inferred from them.

The Skeptical Experience

All existence is precarious and that of conscious animals very poignantly so. Reflection reveals to us how little our survival and the satisfaction of our feelings are under our control. A loved one, a friend, a colleague, is suddenly gone from among us. We speed along the bright highway and must slow down to skirt the patch of blood and splintered glass. We are all standing in line to die, and none of us knows who is at the front or the end of that line. It is only natural that humans should have the psychology of gamblers and of others whose success or failure depends on causes out of their control. We hope for lucky breaks, fear bad omens, cross our fingers, use body english to urge the departed bowling ball toward the center pin. There is a large part of us that knows, despite all the efforts of our critical intelligence, that things are either with us or against us, that we are invulnerable and irresistible or born losers. Most of us oscillate between the two notions.

Behind each of these illusions lies a special psychic experience, best recognized in its extreme form. The first is a kind of megalomania, a projection of our own feelings and values upon the world, a projection so powerful that all otherness and possible opposition to our deepest desires are swallowed up and negated in the limitless universe of our will, of our imperial self. In this condition we may feel we are God, or that we and the universe are one. In a less extreme way, we know the feeling of optimism and self-confidence, the faith that things will work out well for us and ours. A certain amount of this shielding and facilitating animal faith is surely necessary if we are to hold ourselves together and act in a world so full of real danger and defeat.

The contrary experience may be more common, for things more often go against us than not. After a series of disappointments, accidents, losses, we tend to lose our nerve. The world appears hostile to us, or so indifferent to our feelings that our normal aura of egoism tatters and we are left nakedly alone in the universal cold. The extreme case of this experience is depression, autism, and other neurotic and psychotic states in which the sense of oneself as an effective causal agent is lost. In its less severe forms, this sad experience may be at the root not only of value skepticism but of both neurotic and philosophic notions of the unreality of the extended world. The phrase "nothing is true, all is permitted," illustrates how factual and value skepticism are allied, although it curiously reverses the actual psychic order of things. Our felt inability to influence the course of events in our own favor means that, because no action makes any difference, any action is permitted. A world in which all is permitted is a dream world, a world in which nothing is true. Our belief in the existence of an objective external world depends upon our sense of self-worth, of effectiveness. Whether, and in what sense, a value may be derived from a fact will be considered later, but we may here note in passing that our ability to project an external world is, by a primitive psychological derivation, a product of our sense of ourselves as beings with some capacity for achieving the satisfaction of our feelings.

The two experiences cannot be false; no experience can in itself be false. They can, however, prompt us to false conclusions. If we are to neutralize the impact of these visions upon our moral thinking, we must demystify them, assimilate them to our ordinary experience, understanding, and feeling, and show the hiatus between what we actually experience and the theoretical judgments that mistakenly are built upon them. The process is similar to that by which we handle optical illusions and dreaming.

The optimistic experience does not concern us further; it is the pessimistic experience that lies behind most assertions of value skepticism. The assertions are founded upon a notion that values must somehow be "out there," somehow embedded in the structure of things external. The notion is naive, animistic, universal among unreflective or uneducated people, and recurrent in the thinking of the rest of us. The experience of the world as indifferent to our interests seems a direct refutation of our natural egoism and therefore of our values. It is not. Values never were "out there." Further, our discouragements promote a false view of our situation in life. We are not perpetually doomed to defeat on all fronts. If it is ever possible, on any occasion, to do anything that forwards our realization of a human interest, however slightly, then on that occasion it makes sense for us to experience and to state a preference for that thing. Value skepticism is an expectable response to the feeling that every one of my desires has been and always will be frustrated. If that feeling is not supported by actual experience, however, then value skepticism is not a theory of value but the symptom of an illness.

Skepticism in Advanced Societies

The outstanding characteristic of humans, the one that accounts principally for their present apparent evolutionary success, is intelligence. Yet we find that systematic directed thought is hard work. Like other labor, thinking is prompted by and accompanied by fear, hope, desire—that is, by motivations or values. Although we need valuable considerations to spur us to protracted thought, our thinking is much more effective when its internal operation is sealed off from value considerations. We see very well that serious study ought to be as value-free as possible, not only in the study of physics, but also in the study of biology, psychology, society, and even of value itself. We value value-free thinking because it best serves our values.

An unfortunate consequence of this realization has been a general confusion about the status of value judgments. Society trains and employs millions of specialized thinkers, and carefully compartmentalizes and directs their labor; the habits of mind they acquire in training and on the work site spill over into their non-work-related thought. All questions come to be regarded as technical problems; the organizational mission becomes the underlying tacit value system, within which all value questions that arise are seen as instrumental. Questions that seem not to be answerable by polls, computers, physical or mathematical analysis, are felt to be embarrassingly naive.[3] An overt concern with value questions becomes associated with the backward elements of the population or with the meretricious arts of entertainment, salesmanship, and political rhetoric. The mode of life of many of our educated and professional and managerial elites is such as positively to incapacitate them for dealing with open value questions. It is not surprising that they take refuge in some sophisticated form of value relativism or in skepticism.

We are familiar with the many ways in which modern society promotes skepticism about value. Among those ways are the steady erosion of social solidarity, the spread of the assumption that relationships are necessarily adversarial, the privatization of life, and the new legitimation of raw egotism. It is true that the skepticism engendered by modern life is principally directed toward cultural values, and in such a way as to forward the idea that the individual is the final basis of value. But as this takes place, individuals are themselves understood simply as stimulus-response mechanisms, creatures whose values are the product of conditioning, and so not to be taken seriously.

Rationality and Skepticism

There is a curious tension between thinking and valuing. Rousseau thought that "a thinking man is a depraved animal," and that "it is reason which engenders self-love, and reflection that strengthens it; it is reason that makes man shrink into himself—it is philosophy that destroys his connections with other men."[4] Thinking abstracts us from ourselves, distances us from our existential self. When we think at length about astronomical distances and the life periods of galaxies, or when we immerse ourselves in the history of ancient peoples, our mind returns to its ordinary concerns with difficulty. The little areas and years within which our passions exercise themselves seem contemptible by comparison; we see ourselves from a perspective that reduces our lives to those of agitated mayflies. If we were indeed pure intellects, if that impossible were possible, we should truly see that nothing matters. Nothing can matter to a mind without care, interest, or motivation.

Even within our own lifetime we can detect the extent to which rational analysis has eaten away at the chains of conventional morality. Now, as much as in the days of the Sophists, conventional morality has no defenses against the critical questioning mind. Any curious youngster can see at once that the cultural emperor has no moral clothes. Since conventional morality is all that most of us know, it is evident that, when it is all criticized away, there will be nothing left, and so moral skepticism seems the final position.

The central point about rationality and its connection with skepticism is in the very nature of thinking and of valuing. Without feeling-motivation-value, our intelligence cannot stir or persist in motion, cannot find an object on which to work. Yet although it be the slave or the scout of the passions, our intelligence seems somehow unable to see them. Our mind can deal with existences and concepts and with the relationships among existences and concepts, past and future, actual and possible and even impossible. It can even deal with the values of others as natural facts: "The king refused to break his promise, and so was executed." Ask your intelligence: "Should the king have refused to break his promise?" It replies with information: according to this interpretation of Islamic law, yes, according to that, no; according to leading French ethical teachers, yes, under the following conditions, 20 percent dissenting; if you take promising in this sense, yes, in that, no. Our intelligence can consider everything that can be considered, but it cannot conclude, "All things considered, the king ought (or ought not) to have broken his promise." There is something—not particularly mysterious—in a value judgment on which the intelligence cannot seem to get its hands. Those whose world is very largely the world of the intelligence—we may think of ethical philosophers as much as mathematicians—have a strong natural tendency toward value skepticism.

Skepticism, the assertion that there are no warrantable value judgments, turns out to be no more than a feeling in search of proper words and continually finding the wrong ones. If someone wants to insist that there is no tooth fairy, that conventional values are a little ridiculous and certainly not necessarily binding upon us, that life is very depressing, that there are no logical or empirical methods for determining what is of value, that values do not exist "out there" awaiting our discovery—what can we do but agree? But all this does not take us to value skepticism, for we must yet decide what to do, even though that decision be to end it all. For that decision to be made, something must be assumed or known to be better than something else, if only to ourselves.

Value skepticism is not merely an intellectual confusion or a bleak mood. We encounter it in the world as a cynical way of talking that masks some sinister values, that weakens those social inhibitions that make life less dangerous to us all, that scorns moral reflection and so throws the individual back to subjection to his or her raw and immediate passions. Value skepticism may be understandable; in a mature person it may not be forgivable.

CHAPTER 3

The Unique Individual

Whatever their ultimate origin, value judgments are events that occur only in individual minds. The more crucial the decision, the greater the sense of isolation. It is "lonely at the top"; at the level of our personal affairs we are continually reminded that "only you can decide." Some people find such momentary solitudes unbearable. They seek external legitimation for their decisions—custom, religion, authority, advisors. To the extent to which they succeed in escaping personal responsibility, they abdicate a human function: they cease to make value judgments at all.

Because the parroting of value terms does not constitute a value judgment, because evidence of personal decision is needed, it has come to be thought that the essence of a value judgment consists solely in individual commitment. Since "individual" is commonly equated with "unique," it has proven easy for some to conclude that it is only that part of us that is significantly different from all other minds that is capable of making value judgments. This conclusion, as a theory of value, asserts that the origin and authority of value judgments is to be found only in individual humans, each considered as unique.

No other theory is held more widely or dogmatically among the educated young people of the Western world. Yet for all its popularity, it has found no serious intellectual defenders. Perhaps some philosophically inclined writers, perhaps some existentialists, hold and defend this view, but the excessively open texture of their thought makes the determination of this, as of many other questions of which they treat, impossible. When many people hold a theoretical position for which there exists no body of reasoned support, we are entitled to look for cultural and psychological explanation. Before I look into the possible validity of what may be called "value solipsism," I want to consider how anyone ever came to believe in so strange a view.

Many modern intellectual, historical, and social trends, however mutually opposed in other respects, have concurred in forwarding the notion that each person is a moral island. Instances are the apparent radical individualism of most of the early Protestant reformers, the political philosophies of Hobbes and of Locke, and nineteenth-century liberal and economic theory. Modern epistemology began with "I think, therefore I am," with the discovery of the authority of the single thinking ego, and has had only middling success in getting past that beginning; the value solipsism we are discussing is related to the epistemological solipsism that is one of our heritages from Descartes. When romanticism, in all its myriad forms, arrived on the scene, it found new ways of accentuating the loneliness of the individual. The passion for what is unique and special, rather than for the classically typical, the interest in the most ephemeral subjective viewpoints and feelings, the faith in the ultimate aesthetic and moral authority of the sensitive and imaginative idiosyncratic individual—all have strengthened the trend in our youth culture toward value solipsism. To all this we may add a grab-bag of reinforcers: all those factors that have tended to bring conventional social values and models into disrepute; the principled pluralism and toleration of personal deviance; all those things that have privatized our lives and made elementary communication, let alone shared values, increasingly difficult to attain; the deterioration of the principal modern alternative, culturalism. It is a wonder how any mainstream young person could resist a view toward which so many social and historical forces and traditions seem to lead. They are urged to do their own thing, to do it if it is right for them, to consult their own unique feelings.

There are indeed some values and preferences that are appropriately based solely on idiosyncratic choice. If you like vanilla and I like chocolate, it would be absurd for either of us to argue that the other is mistaken. The advantages of taking inconsequential preferences as the model for all value judgments are evident. We can claim for ourselves and for others both the prestige awarded to autonomous actors and thinkers and a right to immunity from the social or legal penalties or pains that usually result from principled heroism. We can claim to live by a morality superior to, because more authentic than, that of society or of conventional people, and also deny that we need to defend our choices. Since sincerity is the prime, indeed the only, virtue, we may not only change our values to suit our present feelings or mood, we may do so without condemning our past value judgments, for they too were sincere at the time we made them. This doctrine seems to promote a sincere toleration more than can any other. There is literally no basis, other than insincerity, on which anyone can condemn or disagree with the values of another. Indeed, members of this sect commonly urge us not to be "judgmental."

Perhaps the case for value solipsism is not fairly made in cold propositional terms. It is not enough to assert that each of us is unique; the point is that that uniqueness is said to be the most important thing about us. The life task of each of us is to come to terms with our essential self or, rather, in the course of a series of crucial value decisions to discover and create that essential self. Real life is dangerous; really living can be terrifying. Many of us are not up to the strain of being or becoming an authentic person. Tensely crouched behind the role-masks that society provides or we neurotically invent, we bargain away for security the only thing worth preserving, ourselves. At length we become hollowed out, nothing but the roles at which we clutch. In the despair and self-hatred that follow from this self-betrayal, we join the effort to crush the few who have not yet succumbed.

After all, it can be said, did not such men as Kant and Rousseau argue that, although my freedom lies in total subjection to the law, that law must be of my own making? How can it be of my own making if I make it under duress or social conditioning? How can something be beautiful, to me, unless I myself see it as beautiful? How can I accept something as good, or right, unless I actually experience it to be so? It follows that, in regard to the relation between my value judgments and those of others, as mine ought not be subject to them, theirs ought not be subject to mine; my value judgments are unique to me and valid for me only.

However persuasive the arguments and intuitions that lead some to this position, we can see almost at once why it has found so few philosophical defenders. Protagoras said, if Aristotle understood him correctly, that "*each* man is the measure of all things,"[1] but Protagoras did not, so far as we know, produce a serious defense of this notion. The objections are very many.

Humans are both unique and similar to each other. Whether it is our uniqueness or our similarity that is to be taken more seriously depends, not on the discovery of some final truth about the matter, but on the context in which the question arises. For example, doctors and psychologists readily concede the physical and psychic uniqueness of each human, but at the same time they must argue that, if each person were totally unique, there could be no medicine or psychology. If people are even to be human, they must grow up as members of a society. A society is a system of communicated and shared values. A society of unique individuals, each with his or her own distinct set of values, is a contradiction in terms. Friendship and community would perish, were we all unique, and we should flee each other in horror and in fear. We are not unique in any important sense; if we were, the human species would soon perish. We may easily tolerate, in inconsequential matters, what Freud called "the chauvinism of small differences," but the major bloodthirsty chauvinisms that plague our species are the best proof that the acknowledgment of difference does not end in the toleration that the moral subjectivists envision. Jealousy, vengefulness, spite, are as authentic as any other feelings. If those who experience such feelings also feel bound to act on them, we can anticipate even more trouble than we have. There need be no quarrel between us because you prefer vanilla and I prefer chocolate, nor even if you prefer a diet of plastic and metal filings—although that kind of uniqueness is intolerantly and savagely punished by nature. However, if your authentic self prefers conflict, torture, and bloodshed, while mine prefers peace, love, and forgiveness, and we cannot avoid each other, then mutual toleration means that you accept my gifts and affection and I accept being chopped up by you. A society that agrees to the validity of individually based values will be unable to enforce any of its laws, for anyone who breaks them can claim immunity on the basis of freedom of conscience. Sincerity, once called "grace," would become the only universally acknowledged virtue. When that happens, as we know from the histories of Calvinist and ideologically dominated societies, hypocrisy becomes universal.

A hypothetical anarchist might concede that some of us display such uniqueness of value judgment that our existence may be dangerous or oppressive to others. He or she might argue, however, that these deviants have had their basic good nature soured or distorted by life in a bad society. Smash the evil institutions and the qualities of brotherly love and mutual supportiveness will flourish in all of us. Quite aside from the degree of probability that we may assign to this scenario, the argument itself tacitly abandons the position it was meant to support. It does so in favor of a particularly dogmatic and improbable human nature theory, one that asserts that all humans, aside from socially induced distortions, have a basically good nature. That goodness guarantees that all or almost all members of the species, in a great variety of situations, in matters relating to sex, property, or material assets, the division of income and of irksome labor, the making of community decisions, and the allocation of leadership functions, as well as in all ordinary personal relations, will—without any need for social conditioning, peer pressure, or special family, religious, or community training—spontaneously act in ways that actively promote, or at least do not impair, the welfare of others. In this smiling uniformity of feeling and evaluation, where every person is simultaneously an ethical wild deuce and a social king of hearts, where is the uniqueness originally postulated? Actual intelligent anarchists will have nothing to do with such puerile dreaming.

The value individualist might concede the need in a good society of a minimum of repression and a maximum of education, socialization, and friendly persuasion. No one can quarrel with the idea that we ought benignly shepherd our children toward gentleness and benevolence and no one's principles are offended by the effort to transform our society in that direction. No one's, that is, but those of value individualists themselves. They cannot make a distinction between mild and violent methods for undermining the individual uniqueness for which they claim the prime position.

Many acts that might seem to arise out of individual value choice in fact do nothing of the sort. We now understand conscience, or superego, to be the expression, not of individuality, but of internalized social norms. Luther, against the pressure of overwhelming forces, arose to say, "Here I stand; I can do no other." But he stood there in the calm assurance, not of his unique personality—his name for that was "sinful pride"—but of his possession by the Spirit, a Spirit that was not his, but God's. Luther urged his listeners to agree, not with him, but with God. Rousseau, who all but invented the modern ideal of authenticity, did not believe that what was unique in himself, or in any individual, was anything but a source of weakness and of error; he thought, unlike some of our contemporaries, that we achieve authenticity precisely by abandoning our chaotic idiosyncrasies and finding our species-normal nature.

> Here is your history as I believe it to read, not in the books of your fellowmen, which are liars, but in nature, which never lies. Everything that comes from nature will be true, there will be nothing false except what I have involuntarily put in of my own.[2]

The values of a truly unique person could be of interest only to him or herself. The interesting moral teachers have explicitly grounded the authority of their revelations outside of themselves. It they had not, why would anyone have listened to them, and would they not have listened to them at the risk of their own unique integrity?

We are not all the same, but we are interestingly unique only to those who love us. If there were unique persons, persons who have no community of values with other people, then, as Aristotle put it, they would be, not human, but either beasts or gods, either more or less than human.[3] We know of the claimants to such uniqueness from our newspapers, but however they speak of themselves as godlike, we know them as sadists, tyrants, terrorists, as bestial. No unhuman godlike creature has yet appeared among us.

The doctrine of value individualism seems well suited to the pampering of trivial egos in a narcissistic consumer society. We see them, pondering in the aisles of the department store about whether they really like the wide or the narrow stripe. We hear them pontificating on the dreary sillinesses they call their tastes and "life style." In their hands moral decision has indeed come down to "vanilla or chocolate?"

A *footnote*: In *Language, Truth, and Logic*, written fifty years ago, A. J. Ayer argued that value judgments are essentially meaningless because they are merely expressions of individual feeling.[4] He seems to be aiming at value skepticism, though his argument actually supports the kind of value individualism just described. It supports either of these only on the assumption he tacitly makes that feelings are idiosyncratic and ephemeral and therefore not to be taken seriously. If, in fact, feelings are the most important component of our being, if they are common to all people and influence action over long periods of time, if their satisfaction is the only conceivable motivation to action—all of which I will argue for later—then Ayer's demonstration moves from what is quite true to what is quite false, by way of a factual error. Values are indeed expressions of feeling, but feelings are not merely individually subjective and ephemeral; they are species-universal and enduring.

CHAPTER 4

God, Nature, Reason

As far removed as possible from the individualism just discussed are those suggested bases for value judgments that transcend not only the individual but also our society and even our species. These bases have been said to be God, Nature, or Reason. Many have thought that if values are to have the authority to command us—and it ought to be no ephemeral or ignoble basis on which we wager the direction of our lives—then they must have a foundation more enduring than the vagaries of the individual mind or state of feeling, less bewilderingly various than the customs and conventions of the cultures, more elevated, or at least more respectable, than our "animal" human nature. Skeptics, often disappointed dogmatists, seem to have begun in this way, as though the only possible position alternative to theirs must be a value system resting on an authority transcendent to things human. The discussion here of each of the three transcendent value bases is brief, not so much because of their lack of intrinsic interest as because few contemporary moral thinkers defend any of them.

God

Whether God exists at all, and in what sense, and whether, if he or she does exist, he or she takes any interest in us, or what kind of interest, are deeply absorbing questions. They are too difficult for us to discuss here. Yet even if we assume that God exists and wishes us well, there are still serious problems in basing a value judgment on his or her commands or will.

The principal problem is that of communication. There are no reliable procedures, no criteria, for determining what it is that God wishes us to do. Even on the assumption that God wishes us to do well there seems to be no method for determining what God's notion of well is, except by arguing that God's ideas agree with ours. This argument not only is blasphemous but renders God's existence superfluous for value theory. Some have suggested that God speaks to us through Reason or Nature. The reasons for thinking so are not good, but if they were, the problem is merely transferred to another area. The Devil that can quote Scripture and perform miracles should have no trouble in deceiving us through our perceptions of Reason or Nature. Many established religions claim to instruct us in God's will. They base their claim on sacred texts, tradition, revelations, and miracles. Without prejudice to the possible truth of any of these claims, it must be said that none of them is authoritative to us and it is an empirical fact that no single faith can show a significant advantage in the conversion of neutral or agnostic persons. Actually all religions concede that more than argument or intellectual understanding is necessary for conversion, and so admit that their arguments are insufficient. We need not, therefore, analyze them further here.

The problems of communication between God and humans have never been satisfactorily solved. Even in the ages of faith it was both a theoretical and a painful practical problem. Luther, when cross-examined by Erasmus about the basis of his religious doctrines, first asserted that Scripture, rather than the Pope or tradition, is the sole source of our knowledge of God's will. Then he admitted that many apparently "holy men" read Scripture differently and so he had to assert the authority of the Spirit within us to determine the meaning of Scripture. Then, in order to save Christianity, he had to reassert the authority of Scripture over the Spirit.[1] The only significant improvement over this confusion was that introduced by Calvin, who argued that "God will not deceive His people," that the gathered congregation speaks God's will with one voice.[2] We can trace the history of this theory of popular sovereignty in moral truth through the sects of Calvinism and then, secularized, through Rousseau, Marx, and Mao and on to recent notions of participatory democracy. Whether religious or secular, the idea that the voice of the people has a moral authority that no individual can have is one that pushes God into the background, that takes us out of the transcendent realm and into culturalist or human nature theory.

Some have argued that the differences between the various religions ought not concern us, for they all teach the same fundamental moral message. If true, such an argument would be impressive, although not conclusive, but it seems not to be true. Even if we could find some consensus among most of the prevailing religions, it would not show us what God wants us to do. It would more likely show that human societies have similar values because they consist of similar humans in similar conditions. There are societies that do not have a God, nor even a tradition of having had one, and yet these societies lie well within the thin value consensus of the religious societies.

There are individuals who say, and believe, that God has spoken directly to them. Those who so believe have solved, for themselves, the problem examined in this book. For those to whom God has not spoken, the problem remains, for when they hold certain values to be the will of God and do so on the basis of God's having spoken to some person other than themselves, they believe not on God's authority but on the authority of that other person.[3] Further, if we begin with an appropriately serious notion of God, and then consider the character of those who claim to have heard from God or of the message they say they have received, we can hardly fail to be struck by the incongruity between the two. There are also logical and epistemological questions about how God talks to humans. As Hobbes put it, how can we distinguish between a message from God and one from our own unconscious or from our underlying culture? If we make the distinction on the basis of the content of the message, then we are using criteria of the truth of the message on grounds other than its supposed origin in God.

Suppose all these problems solved: What motivation do we have to obey a command of God? One notable motivation is the love of God. The number of persons who can be motivated in this way must be very small, much below one percent of believers. The rest must be motivated by the threat of divine punishment and the promise of reward. This brings theistic morality into the realm of utilitarianism, of the pleasure-pain, stick-and-carrot morality of Bentham. In any case, studies indicate that the fear of divine punishment does nothing at all to support actual morality; it can be argued, statistically, that a belief in a future life and future punishment promotes criminal behavior. Believers and non-believers seem to have about equal motivation to behave well toward fellow humans.

The number, variety, and levels of sophistication of the conceptions of God are many, and some readers may find the preceding discussion shallow. However, as we move toward a more generous or imaginative notion of God and of his or her relation to us, we also move out of that area within which we can hope to find an intersubjective notion of how God can support a value judgment. Those who have gone beyond the idea of God as the Gaseous Invertebrate of nineteenth-century atheism or the kindly bewhiskered old man of their childhood must understand him or her as a metaphor for something other than as God as commonly understood. That metaphor has been variously interpreted as our sense of a lost community, or ideal of our higher self, as the heart of a heartless world, as the principle of improvement in nature, and so on. Whatever metaphor we choose, it will be the ground of the metaphor, not God, that will be a claimed basis for our value judgments, and that other ground will be discussed here under some other heading. Besides, although there is no limit or end to unique conceptions of God, these imaginations have no authority for anyone but their originators. Those who cling to such idiosyncratic projections have resigned from serious discussions about the better and the worse, and perhaps even from that human reasonableness that we call sanity.

Nature

The idea that Nature is a unitary system that in some way can serve as a basis and justification of value judgments is old and widespread. Some writers call this idea "natural law," or "the law of Nature." I will continue this practice, although the phrases are used in almost as many senses as there are writers. Locke, for instance, sometimes means by the "law of Nature," "the law of God," and sometimes the "law of Reason."[4] Cicero, and some Stoics, do not make the necessary distinction between a "law of Nature" and a law of human nature. Hobbes, Aquinas, and Samuel Pufendorf are fairly clear in their use of "natural law," but quite different from each other. This is not the place for a systematic study of the history of the meaning of "natural law"; I believe that all the interesting meanings are included somewhere in my systematic study of the possible bases of value. The Nature of "natural law," discussed now, is the universe itself, the cosmos, all things, and not only extended things but all that have some kind of existence.

If we see Nature reductively, as a fortuitous concourse of atoms, then the idea that it might instruct, much less command, us in particular values makes no sense. What must Nature be like if it is to serve as a basis for value judgments? The minimum requirements are that it be unitary, a total coherent system, that it be a system at a level of complexity and degree of organization comparable to that of humans, that it contain or embody a moral code in a fashion that requires that it have some degree of consciousness, that it act in such a way as to enforce its moral code upon us. This is the Nature of primitive people and of children. In fact, so pervasive is this view of Nature, even for the most sophisticated persons in their unguarded moments, that we might fairly consider it to be a part of our elemental psychological makeup. Animism is our natural religion. Belief in teleology, the purposefulness of Nature, is universal among uneducated people. I can assume that my readers are capable of imagining, in some poetic sense, that the universe is a single unified system, even that it is something like an organism, possibly even that it is an organism with values that it is incumbent upon us to obey. Between such imagination and belief, I also assume, there is for them the sort of credibility gap that distances us from the gods of the Greeks.

It might be imagined that Nature unconsciously embodies and enforces values. The tactic abandons the original case. If Nature merely transmits values that it does not originate, then it is not a basis itself, but the transmitter of the values of some other transcendent authority, as God or Reason. Hegel seems to have thought that the Real, or Nature, is the Rational, and Aquinas suggests that the general course of Nature exemplifies the will of God. In either case, Nature is not the ultimate authority.

There is, of course, an obvious sense in which the study of Nature is highly relevant to our welfare. Those unable or unwilling to understand the facts of Nature are doomed to starve, to be eaten, to fall off cliffs, to be ill and unhappy.[5] Metaphorically we may speak of "natural punishments," of the retribution that Nature exacts of those who ignore her habitual courses. Metaphor is not thought, however. The thought suggested by such metaphors is that Nature is a system of facts and relationships; humans are systems of needs and passions; those with needs and passions satisfy them best if they know the facts of the world about them. Natural law in this sense is really human nature theory.

There seems to be no way in which the observation of Nature can provide us with the motivation we need for the formation of value judgments. The history of the study of Nature, the history of science, is in part a demonstration of the uselessness of ascribing purpose or value to Nature, while the history of value theory is in part a demonstration of the fact that our enormously enhanced knowledge of Nature has done nothing to clarify or specify the contents of the "law of Nature," nothing for our ability to understand and discuss value judgments. The desire to find purpose and value in Nature involves a perfectly natural, but completely illegitimate projection of human feelings and motives into a sphere that exists only as a metaphor.

If we ought to live "in accord with Nature," then we ought to seek the "natural" and avoid the "unnatural." But since everything that exists, exists in Nature, how can anything be unnatural? Sometimes the unnatural is taken to be what rarely happens, as the birth of two-headed calves or snow in July. But rarity cannot be a criterion, for four-leaved clovers and diamonds are also rare but are not thought to be unnatural. In fact, those who seek to validate the concept of the unnatural are trying to justify the human sense of unease at certain phenomena that run counter to our expectations or that somehow strike us as sinister. Birth control, fluoridation, pasteurization of milk, the income tax, long-haired men—all kinds of things can produce in some people a kind of moral nausea, indignation mixed with fear. Nature has no connection with this feeling. We do not need to study Nature to find why we see a neglectful mother as morally repellant, as "unnatural." We need to study the feelings within us that lead us to call her unnatural. We will find the source of those feelings not in Nature but in our personal or cultural experience or in our genetic feeling profile. The idea of the "unnatural" is a non-idea; nothing corresponds to it; it is an empty concept.

There is, at a level well below that of the philosophic, a sense in which "the natural" may be taken to be vaguely prescriptive. The contemporary marriage of science, technology, and salesmanship has produced an environment of synthetic materials and foods, wonderful medications, unprecedented speeds and conveniences, not to mention experimental modes of human interactions. Sensible people have learned to detect some of the thorns amid these flowers of contemporary life and have even acquired a general distrust of most of them. The craze for the "natural," in food, childbirth, medication, and general living, has a foundation in the desire to survive and to live well. The conditions of human well-being are flexible, within limits, but the limits are not less real for our not knowing precisely what they are. We do well to have a bias toward less complicated procedures and products that have stood the test of time. None of this has anything to do with natural law theory, for the Nature appealed to by those who currently favor the natural is only the general environment in which our species evolved and to which, minimally modified, it is most likely best adapted. Even this sense of "the natural" has to be taken cautiously, for among the items in our original natural circumstances were presently preventable plagues, starvation, superstition, brutality, and miseries without end. Our capacity to invent and to modify our circumstances is also a human expression of our native intelligence.

Reason

What connection we find between reason and value will depend upon whether we use "reason" in a strict or a loose sense.

The strict sense of reason is that of logical entailment. All reasoning is deduction from definitions; a rational statement is thus a tautology. It is this strict sense of reason that, I will argue, cannot support a value judgment. The less strict sense may not do the job either, but the important battle about reason has been at the level of the strict sense of the word. A rational ethic would be a set of value judgments derived logically from definitions that are intuitively certain. For example: establish the necessary existence of God (from, say, the need for a first cause); deduce from the existence of God the fact that he or she created us; conclude that we ought to do his or her will. Hume considered this argument over two hundred years ago and wondered how it was possible to derive an "ought" from an "is", how, from the existence of one state of affairs, it could follow that some other state of affairs ought to ensue.[6] No one has answered Hume on this matter. A rational ethic depends on a logic that it is irrational to follow. As Hume put it in another place: "It is not irrational for me to prefer the utter destruction of myself and of all those I hold dear to the causing of the least inconvenience to an Indian."[7] It is not irrational because such action or preference does not imply a contradiction. In the strict sense of "reason" something can be said to be against reason, to be irrational, only if a contradiction follows from it. Examples of such a contradiction are: "$2+2=5$," "a married bachelor." A contradiction involves the violation of an intuitively certain principle, as $A=A$, the opposite of which is inconceivable; a thing cannot be and not be at the same time and in the same sense. It follows that facts cannot contradict each other, although statements of fact may, through one of them being false. Similarly, there is no way in which a fact, or a statement of fact, can contradict a value or a value judgment. Note some subtleties here: "I now prefer vanilla" contradicts "I now do not prefer vanilla." The contradiction is, however, a contradiction between two purported statements of fact, not between a fact and a fact, a fact and a value, or even between two values. An example of two contradictory value judgments would be: "vanilla is preferable to chocolate" and "chocolate is preferable to vanilla."

Hobbes argued that to make a promise and to break it is against reason, a saying yea and a saying nay at the same time, a self-contradiction.[8] But there is no contradiction, simply two events, a promising and a non-performing. It is not irrational for me to break my promise. However immoral, unfair, unsafe, illegal, despicable, it may be, it is not, in the strict sense, irrational. Kant seems to have argued that breaking promises is indeed irrational, because the practice, if universalized, would abolish the practice or the meaning of promising.[9] He may be right, but this part of Kant's ethical theory is singularly unconvincing, for he is either appealing to prudential considerations when we were led to think he was talking about rationality or appealing to some implicit obligation—a promise to keep promises—that involves an infinite regress.

The loose sense of "reason" is less troublesome. When I say that "it stands to reason" that you ought not prevent the least inconvenience to a total stranger at the cost of the destruction of yourself and of all you hold dear, all I mean is that I find such behavior completely out of line with what I have come to expect from fellow humans. A person who acts in this way seems to have a set of priorities, or a view of reality, that is completely different from that of other people. If that person were a friend of mine, I should think he had gone mad, and I would probably be right. "Madness," of course, is not a term in logical discourse.

The strict and the loose sense of "reason" can be translated respectively into the "logical" and the "reasonable" or normally expectable. The law recognizes the latter in talking about what, under given circumstances, a reasonable person might be expected to do, and the sense is clearly not "logical" but "sensible." A reasonable person is one with species or culturally normal feelings and views of reality. Reasonableness is a norm and one that is based not on reason but on expectations that have arisen out of our life experience and feelings.

The philosophers who have attempted to derive values by a purely rational process are both fewer in number and more recent than a student might be led to think by some histories of philosophy. Even Plato and Spinoza, as I shall argue later, are not rationalist moral thinkers. Our contemporaries Max Black[10] and John Searle[11] argue that when we willingly enter into a system or vocabulary of values or oughts, or perhaps merely of standardized procedures, we acquire a moral obligation to act in certain ways. For instance, if we play chess, but insist on moving the knight as though it were a pawn, we are disappointing the expectations of our opponent, of the whole community of chess players, and also breaking the very rules that constitute the game of chess. We are rationally obliged, it is said, to play by the rules that we accepted when we entered into the playing of the game.

In Max Black's example, because chess would not be chess unless both parties to the game can be assumed to be trying to win, we have an obligation to take our opponent's queen when doing so helps us to win the game. It does seem as though there is some kind of obligation in this case. The obligation need not, however, govern our actions and we are not irrational in overriding it. We have no obligation to allow the rules of chess to take precedence over the rules of all the other games we may be playing, overtly or covertly, at the same time. We may be mocking an inferior player, amusing a child, angling for a promotion, assisting in a burglary taking place in the house; why ought the rules of chess take precedence over these other objectives? Further, the basis of the obligation that we have to try to win is, when not compulsiveness or competitiveness, a desire to please ourselves or others when we can, or not to hurt the feelings of others, and so on. No trace of a rational obligation survives such analysis.

A less trivial example might be in the alleged obligation we have to observe the rules of the society in which we voluntarily live and from which we have benefited.

There may well be such an obligation; the question is whether it is a rational obligation. The number, complexity, ambiguity, and hierarchical rankings of social conventions are such that, even if we wanted to do nothing but exactly what the conventions demand, we would often not know what course to pursue. Social morality is precise and detailed only at the level of unimportant ritual or fashion. Further, social conventions cannot be as strictly binding as those of chess because they do not constitute society in the same way that chess rules constitute the game itself. The price of social progress, justice, or even social survival might often involve the breaking of old rules and the creation of new ones, and this on a basis that cannot be called strictly rational, but only reasonable or sensible. With all this, even if we live in a static and secure society, which happens also to be a utopia in every sense, we act badly in breaking its rules but cannot be said to contradict ourselves.

Some recent writers have attempted a rational ethic. Peter Singer, for one, argues:

> We can progress toward rational settlement of disputes over ethics by taking the element of disinterestedness inherent in the idea of justifying one's conduct to society as a whole, and extending this into the principle that to be ethical, a decision must give equal weight to the interests of all affected by it.[12]

He concludes that "the principle of equal consideration of interests is a uniquely rational basis for ethical decision making." Now it is true that we must talk the language of disinterestedness if we are to justify our conduct to others, but this fact implies not a principle, but a practical necessity. Crude egoists have small audiences. We can *say* that disinterestedness shall be a principle, an ethical principle, but it will yet have no further force for us than our agreement or its original practical necessity. Whether there is a practical necessity that we give equal weight to the interests of all is an empirical question to which we have no certain answer. Singer is urging us to be not rational, but reasonable. His reasons for being reasonable are, in one place, based upon our biological nature,[13] although elsewhere[14] he explicitly disowns such naturalistic ethical arguments.

Alasdair MacIntyre says:

> From such factual premises as "This watch is grossly inaccurate and irregular in timekeeping," and "This watch is too heavy to carry about comfortably," the evaluative conclusion validly follows that "This is a bad watch."[15]

In his following paragraph, the concept of a watch is said to be a functional concept; a watch is "characteristically expected to serve" a function; "the concept of a watch cannot be defined independently of the concept of a good watch." The argument is beset with ambiguities and difficulties: If the concept of a watch includes goodness, then an object that seems to be a watch but that does not work is not a watch and so cannot be a bad watch. If the concept of a watch includes goodness, then the premises contain a value, although the argument is supposed to show how a value can be derived from a value-free fact. If we can nevertheless understand the goodness of the watch to be a kind of fact, then the badness of the watch is also a kind of fact and so a value has not been derived; "good" and "bad" are not necessarily value terms in all cases. MacIntyre's argument seems to depend upon a confusion of the idea of a watch as a natural physical object and as the embodiment of human purposes. The best explanation of "bad watch" seems to be that we use the phrase not to describe the watch but to express our disappointment with its malfunctioning. The feeling of disappointment follows as a psychological consequence, not a logical consequence, from the facts about the bad watch. It is emotivist theory, not animism disguised as rationalism, which explains the phrase "this is a bad watch."

John Rawls does not claim a rational basis for his value recommendations, but his language leads us to believe that we are being conducted through an elegant rational proof. The puzzle as to just what foundation Rawls eventually does find for his moral theory is solved, it seems to me, by paying more attention to the many places where he speaks from a non-reductive human nature perspective, for example:

> The basic idea is one of reciprocity, a tendency to answer in kind. Now this tendency is a deep psychological fact. Without it our nature would be very different and fruitful social cooperation fragile if not impossible.... Beings with a different psychology either have never existed or must soon have disappeared in the course of evolution.[16]

Rationalism in value theory depends upon the unexamined use of language. We call an act rational when it leads to a desired goal. We say that it is irrational to try to cook a steak by putting it in the freezer, to insult a person from whom we ask a favor. Obviously in both cases we ought to say "unreasonable" rather than "irrational," for what we condemn is a disregard for empirical probability. There is simply no way in which we can reason, logically, from a fact to a value.

This brief chapter can hardly pretend to have demolished claims as ancient and prestigious as those of God, Nature, and Reason. We do not hear much of them these days, however, and so I save my longer arguments for the currently more popular claimants to moral authority, the reductionist human nature and culturalist theories.

CHAPTER 5

An Historical Interlude

All humans are born into and live subject to a complex of natural and cultural constraints. Each constraint is the infliction of a defeat, the denial of outlet to a passion.[1] The passions are all but infinite in their demands; their defeat is common and often necessary. Therefore, we prize whatever capacities we have to arrive at the satisfaction of the feelings, especially of the stronger and more enduring ones. Our two principal powers to enhance the quality of our lives are our ability to understand the world within which our feelings must find their fulfillment and then to make value judgments based on a realistic knowledge of our own long-term feelings. We have some modest success in both these endeavors insofar as our personal lives go. When we can arrive at a common understanding with other humans of what is factually true and humanly valuable, we can even effect improvement in the larger natural and cultural world we share. We can do it, of course, only on the assumption that the better and the worse are discussable matters, that there is a common basis on which value decisions can be made, that different humans can on that basis come to common values and join in political and social action.

Up to this point, I have argued that value judgments either have no basis, as the skeptics claim, or that they do, and that if they do that basis must be found in one, and only one, of a few possible locations: in the unique individual, the culture, the species, or in some realm transcendent to all these, such as God, Reason, or Nature. Most of the options were examined and rejected. Some were easily shown to be untenable; some are not likely to be held by my readers. The consideration of the remaining two options is the principal concern of this book. If we moderns are to find a basis for individual and communal action it must be either the culturalist or the human nature position that provides it.

I expect my reader to be an adherent, consciously or not, of some variety either of the culturalist or the human nature view, or to have no view at all but to be curious about what might be said to persuade him or her to one or the other. Variations upon these two positions, and incoherent confusions of both, divide the intellectual world, dominate whole realms of the social sciences, and underlie the serious talk of most educated men and women.[2] Members of the opposing schools do not refer to each other as culturalist and human nature thinkers. They use a great variety of terms to distinguish their views from those of others and in this variety we can see the lack of any real understanding of what it is that divides them.

Some readers may suspect that "culturalism" will turn out to be a code word for radicalism and left liberalism, while "human nature" will stand for the center liberals and conservatives. Not so. Mainstream liberals do not usually make human nature assumptions, whereas libertarian anarchists, humanist Marxist, and non-Marxist socialists often do. On the other hand, although orthodox Marxists are culturalists, so too are many romantic nationalists, fascists, and intellectual racists. The moral to this apparent confusion is that the association of value and social theory with political and social programs is more tenuous than might be thought. When we translate a political rhetoric into concrete operational terms, we find that so considered it has no special affinity with any of the four possible bases for value judgments. Value bases are very abstract. They do not begin to support actual value judgments until they have been fed facts about the external physical and social world and about the psychology of humans. Those facts are necessary to arrive at the concrete policies that are then related to the abstract value theories. A value theory is not an empirical theory but a paradigm. The function of a paradigm is to serve as a conceptual framework within which useful thinking may take place. We can reject a paradigm that contains inner contradictions or that is hopelessly diffuse, but we can choose between two clear and coherent but incompatible paradigms only on the basis of utility, elegance, and comprehensiveness. Among those concerned with the methodology of the social sciences and with the value formulations that underlie social and political decisions, the central paradigmatic conflict is between what are here called the human nature and the culturalist views. I suggest the following hypothetical history, or "likely story," of how the present difficulties came to be. No part of the value argument made or yet to come depends upon its acceptance.

The Tradition

Until the latter part of the eighteenth century, every major secular political and ethical philosopher, with the exception of Hobbes, based his value theory and method of social analysis upon a variety of the human nature view that I here call the traditional. A more descriptive term for this tradition might be "empirical" or "non-reductive." I will argue later that among these writers we ought to include Plato, Aristotle, Machiavelli, Spinoza, Hume, and Rousseau, along with many others less well known. These earlier writers based their studies and policy recommendations upon a claimed understanding of our species nature. They intended to study humans as they observably are, empirically, rather than in the reductive or abstract fashion of those writers who reason from *a priori* models of human nature. They did not limit their understanding to overt behavior; they did not quantify much; they did not speak, as mathematicians do, only to the intelligent, but to the intelligent who have had some experience in reflecting upon human life. They seem to us now more like good novelists than like our scientific social scientists or academic philosophers.

Until Spinoza in the seventeenth century, none of these traditional thinkers made any serious attempt to justify, or even to explain in detail, the empirical human nature theory they all accepted. They did not imagine that any other way of going about their study was possible. By the time of Hume and Rousseau, however, alternative theories, rationalist, natural right, and culturalist, had appeared. Hume and Rousseau argued against these novelties and in favor of the older view. Their defense is the last we hear of the traditional theory. The intellectual currents of the nineteenth century, reductionist human nature thought and culturalism, swept over and buried from view all traces of the non-reductionist human nature philosophy. It has been neither attacked nor defended for almost two hundred years. It is as though it had never existed. The two views that replaced the traditional one are both traceable in an unbroken line back to two minor thinkers in the late eighteenth century, Bentham and Burke. Neither displays in his writings any awareness of the tradition he helped to displace. Both defended their new views only against the similarly new notions of natural right and of the capacity of reason to determine ends.

Bentham[3] represents a revival and application of the reductionist human nature theory of Hobbes, a theory that had been ardently repressed for the past century. Hobbes's moral and social conclusions are explicitly based on human nature, but on a nature no longer seen as a compound of many motivations, ambiguously related and stratified. He thought that human nature is sufficiently understood when we realize that we are natural machines, able to learn from experience and motivated, ultimately, solely by a passion for personal survival. Bentham is simpler yet, for he spares us the metaphysics and bundles all human motivational factors into the single factor of the desire for the useful, for utility, defined as the preponderance of pleasure over pain. It is this reduction of human motivation to some single passion that constitutes the essential character of reductionist human nature thought. The reduction confers upon us apparent powers of understanding, prediction, and value clarity such as we never had before. It becomes easy, now, for persons of ordinary intelligence and with little or no experience of life to understand and solve the most difficult moral and social questions. The initial flowering of reductionist human nature theory is found in utilitarianism, classical economics, and early liberal political theory. In later years the method has continued on into behaviorial psychology and the other social sciences. Some reductionists, as Skinner, even attempted to get rid of the concept of motivation altogether, but Bentham's postulation of an original urge toward pleasure and away from pain persists in the idea of positive and negative reinforcement.

Burke, on the other hand, completely eliminated all notions of human nature from political and value theory. His motivation in this was based on a mistaken notion that human nature theory implies natural human right, a doctrine he opposed. Against the natural right thesis he argued that our original nature is so completely overlaid by culture that no trace of it can be discovered in the empirical humans about us. In fact, he thought, the attempt to discover our original humanity by imaginatively stripping the people we know of the influence of culture is like trying to find the real onion beneath the layers of onion skin. In both cases, we find, beneath the cultural accretions, beneath the onion skins, nothing. It follows that if human nature is unknowable, we ought to turn to the study of socialized people; we ought to turn from the study of man, which a poet had recently called the noblest study, to the study of the society that makes us what we are. Sociology is to replace psychology. Because societies are so different from each other, humans of the various societies differ from each other as much as do "different species of animals." I and my motivations are to be understood not as simply human, but as, say, French, or Chinese. Value is culturally relative.

It is important to note that the culturalism of Burke and of his successors begins with a reduction more severe than that of Bentham and of his successors. If we are totally a product of our societies, we must think of ourselves as almost completely plastic to socialization. There can be nothing important or interesting in human nature that resists or that itself shapes socialization. Culturalists can be identified by their struggle to maintain the principle of human plasticity, to allow as little as possible to biological human nature; they argue that what is genetic in us is of little or no interest to our study of human action and value.

There are many variations on the culturalist theme, and perhaps no two writers hold that position in precisely the same sense. In fact, because culturalists rarely argue their fundamental position, it is commonly impossible to determine exactly how they do hold it. However, two principal varieties are discernible. The first closely follows Burke, and may include such writers as William Graham Sumner, Durkheim, and Parsons. They study the functional character of societies, at one point in time or in an ideal present. The other group, usually called historicists, may include Hegel, Marx, and Oswald Spengler. Historicists agree that we are the product of our societies but go on to find that societies are themselves products of culturally transcendent historical processes. Few culturalists make unambiguous statements in favor of the organic model of society, yet all attribute some degree of autonomy to the power of culture or to historical forces. They understand cultures or historical sequences as systems of "internal relations," closed systems in which every part is defined by its relation to every other part.

Not all the value thinking of the past two hundred years can be categorized as reductionist human nature or culturalist. A large number of writers have flourished who cannot be understood as adherents of any of the four major bases for value judgments, or even of skepticism. I do not treat of this respectable group here simply because they have no theory to examine. It is an interesting use of the classification proposed that it enables us to determine not only the fundamental starting point of a thinker but whether she or he has such a starting point. I do not mean to deny to these philosophically uncommitted writers a great deal of practical wisdom, sometimes greater than that of some of the others, but only to point out that they do not address the question that is the topic of the book. Sometimes they simply ignore the issue of foundations and speak only from their understandings and experience of what somehow seems to them better actions and values; sometimes they embrace equally two or more of our fundamental categories and reduce themselves to incoherence. The prime example of such incoherence is that of John Stuart Mill, perhaps one of the best minds of the whole modern period. At an early age he came to understand the powerful attractions both of the reductionist human nature and of the culturalist views and he stated and argued both positions accurately. My own awareness of the nature of this radical division in modern social and value thought goes back to a study of Mill's vacillation, to Robert Cumming's *Human Nature and History*.[4] The consequence of Mill's oscillation between the two paradigms, his failure to choose between or to synthesize the two, resulted in his failure to produce either a value or a political theory. His father, James, with but a fraction of his son's ability, managed to produce both—however limited we may think them—within the scope of an encyclopedia article. John Stuart Mill's ambivalent position is now common.[5] It is somehow thought a mark of tolerance to allow something to genetic human nature and something to culture in the attempt to account for human behavior and valuing. For accounting or descriptive purposes, it is not only tolerant, it is correct, to allow more than one cause here. But as has been argued already, if we want not to account for valuing but actually to value, the merging of bases results in a philosophic disaster.

We are at a time where every social science and serious study of politics is split right down the center on the question of whether the object of study is to be the laws of society or of human nature. Public discussions of important policy decisions reveal that a significant part of every educated group is both antagonized and mystified by the unspoken assumptions of the other part. The present confusions are to some extent ideologically fostered, to some extent are historical accidents, but no attempt to paper over the division has met with any success. The division is indeed unbridgeable; our contemporary house of the intellect cannot stand half culturalist and half human nature. It would be enormously helpful to us if we could arrive at a common understanding of the nature of humans and of society and of the relationship between the two. This does not imply that we will be brought to unanimity on particular issues—that is not the function of a value theory—but only that we can be brought to accept and speak a common language of value. Once we comprehend each other, agreement becomes a possibility.

CHAPTER 6

Reductionist Human Nature Theory

There are two kinds of human nature theory, one explained and defended in Part II, and another against which I argue in this chapter. The difference between the two was first set forth by James Harrington, a contemporary of Hobbes, who referred to the latter's reductive, aprioristic method as the "geometrical" and to his own empirical, traditional method as the "anatomical."[1] We turn now to consider the geometrical human nature theories, theories that reduce motivation to some single passion. Parts of this chapter are preliminary to the discussion in Part II.

Human Nature

The geometricians and the anatomists agree that the origin and basis of value judgments, as well as the proper approach to the study of the social sciences, are to be discovered by analysis of species-typical humans, of human nature. Before we begin the analysis of the reductionist human nature theory, we must ask: what is human nature? The phrase has been used in so many ways, has so many diverse associations and connotations, that I would, if it were practicable, abandon it altogether. Instead, I will explain the senses in which it is and is not used here.

In the broadest sense, the nature of any thing is simply the sum of all possible true statements that can be made about it. The broadest sense is of no use to us. We move to a narrower sense: we state the nature of a thing when we list all the characteristics without which it would not be what it is or, in a more practical way, the characteristics that we find interesting or important in understanding what to expect of it in general. Members of our species have existed in large numbers for a long time and in a great variety of circumstances. The only characteristics we all share are those anatomical and psychic structures that are the evolved product of our genes.

Parenthetically, it is interesting to note how often those who speak of our species have sought to find a special essence in it, some ennobling characteristic, as though it were somehow important to establish an objectively qualitative difference between our species and all the others. Why they should do so is a puzzle. It is as though they suffer from a sense of insecurity or status anxiety. Of course we are a unique species; every species is unique. The attempt, however, to establish one or more of our characteristics as somehow transcendently valuable is mistaken. Because there can be no species-transcendent values, the statement that one species is better than another can reflect only the feelings of the species of the evaluator. If we point to our high intelligence as a mark of our superiority, we can mean only either that having it gives us pleasure, a pleasure dependent upon our having certain species-typical feelings, or that it enables us to survive and to gain our ends, that it serves some interests of ours. Yet other species, as the ants, survive very well and in numbers greater than ours, and their prospects as a species in the millennia to come are probably better than ours. This does not mean that we are mistaken in our preference for intelligent species over less intelligent ones; it means that we should realize that our preferences can have no broader base than in our species feeling pattern. Intelligence is an instrumental good. Since species do not exist in order to serve some purpose, we cannot say that one species is better than another in any non-instrumental sense.

Human nature, then, is the sum of all the characteristics that all or most humans share. The reason for the "most" here should be evident. Biological discourse does not have the precise categories of physics. A six-fingered person who shares all our other human characteristics is still a member of our species. We cannot say, exactly, how much variation from the species average or norm is required before we cease to regard a creature as human, any more than we could ever locate, in our evolutionary history, the one person who was the first human. To have a human nature is not to conform to a single ideal type, but to be included in a normal curve of distribution, or rather in the overlap of a great many curves of distribution, superimposed upon each other.

Human Feeling Patterns

Human nature ethical theorists are interested, not in all human characteristics, but only in those that relate to value judgments. They are interested in motivation, that is to say in feelings, and so their study is of the human genetic feeling pattern. Because of the almost universal misunderstanding on this point, it is necessary to repeat it. Students of human nature are concerned with human feelings, *not* with human behavior. It is true that much of our knowledge of human feeling is necessarily based on observation of behavior, but behavior is a consequence of the interplay of genetic feeling and cultural or idiosyncratic knowledge or opinion and so is not simply or even mostly genetic.

Our feeling pattern, like our intelligence and binocular vision, is a fact about our species and from such facts no value distinction can be drawn between species. As we are not better than elephants because we are smarter, so we are not better because we have some feelings they do not have. Similarly, our species-typical feeling pattern, human nature, cannot be used as an absolute standard of value even within our own species. When we complain that some person has no feelings, or abnormal or "unnatural" feelings, we express a preference for those who share the feelings of most of us. Human feeling deviances cannot be considered bad in themselves, any more than can four-leaved clovers or very cold winters. Nevertheless, we do experience very cold winters as "bad winters," and so we may say they are bad in relation to our feelings. Similarly, if we keep this distinction in mind, we may speak of a bad human, a depraved or evil human, as long as we keep in mind that such language expresses feelings that typical humans in our position would have about a person who seems to have feelings that render his or her motivations inexplicable or threatening to us.

If we take the human feeling pattern to be firmly fixed and easily knowable, and if the relationships between particular feelings and the objects that arouse them are also fixed and knowable, then human nature theory should support a rather dogmatic and specific value system. If, on the other hand, we find human nature to be highly variable, scarcely knowable at all, or if there are no constant relationships between recurrent feelings and objects, then the value system we might base upon it would be so vague as to be worthless. The task of a human nature thinker is to show that the latter possibility is not true. He or she does not have to argue for the former. Any degree of knowledge we have about human nature, however slight, will furnish some support for a human nature moral and social theory.

Some knowledge is available. We should be much the same animal, with much the same feelings and problems, if we had four or six fingers, thicker fingernails, different skin color. We would be a very different animal if we were genetic solitaries, as panthers. A simple hypothetical experiment shows that it is our emotional characteristics that are the most significant in our perception of our own species being. Let our genetic characteristics be divided into those that are physical, intellectual, and affective. We are creatures of a certain configuration, we think and we feel, and in each of these categories we are as a species more or less genetically unique. Imagine yourself isolated on a desert island along with two other creatures, both with the rational capacity of a human and fluent in conversation. One of them has the physical appearance of a lion, but the feeling pattern of a human. The other has the physical appearance of a human, but the feeling pattern of a lion. Initially you would find the human-appearing creature, the more acceptable as a companion; soon you would discover that only with the lionlike creature, with the human feeling pattern, could you carry on the kind of conversation that is most important to you, conversation involving feelings, sentiment, value. The part of their nature that humans find more interesting in themselves and in their fellow humans is their common feeling pattern. We could discuss geometry and science with our intelligent lion in human form, but almost all of our poetry and art would be meaningless to it; it would puzzle over our intense concern for our children, our homesickness, our pair bonding and sociality. It would disdain us for our insensitivity to its feelings, of which indeed we can know little or nothing. It is our common feeling structure, not our intelligence or anatomy, that makes us, from our own view, truly human.

Human nature thinkers are concerned with the study of the feeling pattern typical of our species. Their value theories and their social and political understandings are based on their understanding of the normal range of human feelings, taken in conjunction with this or that set of empirical facts about the world and existing or possible social arrangements. Genetic studies of humans may focus either on what humans have in common or on the differences among them. Either study is legitimate, for humans are genetically both the same and different, as a glass of water may be considered either half empty or half full. Human nature theorists should be, in principle, less prone to racism or ethnocentrism, or to any of the other ways of setting us against each other, simply because the usefulness of their theory depends upon the degree to which they can convincingly argue that we are, in as many crucial respects as possible, all but identical with each other.

Human nature theory does not, in itself, determine what we shall value. It commences with the assertion of a common human feeling pattern on the basis of which, and taken in conjunction with relevant circumstances, we can understand why we behave and act in certain ways and value certain things. It goes on to constitute itself as a basis for value theory when it asserts that human feelings are prescriptive for human value and action. This latter point will be discussed in a later chapter.

Reductionist Human Nature Theory

Human nature theory is found, as was said, in two varieties: one we call the traditional, empirical, or non-reductive, the other, first appearing clearly in Hobbes and widespread since Bentham, the aprioristic, or reductive.

The clearest and most powerful statements of the reductionist human nature position, as well as the most severe attacks on the traditional thinkers, are to be found in Hobbes. Speaking of the latter, he said:

> The natural philosophy of these schools was rather a dream than science, and set forth in senseless and insignificant language, which cannot be avoided by those that will teach philosophy without first having attained great knowledge of

geometry . . . . Their moral philosophy is but a description of their own passions . . . . They make the rules of good and bad by their own liking and disliking.[2]

"Knowledge of geometry" involves a mastery of the principles of the reductive-compositive method. This method calls for the reduction, in thought, of a complex situation or object into its essential components and then, still in thought, its recomposition back into its original state according to known general principles. When we have completed the process, we have come to understand the original situation or object. It is in this way that we come to understand a clock, a geometrical figure, a solar system. In Hobbes's own lifetime, Galileo had used this method to discover the fundamental laws of motion; his way of doing so was aprioristic, deductive, and successful. It seems inevitable that someone would be inspired to apply the method to human affairs. Hobbes was that someone; he applied the method in the belief that he had achieved the kind of certainty that can be had in geometry and in Galilean physics. His argument is worth stating, for it best conveys the spirit of all reductionist human nature theory:

1. All things are matter in motion. Whatever is not matter in motion is not real.

2. Some things, organisms, are natural machines, constituted as homeostatic systems, so made as to resist dissolution. They behave *as though* they wanted to preserve themselves.

3. Of these natural machines, some, the higher animals, have the capacity to learn from experience, to acquire prudence. Their learning ability is completely in the service of the basic urge toward self-preservation.

4. Among the natural machines are humans. Humans have the additional ability to reason, that is, to make correct deductions from definitions. Like prudence, "reason is the scout of the passions."

5. The numerous passions are varied expressions of the underlying programming that impels all animals to seek survival. To say that we seek preservation and to say that we seek the satisfaction of our passions is to say the same thing. There can be no final satisfaction of the passions, no final good for us, for the satisfaction of one passion only makes room for the arousal of another, and then another, until we escape from them all in death. The survival at which the passions are directed is always the survival of the particular passionate individual, except in the very few cases where the individual's attachment to or identification with some other persons—"the bonds of natural lust"—is so great that he or she may jeopardize his or her own interests in their behalf.

6. Value judgments are expressions of personal interest or passion and have no other basis:

> But whatsoever is the object of any man's appetite or desire, this it is which he for his part calls good; and the object of his hate and aversion, evil; and of his contempt, vile and inconsiderable. For these words of good, evil, and contemptible are ever used with relation to the person that uses them, there being nothing simply or absolutely so.[3]

7. Hobbes is alone in concluding that the scarcity and insecurity of the means of survival, together with the egocentricity of humans and the perception by each of them of his or her effective equality of power, produces a state of universal war, which he calls the state of nature. Out of that awful condition there is no escape but in subjection to an absolute and arbitrary sovereign.

Hobbes claims to deduce concrete value judgments and a political philosophy from a theory of human nature that reduces all motivation to one, survival. None of his reductionist successors has produced as tight and philosophical an argument, but they have all followed the form he invented. Bentham rests his ethical and political theory on the assumption that humans are subject solely to the complementary urges of pain and pleasure. Adam Smith, speaking as an economist, understands us as thinking creatures driven to maximize our economic utilities and therefore necessarily a bartering and exchanging animal. He went on to make the psychological observation that anyone who does not maximize his investment opportunities must be "perfectly crazy," that is, not quite human.[4] In the same way, Hobbes characterized as mad those who commit suicide or who fail to maximize their survival opportunities. James Mill, in his *Essay on Government,* argued to a liberal and even democratic political conclusion from a judgment that our primary social characteristic is a desire to maximize our pleasure-gaining potentialities, principally by gaining power over others and thus over the product of their labor.[5] Our contemporary, B. F. Skinner, wrote a behaviorist's utopia, *Walden II,* which, except that it substitutes "positive and negative conditioning" for "pleasure and pain," is a novelistic version of Bentham's plan for a model prison system, the Panopticon.[6] David Truman has replied to the attack on the reductionist concept of the rational economic actor by attributing the felicific calculation of that mythical person to similarly competing interest groups.[7] In a manner reminiscent of Sumner and Karl Mannheim, Richard Rorty[8] has produced "antifoundationalism," a curious blend of fashionable culturalist deconstruction with reductionist human nature theory. Humans are said to have one overriding passion, the rage for recognition. All our science, politics, and art are the product of the "strong poets" among us who achieve recognition by imposing their personal metaphors upon us as truth.

Reductionist human nature theorists begin with the postulation of some "self-evident" single human motivation. They then move rapidly and easily to detailed and authoritative value conclusions. No wonder their no-nonsense, down-to-earth approach has enjoyed enthusiastic support from so many. Eight years after the

1651 publication of Hobbes's *Leviathan,* Harrington commented: "There is between the discourses of such as are commonly called Natural Philosophers and those of anatomists a large difference; the former are facile, the latter difficult."[9] Why take a difficult way if the facile way is available?

Objections to Human Nature Reductionism

Harrington's argument against the facile reductionist method is that it works only when the objects of study are simple, as clocks and solar systems are, when their elements and internal relations can be accurately distinguished and the principles involved are few and clear, as in Euclidean geometry; only then does the geometric system produce the best and most certain results. When things are not as simple, as in the matter of the circulation of the blood, then we must turn to the hypothetical-deductive, or "anatomical," method that Harrington ascribed to William Harvey, that he himself used in his political studies, and that in fact has proven more generally useful in science since his day. After patient consideration of the facts and relations in a field or situation, the hypothetical-deductive thinker moves to the proposal of explanatory hypotheses. From these hypotheses, factual conclusions are then deduced and these conclusions are then compared with the actual phenomena.

The reductive-compositive method works best in the study of the grand overriding uniformities of nature. It works less well in "open systems," systems that are subject to a great deal of outside interference, or that are relatively closed but where the number of independent variables is very large, or where the independent variables are few but their relative force at different moments and locations is highly variable or unknown. The reasons for thinking that the reductionist human nature method does not work well in the study of human affairs are so many that it is appropriate to number them:

1. Every reductionist human nature theory reduces human motivation to a single factor. That single factor has, by different writers, been called survival, utility, pleasure-pain, economic advantage, power, eros, and a number of other things. It is evident that no such single factor can ever be shown *not* to underlie all other motivations. We cannot show that Lincoln, Luther, Lenin, and Socrates did not essentially seek only pleasure, or only power, or only survival, in everything they did or thought. Fortunately we need not try. The very fact that we cannot say how reductionists *might* be empirically refuted itself refutes them. Their postulated single motivations are arbitrary definitions rather than statements about humans. As between two reductionist theories, there is no basis on which we can choose which single factor is to be preferred. I take this argument to be conclusive.

2. Reductionists cannot avoid this problem by admitting more than one motivational factor into their analysis of human nature. If there were two or more unrelated and independent motivations, then the theory would lose all or most of its usefulness, for it could not be determined which factor is operating, or how much, in any given instance. A well-known example is to be found in the James Mill–Thomas Macaulay controversy. Mill argues, persuasively, that all of us seek to acquire power over others and that no restraints but the penal laws can contain this urge. Macaulay points out, persuasively, that *many* of us prefer the good opinion of our fellows to gaining power over them.[10] Both opinions have some intuitive support, but Macaulay's more modest claim is the more credible. Mill has the choice of sticking to his principle in disregard of Macaulay's examples or of allowing some exceptions to it. But if he allows any exceptions, his elegant political argument breaks down, for it depends on the assumption that humans seek only power. Again, when John Stuart Mill attempted to save

both the appearances and Bentham's utilitarian theory by conceding that some pleasures are qualitatively different from others,[11] even so small a concession rendered impossible the felicific calculus that is necessary to make utilitarianism a working ethical theory. What made Bentham's theory interesting was his claim that pleasures are quantitatively comparable and that we can thus determine precisely and intersubjectively the better and the worse. Since J. S. Mill's possibly disingenuous emendation, utilitarianism has been able to find no method of establishing and comparing utilities except by tacit reliance on cultural consensus. When Freud proposed that at the deepest levels of the psyche a death instinct might be competing with eros,[12] he was vigorously opposed by the most orthodox of Freudians. They saw that psychoanalysis cannot claim clinical usefulness if it has to account both to eros and to thanatos, if there are two independent ultimate factors accounting for psychic phenomena.

3. Single-factor analysis is not consistent with what we know about the evolution of our own and other species. The lobster may look, to our imaginative eye, like a living pliers, the queen bee like an egg-laying machine, but despite such striking specializations each organism lives in and must cope with a wide variety of circumstances. Different species evolved in particular environments and evolved further in response to changes in those environments. Each of the evolved organs, physical and psychological traits, and feelings of a species comes into being in accommodation with the whole organism but yet in its own right, so to speak, in response to a particular environmental challenge. Each new structure of an organism evolves independently and even in some competition with other such structures for scarce resources. The red comb of a rooster is costly in terms of calories and protein; the comb must pay for these in some fashion and produce a net advantage for the whole organism. Particularly in the case of evolved species-specific feelings, we find them to be a collection

of independent motivations, each of which has proven its survival worth in some situations in which the species has commonly found itself in the course of its evolution. Retrospectively, we can now see that every, or practically every, characteristic of humans and other animals serves gene survival purposes. The feelings of humans and of the other higher animals came into being under the pressures of evolutionary selection, but they are presently experienced as simple imperatives. The feelings are experienced as what they are, not as passions for survival. If it is true that other higher animals have no feeling about survival at all in the possible absence of a notion of death, then we must consider our own alleged passion for survival as in fact an intellectualization of a complex of other feelings. Feelings are independent of each other. They are ultimate and autonomous motivations. The fact that they frequently conflict is what makes moral theory, however difficult, a practical necessity for us when we reflect on how we ought to lead our lives.

4. A mark of reductionist thinking is the common use of "drive" terminology. A drive is the reification of a motive. "Drives" have been driven from the study of comparative animal behavior and from biology in general; it is time we evicted them from human psychology. We observe people acting in a certain way that we learn to call "sexual behavior." Then we see someone acting in the way we have labeled "sexual" and account for that behavior in terms of a "sexual drive." Nowadays we laugh at those in the pre-scientific age who explained that opium puts people to sleep because it has a "dormative quality"—we can see that this is equivalent to saying that it puts people to sleep because it does—and we call "dormativeness" an "occult" word. "Drive" talk is occult talk. People experiencing passions do in fact feel driven by them, and so the genesis of the pseudo-explanation, but it is the particular feelings that urge them on, not a hypothetical drive. Drive terminology has led to such absurdities as the

"hydraulic" theory of the passions. Passions are thought to accumulate in us, like steam pressure in a boiler, and we are then driven to behave in ways that relieve the pressure. There is, in fact, such a phenomenon as "free-floating anxiety," which exists before the object about which to be anxious has been specified, and animals with instincts seem sometimes to accumulate a propensity to enact certain trains of behavior even in inappropriate circumstances. Nevertheless, it is evident that we do not accumulate feelings of curiosity, jealousy, ambition, and so forth, and then release them in order to achieve relief from their pressure. As our eye evolved to dilate in the dark, so our feelings evolved to occur in certain kinds of circumstances. There is no dilation drive in the eye or brain; our passions are not humming away within us like little motors awaiting the time when we will shift gears and connect them to our drive shaft.

Allied to the above elementary error is the one that reduces feelings to their physical correlates. Stomach acidity may be connected with irritability, and testosterone level with aggressive behavior, but they are not in either case the same. A feeling is what it is and not some other thing, as red is a certain perception and not a wave length of light.

In addition to the intellectual objections to reductionist human nature theory, there is another, so common that it ought to be reported. J. S. Mill said of his mentor, godfather, and friend, Bentham, that "his second [disqualification as a philosopher] was the incompleteness of his own mind as a representation of universal human nature. In many of the most natural and strongest feelings of human nature he had no sympathy."[13] From its beginnings in Hobbes and Bentham to the most recent of contemporary adherents, reductionism has aroused comments of this sort, ranging from those in Dickens's scathing *Hard Times* to the contemporary and often incoherently expressed outrage at B. F. Skinner's clumsy reduction of human motivation. It ought not be surprising that this school of human nature theory should appear to know less about human nature than any other, for it makes a virtue of its ignorance of people as they are. It attributes some single abstract drive to humans and then deduces what humans must want to do if they are ruled by that drive.

However little claim reductionists may have on our ultimate belief, however shallow and philistine they appear to most of us, it must yet be admitted that they do present to us a ready means to comprehensive and easily communicable ethical and political conclusions. A few recent writers, attracted to this appearance of systematic orderliness, have avoided some of the problems of single-factor reductionism by an equally arbitrary positing of several or many human motivations. Commonly they offer shopping lists of human needs and wants, beginning with food and water and ending with fulfillment of potentiality or a need for freedom or creativity. With no attempt to discover the deep structure of the human motivational pattern, they itemize as motivations or needs whatever occurs to them. Starting in this random way, they have no means of settling disputes among people with different shopping lists, no way of establishing motivational priorities, therefore no value or political theory.

Contemporary utilitarians have responded to some of the criticisms of Bentham's formulation, but in softening some of the starkness of his thought, they have also blunted its cutting edge. In his utilitarianism we had a fairly good idea of what pleasure and pain are and how they both do and ought to control us. In the newer versions, a medley of subjective or cultural values or rules are introduced and proclaimed to be self-evident. Yet although contemporary utilitarianism has lost the sharp cutting edge of its original, it continues to be a leading theory today. The reason for this is to be found, not in the coherence of the theory itself, but in the general ignorance of any alternative but that of culturalism.

Severely reductionist human nature thinking and scientism go hand in hand. Impatient people with well-compartmentalized minds take to them with enthusiasm. All we can say to them, until they learn to connect the separate parts of their consciousness, is that reductionist human nature theory rests on a tautology and so must be empirically irrelevant.

CHAPTER 7

What Is Culturalism?

We have before us two major and distinct alternative models of the relationship between the individual and her or his society. For one of these models the species-typical human is the elemental reality; culture is the product of the interplay of the passions of large numbers of individuals. The basic laws of society are the laws of human nature. The other model, here called "culturalism," reverses this understanding. Culturalism holds that social laws are more basic than the laws, if there are any, of human nature; society, the laws of society, determine the nature of the individuals who compose the community.

It may seem reasonable to look for some middle ground between these theoretical extremes. Can we, perhaps, assign separate territories to each kind of explanation, or factor both of them into our calculations? Does not commitment to one of them deprive us of the useful insights that the other offers?

For ordinary practical thought, and for much middle-range theory, the use of psychology and of sociology as complementary tools is quite acceptable. However, when we ask for the answer to an important value question, or when we try to do fundamental social theory, we find we must choose; the middle ground is not there to be found. Either model may illuminate the applications of the other, but they cannot divide their authority in final questions; we must decide then which is reducible to the other.

Culturalism as a value theory asserts that the only interesting or important bases for value judgments are to be found in the culture within which they originate. As a social theory it asserts the existence and force of social laws that are not reducible to the laws of human nature. The position is associated with cultural and anthropological functionalism, cultural relativism, current dominant sociological methods and modes of explanation, as well as with historicism, holism, and organicism. All educated people know, more or less, how profoundly culture affects our behavior and the contents of our consciousness. Culturalists are not those who more sensitively and frequently detect cultural influences; they are those who have made a principled decision that no other influences shall be taken into account in value or social theory.

It is difficult to find extended and serious defenses of culturalism; we find, usually, flat assertions of its truth accompanied by a few hurried words of justification. Since the British Hegelians and Josiah Royce, Anglo-American academic philosophy seems almost innocent of any knowledge of it. At least in America, culturalism comes to us from sociologists, anthropologists, and Marxists. As children, if we went to a good school, we got it from these sources as filtered through the minds of graduates of schools of education—which means that it is perhaps as much itself a cultural mood as a theory. Indeed, as culturalists have suggested that reductionist human nature theory is the ideology peculiar to the period of capital accumulation that ended early in this century, so it may be that culturalism is the general type of such current ideologies as monopoly capitalism, the welfare state, meritocracy, and socialism.

There are two principal varieties of culturalism. The first, associated with such writers as Burke, Durkheim, and Parsons, is primarily interested in cross-sectional or static analysis of societies at some definite point in their history.[1] The other, historicism, looks for laws of historical change and is associated principally with such writers as Hegel, Marx, and Spengler. Since few, if any, of the culturalist writers were also serious, consistent, and clear value theorists, we must reconstruct culturalist value theory from its foundations, assisted by a great mass of suggestive culturalist literature. I want to remind the reader, however, that this is a study of ideas, not of persons, that the names of writers are mentioned as an aid to the study of ideas and not for the purpose of explicating the writers themselves.

Before talking about the culturalist ideas, it is worthwhile to take a moment to consider the difference between the conflict in question and the old nature-nurture controversy. The debates are not the same; to the extent to which they are identified, both are distorted. The nature-nurture argument is about the determinants of behavior. "Behavior" is defined as the motion of an organism that can be described without the imputation to it of motive or understanding. The only interesting behavior that is clearly genetic in animals is reflexive or instinctual behavior. Because humans have no instincts (defined as genetically determined, relatively invariant, extended sequences of motion), and since our genetically determined reflexes or tropisms are not interesting to students of human value and society, the nature-nurture discussion about human behavior is at once settled in favor of the nurturists. We can, of course, revive the battle by using vague meanings of "behavior" and "instinct," but this tactic simply transfers the vagueness to our conclusions. The present discussion of human nature and culturalism is not a continuation of the nature-nurture controversy because it is not about human behavior but about human motivation.

We must decide whether human motivation is determined by human nature or by culture. Those engaged in the furtherance of knowledge about the external world do well to learn to suspend belief when confronted with two interesting theories. But although we can and should suspend belief, indefinitely if necessary, we cannot suspend action indefinitely. Value judgments, on the basis of which we act, cannot be suspended pending possible future developments in value theory. If we see the basis of value judgments as either in culture or in the species feeling pattern, we must choose which of the two shall be the basis of our value reasoning.

Culturalist Intuitions

We understand culturalism better as an ensemble of intuitions than as a reasoned argument. The wider our experience and education, and the longer and more seriously we reflect upon both, the more clearly do we come to realize how much and in how many ways culture has molded, modified, almost created, the content of our minds. Culture powerfully influences the way we structure experience, the kind of experience we have, or think we have, and our expectations of and assumptions about reality. As for values, as we see them variously embodied in words, institutions, and attitudes, it is easy to understand how they might be thought to be completely a cultural product. A list of typical value expressions is the signature, it identifies the culture from which it comes. When we see these expressions as functional for the society, changing in time to adapt to changes within it, as almost universally accepted within it and commonly rejected outside of it, we can also come to see values as totally a cultural product, as having no sense outside of their native context.

The roads to such insights are many. When we were very young, we began with the belief that the values and institutions of our narrow social environment were "natural"; that three strikes puts you out and that heavy things fall were seen as facts on the same footing. We soon came to learn that the rules of baseball are only conventions, and then had to learn the same truth about a great many other customs and usages. As we went on to study the language, history, art, and literature of other times and places we reached the point where we could fleetingly see our own society as others must see it, as if it were outlandish, foreign. At such moments we not only see it, we see through it; we understand that all values and opinions, with the possible exception of opinions in physics and mathematics, are conventional. Not everyone in our society goes through this process; it is an experience almost completely reserved to the educated. (This fact suggests a speculation: the poor communications and even hostility that exist between our educated and uneducated classes—the deepest division I see in modern society, and one that is not completely economic—may be accounted for if we see culturalism as the ideology of our new ruling class, and of aspirants to it.)

Each culture, and each historical period of each culture, seems to produce a special and unique state of consciousness, a different account of meaning and of value. We suffer some degree of disorientation, "culture shock," when we move, even in imagination, from one culture to another. Humans are most comfortable with themselves and with the things and people around them when they live in their society with the calm unconsciousness of the medium displayed by fish in water. Very quickly, when our major culture loses its power to orient us to the world and to each other, we move to establish or reinforce mini-cultures of order and value. A group of children at play, a shipwrecked crew, will establish a complex orderliness in their interactions; the group sprouts norms, procedures, definitions of reality. When two or more strangers meet, they meet under the conditions of an assumed common culture, they establish a minimum mutual culture, or they are at war.

Niko Tinbergen,[2] the student of sea gulls, expresses amazement at the contrast between the complexity and functionality of gull behavior and the pitifully small size of their brains. Instinct, he thought, enables these and many other animals to live far above their intellectual means. Similarly, observers of human life, from Aristotle onward, report on the striking disparity between the complex and subtle functionality of societies and the ignorant simplicity of the ordinary people who inhabit them. Most of us live beyond our intellectual means when we flick a light switch or brake a car; all of us do so when we live immersed in our culture's historical accumulation of norms and institutions. Even advanced specialists in these matters, sociologists and anthropologists, continually discover within themselves fresh instances of the cultural determination that it is their business to unmask and to dissolve through understanding. Culture is the human substitute for the guiding instincts our species has long since renounced. The formation of cultures has been called "pseudo-speciation," a term that implies two allied notions, the one that different societies are like different species in that they are unique adaptations to special circumstances and environments, the other that people of different cultures are as profoundly unlike each other as are members of different species. What instinctual animals, notably the social insects, accomplish by evolutionary adaptation, by modifying their very being, so to speak, we accomplish more quickly and precisely by the formation and modification of cultures. It is conjectured that we can do this so well because we have abandoned our "very being," our genetic human nature, or rather our nature is to be understood as consisting of what our own culture has made of us. That is, our pre-social "very being" is no more than our capacity to form culture in response to challenges of the environment; our socialized being is no more than is implied by membership in our particular culture.

Although the analogy of culture to instinct is important to the understanding of culturalism, culture is far more adaptive than instinct; it tells us what to do, and when, and how, with a completeness, subtlety, and flexibility that no set of instincts could match. Well-socialized humans carry on their lives with the confidence, the inner calm, displayed by animals under the control of instinct. Instinct, culture, ingrained habit—they are the automatic pilots that take over when what needs to be done by an animal or human is too trivial to hold its attention, too complicated for its understanding, too important to be left to its own judgment.

Everything about us urges us to the acceptance of social norms and customs. Other members of our group want us to act in ways that they can predict and trust and that do not conflict with their interests. We have the same concern with what they do and with their motives; the pressure is exerted in both directions. "They" outnumber each of us enormously; their influence over us, commencing at our birth, is overwhelming. Our families, friends, associates, these are the principal givers of pain and delight; we must court their approval. There is good reason to believe that we are ready for all this, that natural selection has rendered the young of our species not only able but eager to acquire a very complex socialization very quickly.

It is not enough to note that humans survive only as members of a culture. We must see that they do not become fully human in the first place unless they achieve considerable social integration. The accounts we give ourselves of the wonders of human intelligence are largely true, but in our species, intelligence is all but worthless as an individual possession. Its major use is to master language and the intricacies of mores and institutions. By the time intelligence is ready to be turned to the solution of an individual's problems it has already become more a social than an individual asset. Rousseau speaks of the "right" to society as a right that antecedes all other rights. He means that unless we are members of an integrative society we are not sufficiently human to have any of the other human rights. Studies of autistic children and of "wolf children" and the Harlow studies of young rhesus monkeys support the spirit of his thought.[3]

The intuitions that lead to the culturalist conclusion are a progressive revelation that comes most fully to those who have had protracted opportunities to learn and to think. Because of this long incubation period, we should expect to find, and do find, examples of halfway or vulgar culturalism among the young and the half-educated. Some of them, seizing upon the news that humans are the product of culture, therefore of convention, assume that in this realization they have at once transcended their own socialization. They then go on to speak for some passing conceit, some new cultural fad, as a self-evident and eternal truth. But as those who spoke, a decade ago, of "the end of ideology" are now routinely understood to have been enunciating an ideology of that era, so those who fail to see that the concept of ideology, of culturalism, is a two-edged sword are themselves naive ideologists. Vulgar culturalism is curable only by more culturalism; the truth of the culturalist insight deals with more profound matters than a taste for Coca Cola, a faith in General Motors, and reverence for the F.B.I. The counter-cultural movement of one decade is all too predictably seen in the next as merely another suit of clothes—this is no longer a metaphor—for the establishment. The intellectual experience of those who have transcended vulgar culturalism is that, every time a neutral realm of truth, a realm that escapes the relativism of the culturalist approach, is asserted or suggested, further experience and thought will show that it too is a cultural product.[4]

Culturalists understand thinking, or at least theory, as culture-bound, as an expression of the culture in which it occurs, as therefore having no claim to truth except within that culture. Their conclusion does not follow. There is no reason why the same idea or theory may not have both truth value and ideological use. For instance, all the important concepts of evolutionary theory were taken from classical liberal economics and population theory, and evolutionary theory was then used to buttress bourgeois social theory and practice—yet it seems also to be true. But culturalism is not like other ideas that can function comfortably both as ideology and as truth. It cannot stay its hand from the ruthless criticism of everything existing, including, finally, itself. Culturalism is not, to paraphrase a famous culturalist, a streetcar that can be boarded and left at our convenience. It is more like dynamite, a substance that is very likely to blow up those who use it. To continue with this sunburst of metaphors, each successive culturalist explains, explains away, every preceding alternative to his of her own chosen Archimedean standing place for the discussion of meaning and value, but culturalism is itself an intellectual doomsday machine, an approach that destroys all standing points including its own. If all ideas are to be considered culture-bound, then culturalists must understand the idea of culturalism itself as similarly culture-bound, must understand this understanding of that idea as culture-bound, and so on.

The best argument for the culturalist position is the evident inadequacy of reductionist human nature theory, its only perceived adversary. Culturalism offers us visions of meanings, of massive structures of meaning, that quite cast in the shade the precise but shallow views, the blinkered pedantic empiricism, of the reductionist human nature writers. Such visions, such poetry, go far beyond pedestrian rational and empirical analysis in illuminating, however fitfully, the meanings and potentialities of human life and history. The question we shall examine here is, not whether culturalist insights are valuable or not—they most certainly are—but whether they can function usefully as a basis for value judgments and for an intelligible social theory.

CHAPTER 8

Problems of Culturalism

The intellectual and practical difficulties of culturalist theory are such that it ought to be rejected as a basis for value judgments or as an ultimate basis for explanation in the social sciences. Three interesting claims of culturalist theory will be discussed in the context of the writings of three important culturalist thinkers. If the reader should disagree with my interpretation of what Burke, Sumner, or Durkheim thought, I am willing to substitute for them "Burke," "Sumner," and "Durkheim," characters I invent to maintain certain theses. The claims discussed are that culturalist theory can understand and prescribe for social change, that all values are cultural, and that there are non-reducible social laws.

Burke and the Problem of Social Change

The first and perhaps most lucid of those who have thought that culture is autonomous, that people are wholly plastic to the influence of their society, is Edmund Burke. Earlier writers on moral and political topics had recognized the importance of culture in the molding of human consciousness, yet all of them remained human nature thinkers. Burke was the first to break decisively with this tradition. He asserted that humans have two natures, an original species nature and an acquired social nature.[1] About that first nature, he said, we must remain forever ignorant; we cannot appeal to it in our social or political discussions. When we study humans we find no original nature, only the overlay of their social second nature. The concept of an original nature is useless. We ought, then, to turn to the study of what we can know, to the study of our acquired social nature. This is a possible study, for in everything we do or think we display the character imprinted on us by our society. Indeed, in studying socialized humans we are really studying the society that made them. If our actions and thoughts are to be intelligible to us, they can be so only to the extent to which our culture is intelligible. We ought to turn to the study of society, its rhythms, regularities, functionality, laws, habits, and formation. The final explanation of psychological characteristics is to be found in the culture in which they are discovered; the reverse procedure of former analysts must be discarded. Sociology must replace psychology as the queen of the social and policy sciences. Burke's dramatic conclusion is that, if people are shaped by their societies and if societies are as different from each other as they appear to be, then people of different societies, even of different classes within one society, are as different as are members of different animal species. There is no stronger way of expressing the culturalist principle.

I intend to discuss here only one facet of Burke's thesis, that which has to do with the evaluation of social change, with the ability of culturalists to become policy advocates. How can we, as culturalists, tell what social changes we ought to favor?

Burke has often been denigrated as a reactionary who looked back with longing to an idealized feudal past. Despite the element of truth in that charge, we are interested now mostly in his attempt to get around what seems to be an inherently reactionary tendency in all culturalist thought. Those small, isolated, and "less developed" societies with which anthropologists mostly deal usually find their best survival strategy in a clutching at any achievable equilibrium. For them, no news is good news; change means motorbikes, whiskey, alienation, and relegation to the servile fringes of other cultures. The anthropologists who study them, whatever their politics back home, quickly come to be tribal conservatives. If they cannot actually keep "their" tribes as pets or in a zoolike condition, they display solicitude for the maintenance of at least some of the old ways. Would we have them act differently? Culturalists who deal with advanced societies, however, have not hesitated to assert the desirability of social change. Their problem has been with the production of a normative basis for the transformation of cultural norms.

Burke recognized that "a state without the means of some change is without the means of its conservation." The examples he gives of times when change was necessary are the English Restoration and the later Glorious Revolution, when the English

> regenerated the deficient parts of the old constitutions through the parts which were not impaired.
>
> I would not exclude alteration, neither, but even when I changed, it should be to preserve. In what I did I should follow the example of our ancestors. I would make the reparations as nearly as possible in the style of the building.[2]

Michael Oakeshott, consciously following and extending Burke's thought, believes that political activity

> springs neither from instant desires, nor from general principles, but from the existing traditions of behavior themselves. And the form it takes, because it can have no other, is the amendment of existing arrangements by exploring and pursuing what is intimated in them.[3]

Durkheim, not directly influenced by Burke, nevertheless from his similar principles arrives at a similar understanding:

> New realities, not yet actualized, are as if foreshadowed in these conditions of the present. The future is already there for him who knows how to read it.[4]

"Intimationalism" is the name for this doctrine. Its followers argue: Change in a society neither ought nor can always be avoided. Both institutional and attitudinal changes are sometimes desirable. The desirable changes are to be advocated on the basis, not of rights or justice, but of the survival of the culture. As statesmen or responsible citizens, it is our task to contribute to the making of decisions as to what is to change and what is to stay the same. For instance, are we to abolish serfdom, hold the state responsible for unemployment, abolish capital punishment?

Such decisions involve the modification or even reversal of particular existing cultural values. Culturalists have ruled out doing this on the basis of such external standards of value as a possible genetic human feeling structure. The new values must come from the very body of cultural mores that they contradict.

The culturalists claim to solve this apparent paradox. They say that if we completely immerse ourselves in the traditions of our society, if we come to grasp that immanent spirit that unites all its multifarious nuances and apparently arbitrary facts, we will see how that spirit itself tells us how to deal with new circumstances, how to modify the parts while preserving the organic structure of our culture.[5]

Oakeshott deals with the question of whether equal political right ought to be granted to women. He finds in his society one tradition that assigns a greater degree of political responsibility, and therefore of right, to males, and another that insists on equality for all. Faced with the demand for equal rights for women, Oakeshott's statesman intuits that the tradition of equality is stronger or more basic than the tradition of male political monopoly, that the latter is, indeed, rooted in ephemeral economic and social circumstances. Oakeshott concludes (some decades after the fact) that women ought to be allowed to vote. The intimationalist oracle has been consulted and has spoken, not for any abstract rights of women, for culturalists cannot speak of rights except as legal or conventional, but for the practical political equality of women.

The merely incantatory character of the intimationalist solution is evident. The method will succeed, or at any rate gain acceptance, only on condition that the power to invoke and enforce the intimations is reserved to a small homogeneous elite who have the leisure and priestly qualities to have internalized the sacred cultural history and mores and the social prestige to overawe those with competing intimations. We might as well consult the stars or the entrails of birds. If we consult instead Livy's *History of Rome*, or Machiavelli's commentary on that history, we find that intimationalism and political hokum have a long historical association.[6]

Every culture contains within itself myriads of arbitrary social facts, fantasies, myths, and divergent moral and theoretical principles. A seasoned and successful culture will come to contain every imaginable principle, value, or fact in one form or another. The problem for intimationalism is the embarrassing plenty of possible intimations and the mutually contradictory character of most of them. There is simply no way of making a choice among them without a standard based outside them. Our own supposedly intimationalist Supreme Court is well known to have abandoned that method in favor of such external authorities as John Locke, Herbert Spencer, the ballot box, and current sociological textbooks.

Yes, there is such a thing as "national character," and the more sympathetically we understand the enduring moods, the ethos, of our society the more likely we are to produce sensible proposals for change that do not unnecessarily and dangerously tend to dissolve the implicit contract that makes us a people. Such proposals, however, are defensible on broad utilitarian grounds only. The claim that they are the product of a mysterious intimational process is merely obfuscatory. Burke is himself more sensible than is his theory. His practical alternative to natural right theory is not ancient prescription but present convenience.[7] Most commentators have noted that "convenience," as used in his writings, readily translates into "utility," a concept that can be defined only in the context of a theory of human nature.

The intimationalists are quite right in arguing that an adequate scientific understanding of society is simply not to be had. The path of the social engineers is littered with the skulls and bones of unintended consequences. Culturalists are right in reminding us that societies are subtly articulated structures of which we have little systematic understanding, that uncompromisable principles of right and justice are poor guides to public policy, that human nature theory is too general to be effective in the analysis of concrete political complexities. All this is negatively true, but none of it contributes to give us an inkling about how to identify and promote useful social change. Intimationalism does not work. It corresponds, as an illusion among culturalists, to the incoherence of "incrementalism" (the idea that we ought to eschew theory and simply solve each problem as it arises on the basis of obvious technical procedures) among recent reductionist human nature thinkers.

There is another route, quite different, that some culturalists may take to the solution of the problem of social change, but it is available only to historicists and so will be considered in the next chapter.

Sumner and Cultural Relativism

A popular variety of culturalism is best represented in the writings of the anthropologist William Graham Sumner. His analysis begins with a consideration of hypothetical early humans:

> Pleasure and pain . . . were the rude constraints which defined the line on which efforts were to proceed. The ability

to distinguish between pleasure and pain is the only psychical power which is to be assumed.[8]

It is important to our understanding of all varieties of culturalism that we note the extreme reduction with which Sumner begins. Seeking pleasure and avoiding pain, the earliest humans survive by forming habits that are useful to those ends. People join with other people in societies in which individual useful habits become social habits, customs, folkways. Succeeding generations know and adhere to the folkways, not as a result of their own experience of pleasure and pain, but as a consequence of their socialization. The folkways become the value authority and completely supersede the original "external" criteria of pleasure and pain. The imagined first generation might discuss among themselves whether something is to be called good or bad, on the basis of utilitarian criteria, but succeeding generations can only discuss whether or not that something is customarily called good or bad. (Sumner does not consider whether socialization itself is possible without negative and positive reinforcement.) The very meaning of "good" and "bad" is for them what society, the folkways, says is so. As Sumner puts it:

> The word "moral" means what belongs to or appertains to the mores.[9]

> Philosophy and ethics are products of the folkways. They . . . are never original and creative; they are secondary and derived.[10]

> There is no permanent or universal standard by which right and truth in regard to these matters can be established and different folkways compared and criticized.
> Every attempt to win an outside viewpoint, from which to reduce the whole to an absolute philosophy of truth and right, based on an inalterable principle, is a delusion.[11]

This is the culturalist position on the status of values. They are entirely cultural products. Sumner is aware of some of the problems that may arise. In time,

> the mores then lose their naturalness and vitality. They are stereotyped. They lose all relation to expediency. They become an end in themselves. They are imposed by imperative authority without regard to interests or conditions.[12]

Finally,

> the goodness or badness of mores consists entirely in their adjustment to the life conditions and the interests of the time and place.[13]

What are we to make of this?

First, the radical reduction of human nature with which Sumner begins is necessary to any culturalist theory. It is to be found in all the writers. How else can they make room for the action of society on people if people are not first previously assumed to be almost totally plastic to such action,[14] if human nature is not held to be free of any resistant elements that might significantly constrain, modify, or supersede the action of culture on the individual? Sumner seems more reductionist than Bentham, for although both hold that the ability to distinguish between pleasure and pain is "the only psychical power which is to be assumed," Sumner restricts the psychical power to ancestors who have only a hypothetical existence; if their successors can distinguish between pain and pleasure that ability can no longer guide their actions or thoughts; it becomes quite useless. For Bentham and the utilitarians in general, on the contrary, people continue to experience pain and pleasure up to the present day and use that experience as a basis for making transcultural criticisms of existing mores. Bentham is well, and sometimes angrily, aware of the influence of habit or culture over attitudes and behavior. His plea is that we escape from such foolishness and judge everything in terms of its consequences for our experience of pain and pleasure. But the continuing ability to make value judgments on the basis of pain and pleasure constitutes an "outside viewpoint," a "permanent and universal standard," and Sumner and all culturalists must deny this capacity if they are to maintain their thesis. Sumner is well aware that, if he wavers on this point, his position collapses into utilitarianism, and so he states and restates his denial of "outside forces" with the firmness and clarity required to make his position interestingly distinct. We ought not write Sumner off as a crude forerunner of a later, more sophisticated culturalist theory. He gives us one of the very few thoughtful statements of that theory.

Second, Sumner says that the mores of a culture cannot be criticized. They cannot be criticized from within the society because they are themselves the only bases for value criticisms. There is, he says, no external or objective basis for discussing them. Neither can they be judged according to the standards of other cultures, for the standards of each culture apply only to itself. It is a mistake, he thinks, to discuss such questions as "ought the dead be burned or buried?" as though there were some answer true for all humans. The correct formulation is: "The Persians ought to bury their dead and the Greeks ought to burn them, each society guided by its own customs." The internal problems of this formulation are evident. Suppose that my culture condemns certain actions as evil or disgusting; what am I to think when I see aliens performing those actions? From Sumner's doctrine it follows that I ought not condemn them, for the values of my culture do not apply to theirs. It also follows that I ought to condemn them, for the values of my own culture are by definition imperative upon me; not to condemn alien practices would be immoral. Various uses are made of this curious ambiguity. Cultural relativism has been used to shield the newly discovered primitive or less developed cultures from the arrogant cultural and other imperialisms of Western societies. Exotic customs and values are held to be as good as those of the more familiar societies. Sometimes this equality is argued for on the basis of functionalist or utilitarian considerations, but the culturalist position is bound in principle to argue only from the cultural relativity of all usages of "good." At home in the advanced societies, however, quite a different tack is usually taken. Once we see that all values are equally valid, equally merely conventional, we see that none has any authority over the liberated mind. Cultural relativism simultaneously asserts the truth and the falsity of all possible cultural values, while it denies the possibility of any other kind of basis. We cannot take such confusion of thought as constituting a seriously intended ethical theory. This is not, by the way, to say that primitive cultures ought to be subjected to the criticism of current mores of the technologically advanced societies, nor that the conventions of the advanced are superior. It is not the value judgments of cultural relativists that are attacked here, but their mistaken way of justifying them.

Third, anthropological or sociological culturalism sometimes calls itself "functionalism," and goes on to justify social mores on the grounds of their functionality. Sumner describes the mores of the hypothetical first humans as functional for them, functionally producing pleasure and averting pain. "Functional" here means "good for"; and the "good" in "good for" is a value term. Either functionalists intend this "good" as defined by each culture, with the presumption that it will be defined differently by each culture, or they mean it in some transcultural or objective sense. From the first definition it follows that the meaning of "functional" will have to be different in each society and therefore not usable by one society to describe another. It also follows that to say that a value is functional for a society is pointless; all that can be meant is that, say, the Thais call modesty a good and that they think that it is good that they call modesty a good. The question of whether it is indeed a good, a culturally transcendent good, or functional even for them, is now seen as vacuous. If "functional" is taken to have some transcultural or objective sense, then the culturalists have found a value that is not culturally relative and so have denied their own major thesis. Their tactic against this sensed problem is to accept an external standard and then to minimize it. A common such minimum standard is "survival"; we admit a very little human nature into our calculations when we allow that everyone seeks to go on living. However, if by survival is meant mere life and breath, unqualified, then very few customs are going to be found to be strikingly functional. Humans can survive and even increase their numbers under what all agree are the most appalling conditions. It is not at all unlikely, in fact, that survival, implying increase in population, may in modern days be incompatible with happiness. If we say that all existing societies are functional, as proven by their mere existence, then we do not mean much by "functional." If survival and functionality are meant to imply more than brain waves and cell division, we want very much to know how much "more" is meant, how that "more" is arrived at and also how, once all that has been explained, the resulting coherent theory differs from human nature theory. The culturalists have profound insights into the actual complex functionality of cultures, but they are mistaken in thinking that these insights contribute to the coherence of their value relativist thesis. The very notion of functionality is subversive of that thesis.

Fourth, Sumner and many other culturalists present us with a choice between absolute moralities based on "unalterable principles" and their own value relativism. It is a false choice, grounded on ignorance of alternative value theories, very few of which assert the existence of absolute standards or inalterable principles. Ethical theorists tell us how to go about determining what sort of thing is better to do, what sort of life is better to live. Culturalists have written, not in the context of a knowledge of actual value theory, but as products of their own society, in which morality is popularly associated with the rigid and absolute demands of the superego or of some of the more old-fashioned established religions. Anthropological culturalism stands convicted of cultural blindness, of not engaging in self-examination or self-criticism.

Fifth, the reader has probably noticed, in the passages from Sumner's writings here cited, that he rather casually blows up his own thesis. The very mores that he says cannot be criticized from an external standard, he criticizes from an external standard. He criticizes them from the standpoint of "expediency," "naturalness," "vitality," "interests," "conditions," "rational considerations," and "adjustments to the life conditions of the time and place." Except for the mysterious "naturalness" and "vitality," all these terms are translatable only into terms taken from the vocabulary of the human nature writers. Sumner does not inadvertently betray his own theory; the contradictions are inseparable from it.

Finally, the intuitions upon which cultural relativism depend are not false, and having them does credit to the sensibilities of those who use them. Many people do in fact often act as though the social norms they have internalized are not affected by their actual experience of the world. We see this most clearly in the phenomenon of cultural lag in our own and other societies that undergo rapid social change. Who is so imperceptive as not to have noticed it in her or himself? Particularly in stable and "primitive" societies we find those who seem like sleepwalkers in life: their all but total subjection to the traditions of their society could lead us to find some truth in Sumner's description of all people. Yet a description of how some people acquire their values and live by them does nothing to tell us what the nature of value is, does nothing to illuminate our own consideration of how we shall live. When we know that some man defends his village because tradition demands that he do so, we may yet inquire under what circumstances it is or is not a good idea for him to defend that village.

Durkheim: Social Laws and Organic Theory

If the culturalists are right, then our proper study is society. When we study society, as when we study anything, we look for lawlike regularities. We look for irreducible social laws. Can we find them?

Gresham's Law, that bad money drives out good, seems to be a social law, for its consequence is not intended by anyone. The law states that if two coins of equal face value, but of different intrinsic value (silver dimes and silver-faced dimes), are circulated, the coins made of the more valuable metal will tend to disappear from circulation. Gresham's Law seems to hold for many societies, perhaps for all in which coins are used. Yet it is not an irreducible social law, because the explanation of its truth is derived, not from an understanding of society, but from an understanding of psychology. What makes it true, if it is true, is not something about society but something about typical humans—possibly their tendency to maximize what they see as an advantage. In the case of such a law as this, the repeated and extensive, not necessarily unanimous, activation of a typically human psychological tendency produces a general effect not intended by any one person and possibly—as when someone shouts "fire!" in a crowded hall—opposed by all. Certainly, at least some uniformities that are called social laws are reducible to psychological laws.

Suppose the generalization "elites tend to be taller than nonelites" to be true. We might understand this fact to be the consequence of elite control over resources, with the result that they eat better and so are taller. Other laws are involved here, as for instance that eating more or better food makes people taller, that people eat better or more food when they can, that societies do not produce enough or good enough food at an affordable price so that everyone can be tall, that elites will take more than their share of a scarce resource when they can, and so on. These laws are psychological, agricultural, economic, biological, but not social in the culturalist sense. There may be yet other reasons for the greater height of elites. If humans value height in their leaders, we would expect elites to be taller. This gives us at least three psychological and two biological explanations: parents feed their children as well as they can; elites favor the co-optation of their own children into elite status; populations prefer tall leaders; good food promotes height; height is hereditary. We do not need a social law to explain the alleged greater height of elites.

If such instances seem trivial, we may go on to consider such supposed social laws as that "in mature capitalist societies, the rate of profit tends to decline," "the condition of the life of proletarians is such as to produce in them a common consciousness of their class interests," "societies dependent upon irrigation tend toward political despotism." All three apparent social laws are rather easily reduced to statements about species-typical feeling propensities in humans. The proposition about the rate of profit, a product of the school of classical economics, is arrived at by considering the probable outcome of the interaction of rational interest-maximizers in the marketplace over a long period of time. If the proletariat are defined as a group of people whose condition of life is very much the same, who are in constant interaction with each other, and who are being treated badly by some other group, then it is psychologically probable that they will arrive at a consciousness of their common class interests. The conclusion is a classic case of the human nature approach. If people have a common feeling pattern and a common perception of the facts, they will come to similar value conclusions. Large-scale irrigation, such as was necessary to maintain the populations of ancient Mesopotamia and other ancient river societies, requires central control for the maintenance of the system and for allocation of water. Those who have that control can be expected to exploit it for political purposes; those who are subject to that control, whose economic life is completely in the hands of others, will necessarily be politically subject to those others. The reasoning depends completely on a knowledge of some facts about nature and about human feelings. There is no "social law" that is not completely reducible to non-social laws, and without loss. Of course some of the reductions suggested may be mistaken, but it is equally true that some of the so-called social laws may also be mistaken.

There are no social laws. Laws that are commonly referred to as social are reducible to generalizations about the probable resultant of the actions of large numbers of humans who are presumed to have similar feelings in similar situations. The question of the existence of social laws has been debated for some years in various philosophical journals. The debate (called the "MI," or methodological individualism controversy) is between culturalists and (mostly reductionist) human nature thinkers.[15] As of now, the culturalists have been unable to produce a single clear example of a non-reducible social law. That the methodological individualists may also be mistaken, on quite other grounds, is another story.

Whether we think there are social laws or not depends not on our study of facts but on our idea of what we think a society is. Reductionists believe that society is nothing but a collection of individuals, individuals who are to be understood in terms of one principal motivational factor. Their idea of society is modeled on the theory of enclosed gases. We understand gases—their expansion and contraction, the way they shape elastic containers—in terms of the average velocity and frequency of collision of the individual gas molecules. Hobbes's model of society, Ricardo's model of the marketplace, Malthus's model of the interaction of arithmetically increasing food supplies and geometrically increasing populations, are such reductions. It is not difficult to sympathize with the culturalists' disdain for classical economics, utilitarianism, and other shallow analogies of human society with enclosed gases. If we insist on thinking of society using this model, we ought to think of a gas in which the molecules are of different and varying size, speed, and weight, in which they form bonds of affection and loyalty, in which they combine in religions, nations, and interests, in which memories of the past and anticipations of the future influence present behavior, and in which those memories and anticipations are somewhat different for each molecule, and so on. Society is not very much like an enclosed gas. What is it really like? Culturalists believe it is a system, a lawlike system, a system that cannot be adequately understood simply as the sum of the interactions of its component parts.

What would have to be true if social laws were not reducible to other laws? Society itself would have to be a system that is not so reducible. We have few models of such a system. It does not help much to think of society as a crystal or a field, and whether it can be thought of as a natural cybernetic system or system of internal relations, in which every part is defined in terms of its relation to the other parts and to the whole, may not matter, since these can be understood to be varieties of the two familiar models, a mechanism and an organism. Metaphysically, it can be argued that there is no such thing as an organism, that all such entities are in principle reducible to the laws of masses in motion. Metaphysically, it can be argued that everything is an organism, and that every part of that everything is in turn an organism. All that concerns us here, fortunately, is what model of society is necessary for the culturalist hypothesis. It is tempting to consider whether societies ought to be considered on no analogy at all, but simply as what they are, a unique kind of thing. The trouble with this verbal solution is that we do not know how to understand unique things. If society is a unique thing, then we must admit that we do not know anything about it as a system. A social philosopher who admits this possibility ceases to be a social philosopher.

The only way of understanding the culturalist thesis is to assume that the organic analogy tacitly underlies it.[16] If some culturalists deny their organicism, they have not let us know what other model they assume.

We say that organisms are more than the sum of their parts, as a human is more than the sum of his or her cells, and that the parts themselves are constituted to be what they are in virtue of their membership in the whole—as in Aristotle's remark that the hand severed from the body is not, strictly speaking, a hand at all but a lump of hand-shaped flesh.[17] It has been suggested that the whole idea of an organism as different from an extraordinarily complex mechanism is nothing but the result of the combination of human ignorance with human imagination and modes of perception. However that may be, the practical necessity of the idea of an organism is indisputable. The question is whether we can usefully think of society as an organism, and whether we must think of society as an organism to explain what we observe in human behavior. It is true that the parts of societies, individual humans, are not in continuous contact with each other, but some zoologists have suggested that we best understand colonies of social insects, as ants and bees, if we consider them as a single animal, despite the physical separation between their members. We can imagine human societies as such dispersed organisms. Language and gesture would perform for humans the functions that scents and postures perform in organic societies of social insects. Whether a society is an organism or not, it is certainly imaginable as such. The crucial question is what we can do with this metaphor once we have coined it. F. H. Bradley said that

> what we call an individual man is what he is because of and by virtue of community, and that communities are thus not mere names but something real. . . . The "individual" man . . . is, we say, a fiction. . . . The "individual" apart from the community is an abstraction. . . . Man is a social being, he is real only because he is social.[18]

As society is seen as more real, more autonomously a system, as in charge, so to speak, the individual is necessarily seen as unreal, ghostly, passive.[19] It is all very well for the culturalists to speak of others, "the masses," "the bourgeoisie," "the natives," as social robots, but what do they have in mind when they think of what they themselves are doing and thinking, when they speak directly to us and say that they and we are puppets of our time and place, confined to the thoughts and passions assigned to us by our society, creatures who are to be understood, who must understand ourselves, not as actually having ideas that might or might not be true, but as having only those ideas that are appropriate to our time and place? How does culturalism rescue itself, its own enunciations, from the universal relativity? What does it mean to give reasons for believing in culturalism, as opposed to indicating its cultural appropriateness, as well as the cultural appropriateness of so indicating?

If society is an organism, then there should be social laws, and if there are social laws, then society must be an organism. Durkheim is recommended by culturalists as presenting the classic extended argument for the existence of social laws. That argument is most completely represented in his book *Suicide*.[20] His choice of the topic was deliberate. Of all the actions of humans, suicide might well be thought the most utterly private and psychological, the least likely to be subject to social law. But

Durkheim found that suicide does not occur at random in a population. Suicides are more likely to be Protestant than Catholic, urban than rural, single or widowed than married, widowers than widows, persons who have experienced rapid social mobility than those whose style of life has remained unchanged, and so on. He discovered also that all these risk factors are not a mere miscellany. They have one common trait, that of association with a lesser degree of social integration, of what he called "solidarity." Failure to achieve membership in a stable and closely knit supportive and orienting group, failure to be deeply involved in shared cares and responsibilities, predisposes a person toward self-destruction. The argument, carried on over hundreds of pages and replete with statistics, is most impressive and I do not propose to quarrel with any part of it but its conclusion. A better demonstration of the existence and power of culturalist nonreducible social laws has not been made. Readers learn to discard their naive images of potential suicides, pondering whether to be or not to be, and instead see them as passive victims of vast social forces that direct their energies against themselves.

It is important to see that the culturalist emperor has no clothes. Durkheim makes no case for the existence of nonreducible social laws. The actual thrust of his mass of evidence and argument is that human nature is such that humans require a great deal of social integration if they are not to suffer psychological trauma. That is, his work has a psychological rather than a sociological conclusion. It shows just the opposite of what he set out to prove. Studies of whole subcultures that have drifted into anomie, even studies of rhesus monkeys, come to conclusions similar to those of Durkheim, and, particularly in the case of the monkeys, there is no possibility of the involvement of social laws. Social life is necessary to our psychic integration; without it we disintegrate; life may not be worth living. Durkheim's law of suicide and Gresham's law of specie circulation are on the same footing; they are both the product of statistical analysis of events that are the consequence of species-normal human emotions.

We may note in passing a tension between the culturalism of Durkheim and that of Sumner. Sumner's attention is on the differences, the conceptual and value gulfs that divide one society from another. From him we would expect different social laws for different societies. Durkheim, on the other hand, tends to assimilate societies to each other for the facilitation of the discovery of social laws that are common to all of them. The contrast is only interesting to us here insofar as it raises questions such as: if society forms people, can it form them so as not to need social solidarity, to care nothing for sex, affection, children, friendship, and so on? If it can, then Durkheim is wrong. If it cannot, then culturalism is wrong.

The most serious charge against culturalism is that it cannot support a value judgment or a political program. Some culturalists readily concede the point and in fact assert that, although all values have a cultural origin, they have in fact no prescriptive force except for those who happen to accept them. This form of culturalism is almost identical with value skepticism. Nevertheless most historicists and some culturalists deny that they are value skeptics. The argument of the historicists will be discussed in the next chapter. Here we will consider Durkheim's denial.

Durkheim argues that humans ought to seek social solidarity, total immersion in the network of social mores, values, views, of their society, because it is their major defense against misery and self-inflicted death. Social morality enforces itself, not merely through penal laws and public opinion, not only through the pangs of socially induced conscience or superego, guilt, and shame, but also through the sanction of the statistical incidence of suicide and the lesser but terrible pains of those who almost, but not quite, commit suicide. The pressures on us to conform are considerable. There is another kind of motive, love. I might well feel affection for and loyalty to a society that had made me a fully developed person, that had been both father and mother to me. Socrates argues this point very well where he opts for obedience to the laws of Athens even at the cost of his own life.

Durkheim's argument does not work. Socrates, for instance, argued for obedience to the laws of Athens, but not for acceptance of Athenian values.[21] His argument is not culturalist, but from human nature, as Hume recognized when he said that Socrates arrived at a Tory conclusion by means of Whig arguments.[22] Durkheim's argument depends upon a highly developed notion of human nature, of innate human motivations. Society calls upon those motivations; it does not create them and it cannot operate in disregard of them. Durkheim finds a value standard in the concept of "health."[23] The same problem arises here as in the case of "functionalism." If health is culturally defined, then there is no standard; if it is not, then a human nature basis has been introduced. The culturalists commonly try to finesse this issue; when "survival" is seen to be too incomplete a description of what society offers they substitute some term, "functionality," "health," or "fulfillment of potentiality," that more satisfactorily meets our objection to the severe reduction of human motivation that "survival" implies. Yet when we examine the less objectionable words and phrases offered, we find that a whole human nature theory has been smuggled into them. The culturalists who argue that neurosis and psychosis, and therefore health and social solidarity, are culturally defined must needs be value nihilists, although none of them that I know has sufficiently transcended her or his own cultural conditioning to realize this fact.

Conclusions

At one time Greeks burned their dead, while Persians buried them. When each learned of the practices of the other, they were properly shocked—but then all foreigners are immoral. When, as a consequence of talking to Sophists, each became more sophisticated, both understood that there is no intrinsically proper way to dispose of dead humans; there are only culturally approved ways. See the first generation of liberated Greeks and Persians beaming tolerantly at each other's quaint local customs. See those smiles fade as a second-generation entrepreneur suggests that, since it makes no difference, why not turn an honest drachma by converting inoperative parents into catfood? A courageous functionalist, unable to find this detrimental to survival or health, conceding that it makes for efficiency, that is, functionality, will be forced to agree. There are reasons based in human nature, I shall argue, for not making so practical a use of our dead, for not accepting Swift's modest proposal, for not favoring universal sexual promiscuity. Those reasons are not stateable in culturalist terms, for they rely on complex human feelings that may be reinforced or repressed by culture but that cannot be eradicated without insupportable loss.[24]

It is a curious illustration of the power of culture over intelligence, of the divorce of theory from practice, that twentieth-century culturalists—how many of them seek social solidarity through voluntary bondage to convention?—whom we might expect, on the basis of their principles, to be the most abandoned of persons, have instead been in general models of personal rectitude and of social idealism. The power of ideas, even over the most activist of intellectuals, has been much exaggerated. It is probably true, as they say, that "no girl has ever been ruined by a book." that if you bring up children "well," you can trust to their "instincts" (socially specified) to rescue them from the consequences of their liberation from formal restraint. On the other hand, the intensifying war between the uneducated, conservative, non-culturalist masses and the liberal culturalist meritocracy may have roots in the confused perception of the former group that culturalist rhetoric and the increasing disorder of their own social and moral lives are connected.

Hume distinguished between social and personal morality. Personal morality is the set of rules we make for ourselves in the process of thinking about how to live our lives in accordance with our species-typical passions; it is justified by how well it works to that end. Social morality, he thought, is justified by its contribution to the general welfare, a welfare in which we have an interest both as members of society and as a result of our natural sympathy with other humans. It follows that social morality is ultimately a product of personal morality and is subject to criticism from the standpoint of species-general feelings. The culturalists agree with Hume that social morality is ultimately justifiable only in terms of the general welfare, what they call functionality, although they have left themselves no usable basis on which to define what functionality is. For them, personal morality is nothing but internalized social morality and it therefore cannot serve as a basis for the criticism of social morality.

A practical paradox follows from this view of theirs. The original culturalist philosophers, mature, at least moderately well-to-do, and deeply socialized into the general value outlook of their society, could hold the intellectual belief that all values are expressions of cultural utility and never imagine that this belief had any relevance to their own deeper personal or social values. With the influx into a diluted higher education of such great numbers of our young people, however, the awareness that values are merely socially functional has had an explosive effect. Social values so understood lose all imperative quality. For the great majority of weakly socialized young people, obedience to any moral rules at all becomes a question of personal choice, that is, of immediate passionate interest. The sacrifice of some immediate passionate interests that every society must ask of its members no longer seems tolerable, especially since those sacrifices, given the differentiation of the population into various ages, sexes, and capacities, cannot be assessed equally. The evolved complex pattern of feelings that in human nature theory makes the practice of social altruism a sensible procedure for us can have no place in the reduced culturalist model of human nature. Passionate young people conclude from culturalist theory that social morality is a fraud perpetrated upon them, and further that there is no other kind of morality. Culturalism liberates people from the chains of convention and offers them no alternative guide to action. Unquestionably, the revelation that mores are merely functional is liberating: it liberates us from all control but that of the penal laws and whatever power of public opinion survives in contemporary cities. Yet, as Burke put it, before we congratulate a man on his newly acquired freedom, we ought to have some idea of what he will do with it. According to culturalist theory itself, a person or a society liberated from morality is not at all enviable.

Culturalists cannot make the slightest contribution to the making of a value decision, cannot advise even themselves on how to live their lives. If they advise on the basis of their ultimate pleasure-pain principle, they are taking Bentham's utilitarian position, which they have rejected. If they attempt to speak of humans as more complexly motiviated than Bentham allowed, they land in the non-reductionist human nature position. If they conclude that we ought to follow the laws and customs of our society, we must remind them that they have themselves discredited them.

Culturalists will not lightly abandon what they believe to be the conclusions of hard-won intuitions about social and political reality. Particularly will they not do so if they believe that the alternative to their view is some contemporary version of reductionist human nature theory, a theory that they rightly believe to be shallow. If we would persuade them, we must show that reductionism is not the only alternative to culturalism, that culturalist intuitions can be quite true and yet not involve the culturalist conclusion, that it is culturalism that is outmoded, a barrier to social and political change, an inadequate support for the value judgments that they too want, need, and are entitled to make.

Not all of this can be done here. It is easy to point out that the culturalist thesis does not follow from culturalist intuitions, simply because no thesis follows from a perception. Those who see the stick projecting from the water as bent indeed see it that way. We ought not try to persuade them that they do not see the stick as bent, only that it is actually not bent. Culturalists have a complex of visions, models of the relation of humans to the society in which they live, of the way in which the mutual relations of humans constitute the society, of how in turn the society constitutes the meaning of those relations, and of how this or that fully developed human consciousness cannot be understood to exist but in the context of this or that culture. They see how the history of past human relations in the context of special physical environments comes to create an ethic, a consciousness, indeed a unique living language, and how all this, for most people, most of the time, is a kind of deterministic network. Only shallow and uneducated persons fail to see, at least on occasion, the people around them, and sometimes even themselves, as marionettes, ventriloquists' dummies, mindlessly gesticulating and chattering in the hall of mirrors that is their society. So powerfully suggestive are these visions that culturalists cannot bring themselves to believe that anyone who disagrees with their theoretical conclusions can have shared their insights. They have some basis for this opinion, for their principal opponents have been the sect of reductionist human nature thinkers, a group noted from their beginning for their lack of imagination, for the tunnel vision of those armed with a self-evident simple truth. We ought to accept the culturalist visions; we should be the poorer without them.

What is opposed here is the dogmatic, useless, and socially dangerous conclusion that is mistakenly derived from those insights. Culture is not autonomous; it is a human product. We must produce and maintain a culture if we are to survive as humans. We are biologically programmed to live in some culture. Culture is not, however, ultimately our maker. Humans make culture and each culture must answer moment by moment and age by age to the complex demands of the passionate creatures who made it and live in it.

It can fairly be said that for a good part of this century the culturalists have carried the torch of progress and enlightenment. Not to be one of them seemed to be to identify oneself as of dubious moral sensitivity, intelligence, or education. But, in recent years, they have been plagued by the weakness peculiar to those philosophies that are merely critical; finally the game of seizing upon the contradictory strands of conventional thought is played out and someone asks, "What *is* true? What *is* to be done?" The popular wing of culturalism tirelessly plays at pop sociology, invents new variations on the theme of "The Man in the Grey Flannel Suit" and Chaplin's "Modern Times." The esoteric wing, excruciatingly profound, loses itself and all possible readers in a bottomless pit of unintelligible jargon. Between these eccentrics there is no body of sober culturalists to speak to us reasonably about understandings or programs that might be of use to our society or to us.

The culturalist and human nature views are curiously asymmetrical. Culturalists cannot admit that any significant part of what we are follows from our species membership; they see that any such admission would endanger their whole position. The human nature writers, on the other hand, can concede everything to the culturalists but their ultimate conclusion. The former need not, for instance, claim that even one item of human *behavior* is genetically determined. All they need do is argue that cultures can direct but not create emotions, that only emotions, feelings, can constitute a motivation, that culture is a product of human feelings, utilizing human intelligence and knowledge in the given circumstances. It is this asymmetry that accounts for the fervor of condemnation with which culturalists have greeted the assertion of the slightest genetic influence in our lives. It is as though the culturalists are becoming uneasily aware that all they ever had was a romantic rhetoric and that the rhetoric is becoming threadbare.

CHAPTER 9

Culturalism as Historicism

The culturalism considered so far seeks to find the laws of societies in general or the laws of particular societies at some particular time. It studies human societies as one might study a single ant colony or make a comparative analysis of several colonies. Even when conducted on the mistaken assumption of the existence of irreducible social laws, or of the literal truth of the organic analogy, such studies have proven useful to our understanding of society.

There is a variety of culturalism that seems quite the reverse of useful. Historicists agree with other culturalists that persons, institutions, ideas, and values must be understood as products of their times and places, but they go on to assert that these times and places, these cultures, must in turn be understood in terms of the irreducible historical laws that produce them. They find three levels of analysis, the individual or psychological, the cultural, and the historical. The third level, the historical, is the ultimately determinative and explanatory system. As the culturalist says that the individual cannot be understood except as a product of culture, so the historicist argues that a culture cannot be understood except as a product of historical laws.

Not all of those who write theories of history, even when their theories are large scale and claim to be predictive, can be called historicists. Spinoza,[1] for example, believed that there are stable human passions and propensities that make it possible for us to predict that in the future we will be more prosperous, enlightened, and free. He did this, of course, as a human nature thinker who believed that freedom and enlightenment, defined in relation to a constant human nature, confer competitive advantages on the individuals and societies that promote them. What constitutes historicism is the belief that there are laws of history that are reducible neither to the supposed culturalist laws of society nor to the laws of human nature. Rather, historical laws autonomously determine both social laws and human nature. Historicism demands much of our imaginative powers. To share its vision, we must begin with the culturalist metaphor of the social organism, an organism that imposes its patterns on the individuals who compose it, that shapes their nature to suit its nature. Then we must conceive that at least some such societies are parts of a temporally sequential system, a system that determines their particular moments or phases, as well as their patterns of change. The laws of history are taken to be actual powers, to be real; social laws and cultures are their partial manifestations, as individuals in turn are partial manifestations of cultures. Historicists discover from the examination of historical data evidence of an internal logic or deep structure, the kind of "logic" or morphological structure we attribute to a good play, a work of art, or an organism. On the basis of a knowledge of that deep structure, they say, we can gain a profound understanding of the past in terms of its partial culmination in the present, of the present in terms of its emergence from the basic historical processes of the past, of the future in terms of the force of the historical laws identified.

This notion that history has a kind of logic or necessity has deep roots in our species psychology. We readily find meaning in all about us. Our symbolizing powers and mythologizing proclivities weave stories about every natural thing and event, myths that function to orient us to the world and to each other. The stories are not always pure fantasy. We do indeed review our own past lives with a comprehension not possible to us before. We do even better in the review of the past lives of others, of our parents, of our historical predecessors, for all of us are subject to massive constraints and influences of which we are only partially aware. We learn to look for signs of large-scale processes that will explain particular events and then for an overarching law that will include all those processes. No one has ever looked for those processes and for that law and failed to find both. A major function of the human mind is to form gestalts, to make sense of and find patterns in aggregations of diverse data. Since long before Polybius's cyclical law of history, historical data have proven docile to regimentation into theoretical systems.

Most contemporary historicists are Marxists and tend to judge a whole work solely on the basis of where it stands on the truth of Marxism as they understand it. The present argument against historicism, which is also an argument against Marxism as I understand it, will not please many of them. Some schools of Marxism, however, have reinterpreted Marx in a humanist, human nature, sense. These may find here some elucidation or reinforcement of their position. I suggest that in fact human nature theory is a much more usable basis for social and political theories of reform or even revolution than is historicism.[2]

Problems of Historicism

The general criticism of culturalism already made applies to all its varieties, including historicism. What follows is particularly directed at historicism.

A historical law is the statement of a regularity. The recognition of a regularity is sometimes accompanied by explanation, by an account, sometimes not. When it is not, as in bare correlation—the level of the water table in Texas varies inversely with the level of political participation in Nepal—we are interested, but not enlightened. We believe in but do not understand the regularity. Historical laws are said to be, not mere correlations, but laws accompanied by understanding. What kind of understanding accompanies the grasp of historical laws? What is being asked for is, not inductive or deductive evidence or proof, but information about how the laws of history can be communicated and grasped.

The rich metaphors of colloquial language—"I get a kick out of you," "her career is going down the drain"—are analogies from common experiences. Science and the learning of science also proceed by analogy, as does all thinking about new things. The heart is like a pump; the solar system is like a clock; a political system is a feedback system, like a thermostat. Analogy moves our understanding from the known to the unknown. It tells us that an idea we knew in one context is also true in another context. Analogies may be more or less legitimate. We may push them too far: the heart is not quite like a pump in some important respects. An analogy may be misleading: "love is nothing but chemistry" builds an overall falsity on a kernel of truth. We may analogize from what is mistakenly thought to be known, or from vague concepts, and produce nonsense.

Hegel[3] and Spengler[4] offer us analogies of the latter sort, analogies that appear to move from the known to the unknown, but that in fact move from the familiar but unknown to the unfamiliar and unknown. The metaphor by which we come to think we understand Hegel's march of Spirit through time is based on the analogy of that march to the growth of consciousness in a mind such as our own. Since neither Spirit in its beginning nor we in our infancy are presumed to have had the intelligence and knowledge to make a conscious decision to become what each of us is now, the underlying analogy turns out to be to the biological maturation of a thinking organism, which in turn depends on our images of maturing organisms in general. We are familiar with maturing organisms; the process seems natural and expectable. When we interrogate someone who uses the acorn-oak example in an analogy intended to explain something, however, we find that in fact he or she has no idea of how an acorn becomes an oak, that he or she is appealing to our sense of familiarity with a process that in itself is, for most or all of us, completely mysterious. Hegel's analogies make us feel at home with the idea of Spirit marching through time, but he has given us no account at all of that process. Worse, the maturing organism, Spirit, of which Hegel tells us, is unique, and so we know nothing of its species characteristics from experience with many examples of it. We cannot guess where it came from, where it is going, when it will end, or how to interpret its past behavior in terms of its fleeting present. Our feeling that we understand the march of Spirit is an illusion. We do not attach any meaning to it at all; our dim image of it draws on our innate mythologizing talents. This is further complicated by the fact that what is said to be marching is neither a material substance nor those elements of the world of thought that represent the structures of the material world but an idea that is thought by no one and that shapes the material world to its end. That an idea should have ends is just one more complication.

Spengler avoids this problem, in part, in that each of the many civilizations he studies is similar to the others. They are all to be understood as members of a single organic species, and so we know the life span and future career of our own civilization by comparing it to other civilizations that have gone through their cycle of birth, maturity, and decline. But although Spengler's historicist theory is more psychologically persuasive than any other, it yet rests on an analogy that we do not understand. He offers us an interesting correlation rather than an intelligible law. The feeling we get in reading him that we have discovered the inner dynamic of civilizations is an illusion.

The flamboyant romantic historicist system-builders of the nineteenth and early twentieth centuries saw no difficulty in resting their systems on vague intuitions and plausible correlations. In the more critical mood that now reigns, we demand a more clearly stated basis. We cannot find it in Hegel or Spengler, for their analogies depend on an exploitation of our native uncritical animism, on the assumption of teleology, of the existence of an immanent purposefulness both in nature and in the world of concepts. Contemporary biologists, the contemporary mind in general, can make no sense of the idea of immanent purposefulness.

Marx's laws of history are more difficult to understand. They cannot be of the type of Gresham's Law, for they are said not be reducible to statements about a transcultural human nature. Neither can they be considered to be very general versions of nonhistoricist culturalist social laws, for these depend for their operation on the relative stability of our second or socialized nature and on the assumption that each society is a relatively closed system.

The locomotive of psychological laws is our passionate species nature; that for social laws is supposed to be our culturally induced passions. What is the locomotive of Marx's historical laws? They are said not to be reducible either to our complex passionate human nature or to culturally induced passions. They cannot derive their energy, as Hegel's laws do, from some postulated ideal superorganism, for Marx's materialism rules out that source. We are driven to the hypothesis that Marx's laws of history are meant to be simply descriptive, as are the "laws" of evolution or gravitation. Philosophical Marxists resist this assimilation of Marxist laws to ordinary scientific laws, for reasons too complex to consider here, but no other intelligible account is available. If Marx's historical laws are scientific laws, what are they about, what forces make them work? Many commentators have agreed that Marx's ultimate intelligible historical force is the evolution of technology.[5] "Technology" must be taken broadly, of course, to include superstructural institutions and facilitating attitudes and skills, but since these are themselves understood to be the product of the development of the means of production, it ought not be taken too broadly.

Studies of history, and historicist theories of history, do not exist in a vacuum. They must assume, for instance, the stability of the underlying laws of nature, of physics, chemistry, and biology, including human physiology and some psychology. If the laws of history are seen as simply arising out of the complex interaction of all these, and reducible to them, then we should expect, in the absence of immanent purpose in nature, to find random or repetitive movements in history. This is just what Marx does not find, and so we must search further for the cause of the direction he discovers in history. The analogy of organic evolution has been suggested. In that case, we want to know what the selection criteria were and how they are enforced. The only way in which we can make the evolving machine metaphor work is by the assumption of humans as their "natural environment," humans who actually conceive and build the machines, who operate and maintain them for purposes of their own, who desire the product of the machines, and who select them on the basis of human criteria of efficiency and productivity. Just as the background stability of physical and psychological laws must be assumed if we are to know history at all, so the stability of complex human motivation, a stability extending over different historical periods, must be assumed if we are to use the evolving machine theory. How that theory can claim to be independent of a human nature theory that it requires at every point, if it is to work, is a puzzle.

If the events of history have an overall structure that we can analogize to that of a play, a play that has artistic coherence and theme, in which the end is felt to follow necessarily from the beginning, then we want very much to know the plot. The number of possible historical dramas is without limit. Does the universe have a death wish and has it produced the human species as the unwitting means to its destruction? Is the play a comedy, a tragedy, a farce; does it have a point that humans perhaps could not understand or have not yet imagined? What criteria do we have for choosing among competing historical theories?

Historicists have two ways of determining the plot of the historical drama. One is the rational, rational deductive, or reductive-compositive method we find in Hegel; the other is the empirical, hypothetical-deductive method that Marx seems to intend to use. Hegel reduces the natural world to concepts. The concepts are then converted into active forces that re-enter the material world and engage in interaction with each other, interactions he illustrates from the world histories current in his day. This is done rather skillfully; if we can forget that real critique of pure reason, Hume's demonstration of the necessary failure of all attempts to reason from *a priori* concepts to the world of experience, then Hegel's historical theory, aside from some absurd details, can almost convince us. In a sense the Real, for us, is indeed the Rational, for we survive as a species on the basis of our ability to find our environment intelligible. Reason is observably marching through time in the sense that, with the growth of science, the world has become increasingly rational, intelligible, to us. We in turn become increasingly rational in apprehending the rationality of the world. Hegel cannot get a value theory out of such fancies, however, for reason and intelligibility can have value only to passionate thinking creatures.

Marx claims to have created a science of history and considered himself to be, despite some allegiance to Hegel's dialectical method, an empirical scientist. His laws of history are not deduced from pure concepts but are supposed to be discoverable through an examination of the events of history. Yet although he postulates four to six important stages of history and claims that his historical laws account for the transition from each to the next, he actually examines and attempts to account only for the transition from feudalism to capitalism. The historical laws do not seem at all helpful in accounting for the other transitions and later Marxists have shown little interest in arguing that they are. This is not an acceptable procedure. Highly general theoretical explanations, which apply to but one instance, are called "ad hoc" theories.

In his "demystification" of Hegel, Marx appears to want to dispense with the notion of immanent purposefulness, of teleology. But if he indeed does so, he loses any chance he might have had of discovering the plot of history: how else could it have a plot? Nevertheless we find in Marx two ways, each incompatible with the other, of arriving at a knowledge of the plot of history. In the first way he proceeds from the assumption that social superstructures, that is, social ideas, institutions, and values, are necessarily the product, a reflection, of the realities of the prevailing mode of production. From this it follows that cultural changes, including our consciousness of ourselves and of the world, are the product of changes in the mode of production. Changes in the material mode follow from technological innovation. The driving force in history is therefore the steady tendency of machines and other physical aids to production to improve themselves. True, they require the service of humans to do this, but they have already created the social conditions that in turn create the human consciousness that desires, constructs, and services them, and so they truly make themselves. Even in our day we speak metaphorically of this self-improvement of machinery in biological terms when we refer to the newest "generation" of computers and missiles. Marx, in reifying this metaphor, has reintroduced teleology.

The notion that human consciousness is at least partly determined by our relation to the production process is very old. Aristotle,[6] Machiavelli,[7] and Harrington,[8] to mention but a few, argued that certain kinds of property divisions, supported by an agrarian law, are necessary for the establishment and maintenance of good social and political order. Marx is in this tradition when he predicts that certain desirable results will follow from the abolition of private property in the means of production. Unlike the others, however, Marx has no basis for his prediction, for without a theory of human nature, a developed human psychology, he cannot predict what the proletariat will do once they have expropriated the expropriators. The fact that his prediction has proven wrong in each of many trials is not the present point, which is that historicist and human nature explanations cannot simultaneously serve as ultimate modes of explanation. Physicists knew they were admitting theoretical incoherence when they said that light is a wave on Monday, Wednesday, and Friday and a particle on the other days. Historicists cannot legitimately reduce our species nature to the vanishing point, to allow full play to historical forces, and then suddenly introduce a full-blown human nature theory to explain how the proletariat will act under certain future conditions.

Only in the post-feudal Western world has technological change been a normal and expectable part of life, a process that visibly and uncontrollably eats away at "superstructural" institutions, ideas, and values and creates new ones. The Reform Act of 1832 does indeed seem somehow to follow, in a dimly perceived way, from the invention of the steam engine. There is no reason to believe, however, that the role of uncontrolled technological innovation as the major cause of social change is the norm or even that it will continue. Some past civilizations have controlled technology for political ends. Increasingly in the twentieth century, governments and great corporations, sometimes in concert, have acted to direct or manage technological change. Whether or not we approve of that control, it nevertheless acts to remove such changes from the realm of blind necessity. When technology comes under the control of other powers, it is negated as an historical force. Politics can and may replace economic forces, as Marx himself recognized in his *Eighteenth Brumaire*.[9]

Marx's other answer to the question of the plot of history contradicts the evolving machine thesis. Assume that humans can be credited with a full range of complex feelings and propensities, powerful and enduring enough to shape cultures (although not as they would). Assume that our nature includes a desire for equality and sharing, an indisposition under decent conditions to reach for power over others, a capacity and a willingness on the part of most of us to understand and to control our own societies for the good of all, and a reliable and natural commitment to social and human solidarity. It follows that the history of humanity and of technology is the history of the gradual creation of the material conditions under which our natural traits can flower without the atrocities and deprivations, the false consciousness, the psychic and intellectual deformation, produced by the struggle for scarce resources. I need not comment on this theory. The Marx of this theory is not an historicist. He is not even a Marxist.

This raises the question of the use of historicist theory in predicting the future. Marx and Hegel agree that the owl of Minerva takes flight only when the shades of night have fallen, that our historical vision can only be retrospective. In fact, they would say, even our retrospective vision is flawed by the false consciousness that necessarily distorts all thinking that pre-dates the final freeing of humanity. The dialectical method of analysis they favored rules out the use of ordinary extrapolative or comparative methods of understanding the past and predicting the future, but it is itself so vague that no two dialecticians, operating independently of each other, have ever used the method to come to the same conclusion. Yet both Hegel and Marx broke the historicist rule against prediction. What could they do? The function of political philosophy is not to understand the past but to deal with the present, to advise us in our major political actions. Both philosphers so advised us, in spite of the fact that political action makes no sense unless we have a rather good idea of the probable consequences which that action entails for the future. Marx and the Marxists have been particularly oriented toward policy recommendations, and therefore toward prediction. After well over a century of testing their long- and short-term predictions, we have some idea of how good they were.

There is a conceptual problem for all the empirical sciences that runs as follows: through any two or more points on a graph (given any two or more pieces of information about a process), an infinite number of curves may be drawn (an infinite number of mathematical equations or empirical generalizations may be made). The physical sciences are rescued from the skepticism that follows this fact by what has been called "coherence theory." A single empirical generalization in a science is supported by its coherence or compatibility with a great many other allied generalizations. All of these are in turn brought together under the umbrella of an overarching paradigm or untestable general model of reality. The model is justified by its general explanatory power and its heuristic value in promoting further successful research. Historicist theories find no such support. Each must compete with the others, and with non-historicist theories, for intellectual dominion over the infinite sea of historical data. Each takes out of that sea what facts it needs to construct its thesis; none can fail to find the support it needs, for there are enough facts and factual ambiguities to support the most widely divergent historical theories. Facts that do not fit are rejected as unimportant or as falsely understood. Each historicist theory is itself the judge of the meaning and importance of the data it uses. Every historicist theory is therefore self-confirming and irrefutable. This is another way of saying that all such theories are useless. In fact, the most enthusiastic attempts to integrate historicist principles into other spheres of practical and theoretical knowledge have failed. Where the attempt has been particularly forceful, as in the legislation of Lamarckian environmentalist theory into plant breeding, the consequences have been disastrous. Historicism has but one practical use: the support of propositions that would be patently absurd on any other basis. Historicism comes to seem reasonable when language that implies it is uncritically accepted into common use. Such phrases as "historical necessity," "the verdict of history," and even "historical development," "developing nations," and "cultural evolution" imply the reality of historical laws. These metaphors are harmless only when understood to be merely metaphors. We easily describe the French Revolution as the product of "historical forces," as inevitable because "the time was ripe" for it, but all we can mean by saying so is that, like every other event, given the fact that it did occur under a certain set of circumstances, it had to happen under those precise circumstances. The same can vacuously be said of whatever word will end this present sentence, of the fall of the dice at a certain number. There are no "historical forces." Human events are presumably determined, but they are determined by the vectors of the forces of species-typical human feelings evoked in many individuals in the context of complex current circumstances and shared interpretations of past experience. All this adds up, from the standpoint of our possible knowledge, to the existence of historical probabilities. We have a passionate interest in the assessment of these probabilities. Those who claim to have a system for determining them on the basis of historical laws, laws that not only explain but evaluate the present and the future, will always find adherents. Yet the "verdict of history" on any past event has not, and never can be, finally achieved. The historicists are quite right in reminding us that each historical period rewrites the history of all the past and that it does so because our vocabulary for discussing the meaning of our lives is powerfully influenced by our common perception of the unique characteristics of our present times.

A "developing nation" is a relatively unindustrialized nation that is in process of becoming something other than it was, either more like "us" or more like "them," or perhaps something in between. That such nations have certain common experiences, as do army recruits or people learning to drive a car, does not imply the existence of either historical or social laws. A society is not like a plant that grows according to some immanent necessity. It is tempting to analogize from organic evolution to the adaptive changes of societies, and so the phrase "social evolution." As commonly used, however, the phrase implies goal orientation. The scientific sense of evolution is, of course, that of adaptation of organisms to present conditions, not change toward some higher or final state of being. Evolution is not a play, has no dramatic unity, no goal, recognizes no higher or lower forms of life. "Social evolution" resonates impressively, but it is a phrase that is either trivial or misleading. It is trivial if it asserts that societies change when circumstances change, misleading if it hints at something more than that.

Historicists lay claim to special competence in the understanding of social change and the formulation of social policy. We noted above the difficulties with the "intimationalist" method of the culturalists. So placid a method is not for the historicists. Their social changes are described in terms of revolutions, of new societies ripped from the womb of old ones. Their "world-historical men" or rising classes smash institutions, reverse attitudes, create new kinds of people.

Policy advocacy is a very awkward theoretical problem, for it involves a claim to knowledge of present and future facts, processes, and values. Historicists are bound to be very modest about their ability to foresee the future, and so cannot see how actions will turn out, even though their historicist values are completely determined by how in fact things do turn out. To the extent to which they claim to be empirical scientists, they are bound by the fact-value disjunction; as culturalists they cannot extrapolate values beyond their own presumably historically determined attitudes. There is only one way out of this trap, and both Hegel and Marx take that way. They solve the problem of value by the assumption that historical change is inherently progressive.[10] This means that later times are better than earlier times, and this, not merely as a matter of historical observation, but in a necessary metaphysical sense. The solution is similar to that offered by those, such as Augustine, who make God the final arbiter of value. As these latter define good as that which God commands and insist that good has no other meaning, can be determined only by a knowledge of the will of God, so the historicists define the good as that which actually happens, the better as that which happens later. The best can be determined only by a knowledge of the goal of history. Historicism is essentially a nineteenth-century phenomenon. The roots of the unargued assumption that progress and change are the same and that both are necessary are to be found in the misconception that evolution is necessary and progressive, in the optimistic Enlightenment rationalism that then yet lingered on, and in the life experience of those who lived through the explosive expansion of the Industrial Revolution. Marx's sensible scientific materialism is applied soberly in his studies in political economy, but when he arrives at value theory, he relapses into his latent Hegelian optimism, joins Hegel in the assumption of the long-range identity of "good" and "later."[11] The bourgeois supporters of the divine right of kings as against the rural aristocracy and the modern intellectual supporters of the destiny of the proletariat now appear equally as progressives. "Morality" is completely summed up in "progressiveness." To be moral is to forward whatever our historical theory tells us is a nascent fundamental change. However much actual misery that change may produce ("the worse, the better"), it is yet a necessary, hence desirable, stage in the inevitable progress toward a good known to be good because it is later. Among the Marxists, only Marx and a few others seem to have realized clearly that this means being retrospectively opposed to peasant uprisings, to Luddites, and to the pathetic resistances that backward societies make to the imperialisms of the advanced nations. No sentimentalist, Marx backed the Americans in the Mexican War and was angrily bloodthirsty in his attitude toward the national aspirations of Slavs and other minorities and ethnic groups. The Gulag Archipelago, the Cambodian genocide, the concentration camps of the historicist Nazis, are not unfortunate deviations from an ideal; they are expectable consequences of it; nor is there, within historicism, any theoretical or principled basis for condemning them. Politically activist historicists remind us, truly, that you cannot make an omelet without breaking eggs. No other political theory claims that if you break enough eggs you will certainly get an omelet. It is not now necessary to argue against the belief that the later is by definition better than the earlier; it need only be stated clearly to be disbelieved. Contemporary Marxists are careful not to state it clearly. When pushed for a value basis for their policy recommendations and ultimate goals, they extemporize whatever human nature assumptions serve their immediate purpose, then return at once to their traditional rejection of all human nature theory. Contemporary Marxist literature shows that thoughtful Marxists are well aware of the theoretical difficulties of their advocacy of value judgments. Yet in the current flood of Marxist theorizing, there is not a single serious account of how those difficulties may be surmounted. It is probable that both the practical failures of Marxist regimes and the Marxist failure to produce even a theory of democratic socialism find their explanation in this incoherency.[12]

Although the belief in necessary progress is actually the only value basis that is both intelligible and consistent with historicism,[13] some contemporary historicists downplay or deny that belief and assert instead the force in history of the underlying desire in us for Freedom. Hegel and Marx sometimes seem to support this notion. In Hegel's writings, the goal of History is the victory of Reason, of Spirit, over the blind necessity that governs unintelligent matter. Humanity is to be the chosen instrument of Reason and will achieve Freedom in the knowledge of and transcendence of necessity. In Marx's writings, the notion of Freedom (we do well, in English translation, to capitalize words whose implied profundity paralyzes our intelligence) is similar but more obscure and ambiguous. In his stubborn resistance to the inherently alienating force of the division of labor, Marx appears to mean by Freedom the absence of all limitation, all specialization, partiality, or constraint, the absolute unconditioned freedom that few but Augustine have attributed even to God. At other times he has ambivalently in mind a conflation of the asocial freedom of humanity in the state of nature as described by Rousseau in his *Discourse on the Origin of Inequality* and the other freedom described in Rousseau's *Social Contract,* a freedom that involves total subjection of each to all, a submission to the social "chains" that it is the object of that work to explain and to justify.[14] We do not know what to do in order to pursue one or all of these freedoms. We are not at all sure that we would like them if we possessed them. Later Marxists have demonstrated the ambiguity and obscurity of Marx's concept of Freedom by interpreting it to mean whatever they happen to value: a higher standard of living, the abolition of the exploitation of man by man, economic security, creative labor, and so on.[15] Both Marx and they have a problem here, for once we have met the bare survival needs of a person considered as a generalized animal, what is good for him or her requires an explanation based on a notion, preferably a responsible notion, of human nature. "Freedom" cannot be defined, as can "a circle" or "hydrogen," in pure abstractions. Whatever we decide it is, it will be relative to the nature of the creature that is to have it. Marx and the Marxists, as historicists, cannot allow to human nature the determinate character it must have if it is to support an adequate notion of freedom.

The essential notions of historicism are not ideas that can be applied selectively or at convenience. Those who adopt these overall notions must take pains to show how their own particular views and values can be accommodated within them. Bertrand Russell's solution to the paradox of the Cretan who says that all Cretans are liars, to the generalization that all generalizations are false, is the positing of privileged zones for the intellect: a statement about a class is not itself a member of that class. Historicists cannot evade the paradoxical implications of their position as easily. Some have gone so far as to imply that statements of ordinary fact, as well as of scientific law and theory, are cultural or ideological products. Some believe that even our sense organs and rational processes are similarly influenced. Here we are concerned only with the minimum historicist belief that our ideas of the social and political process, and of the values connected with it, are socially and historically relative, and totally so. We see that every historicist claims a special exemption from her or his own rule and finds a place in time, her or his time, at which the truth can, for the first time, be seen. Each such writer "unmasks" all earlier writers as covert ideologists. Unmasking is a revelatory method whereby the substantive issues can be completely ignored. We need pay no attention to the question of whether our victim is making true statements or not, whether her or his actions were humanly appropriate or not. Like some Freudian analysts we may treat all statements and actions as symptoms of a deep structure governing the patient. Of course deep structures do exist, despite the positivists and reductionists, but at that point where our sense of the importance of one of them devours our sense of all the others, along with our sense of the rule of contingency in history and in ordinary life, we have become one-eyed fanatics, have lost that openness of mind necessary to human communication. As historicists we understand humans as products of their time. We tease out the historical and cultural threads on which their minds and feelings dance. We know them as they could never have known themselves. After us will come those who will perform the same service for us—unless we argue that we and Truth were born at the same moment. Finally, ironically, we will realize that both culturalism and historicism are products of their time and place, are the ideology of classes and interests of which Hegel and Marx, now long gone, could have known nothing.

It does not follow from these critical remarks that we ought to stifle all thought about historical uniformities or disregard the suggestions made about them by the historicists. It does mean that we should recognize the modest limits within which we can responsibly generalize and the fanciful or ideological character of all but the most limited theories of history. We all experience insights such as that of Blake:

A dog starv'd at his master's Gate
Predicts the ruin of the State.[16]

Such insights are powerfully and poetically true, true of some possible world that bears some relation to our own. Yet any actual dog may only appear to be starving; it may not belong to the man behind the gate; the man may be unrepresentative of the rest of the population; internal resources or external influence may intervene to save the state; possibly it was the ruin of the state that foretold the starving of the dog. Anyone who has followed the political, economic, and social punditry, Marxist and not, of the past few decades, will take a very reserved view of our supposed capacity to understand even our present.

We ought not take the anti-theoretical line of those who oppose theories of history simply out of fear of the totalitarianisms of the left or of the right—as some think was the case with Karl

Popper—or of those "running dogs of the monopoly capitalists"—as some would characterize the positivists or blinkered empiricists. On the contrary, we need historical theories, theories based on surmises about present tendencies and analogies from similar past situations. We need sophisticated, imaginative, and informed scenarios of possible futures. Practically all we do is directed toward the near or distant future; we ought to do all we can to improve our chances of realizing our dreams and of forestalling the realization of our nightmares.

One historicist theory of history, Marxism, has for curious reasons crowded almost all others from the scene. There are other theories of history that are equally interesting and that have no taint of historicism. Lynn White's notion[17] that military technology determines social and political structure, and that changes in that technology produce major social and political change, is an example of a good explanatory system that fails to gain attention, not for lack of intrinsic merit, but because it grinds no ideological axe. Among White's examples, not all original with him, is the relation, in Athens and Sparta, between democracy and a well-manned navy on the one hand and between oligarchy and reliance on a few highly trained soldiers on the other. Similarly the invention of the stirrup and the consequent military indispensability of the mounted knight produced the medieval manorial system; cannon demolished the fortresses of the rural feudal aristocracy and produced the nation state; the mass armies of the nineteenth and early twentieth centuries required democratic institutions. We are led to wonder if democracy can survive the present trend toward reliance on small numbers of military specialists. I do not know how well this historical theory will stand up under criticism, but it is interesting, empirical, non-historicist, and predictive, and it shows the range of what can be done with generally acceptable methodological tools.

The appeal of the culturalist and historicist views is the feeling of power and of deep insight that they offer us so cheaply. Historicists particularly enjoy the advantage of a magic key to the easy comprehension of the most complex human events, past, present, and to come. Some first-year college students can confidently affirm that Aristotle is a reactionary; they know, and it is all they need to know about him, that Hobbes is a bourgeois ideologist; that the Albanian regime and the Palestinian cause are "progressive"; that the Chinese (until recently) possessed the political idea that should be a model for all other societies. Historicism is the opium, the quick fix, of the lumpen-intellectual classes.

Just as it is easy to overdo our condemnation of the reductionist human nature thinkers—James Mill's democratic system of checks and balances is a great improvement over George III—we can go too far in our condemnation of historicists. We go too far as soon as we imply that the attack on the historicist principle washes over onto the social, political, and economic ideals or practices of those who hold it. Nothing in what I have said implies that it is either a good or a bad idea for working people to seize control of the means of production and establish socialism and then communism. What has stood in the way of such supposed improvements, as well as in the way of somewhat different ones that appeal to others, what has stood in the way, perhaps equally with those interested groups who benefit from the ill fortune and mistreatment of others, is the language of historicism. The goal of this book is the rediscovery of a vocabulary in which all of us can find a common ground for the discussion of politics and of value; if the discussion leads to a fight, at least we will know what we are fighting about. What needs to be discussed are value priorities and social and political realities. Of all the present obstacles to that discussion, historicism is the greatest. It has spawned an obfuscatory rhetoric, sprinkled with talismanic untranslatable Teutonisms, scatological characterizations, and the gratuitous vulgarity and paranoia of the adolescent in revolt. Its language, like that of some other religious cults, and recent intellectual movements, can be understood only by believers.

If we could create, out of the current unnecessary verbal and conceptual confusions, a common language of value and a common basis for talking about society, we would find that the present radical division between the educated and the uneducated would narrow; popular and intelligently conceived movements for the correction of what is evil, unfair, and dangerous in our collective life would become possible. The quarrel here is, of course, with contemporary historicists who have sold their aspirations and solidarity with the rest of the human race for a mess of pretentious jargon, who have attempted to corrupt the language of political discourse to the point where the defeat of all intelligently conceived change, along with their own programs, would be assured. But I digress.

Once historicism and culturalism have been unmasked, the Burkeans can go on warning us about the real dangers of unintended consequences and the fallacy of the abstract theory of natural right; the culturalists can ask that we take a more imaginative and humane view of the other, less powerful cultures and remind us of the importance of a tempered respect for elements of our own culture; the communists can make their case for revolution and socialism. This time, however, we will understand each other, will be able to talk about real humans and real problems. The political scene will look less like a convention of patent medicine salesmen or a religious war, more like that town meeting of our imagination, a meeting where an informed and reflective citizenry learn to grasp different views and make responsible decisions about the way in which they shall live.

Part II

CHAPTER 10

Traditional Human Nature Value Theory

Among secular moral philosophers before the seventeenth century, the complete non-reductionist human nature basis of the origin and validation of values seemed too obvious to need defense. Since Hume and Rousseau, that theory has been either unknown or thought to be too absurd to merit argument.[1] However obvious it may once have been, and may again be in the future, contemporary value thinkers do not find it so. Indeed, they do not seem to see it at all, even to refute it. This state of affairs is, I believe, partly the consequence of a commitment to alternative bases, and so the need for the arguments in the first part of this book. Partly it is the result of the notion that the human nature basis is somehow ruled out by "the naturalistic fallacy," or by the "is-ought" or "fact-value" gaps, the irrelevance of which is shown later. My own readings and discussions have suggested yet other reasons for the present puzzling ignorance. The celebrated "two-cultures" split between the sciences and the liberal arts has produced two strains of value thought, the one uselessly ethereal or abstractly logical, the other crudely reductionist and often even vulgar. If we are to have an adequate idea of human nature, we must understand both nature and humanity, both thinking and feeling.

The remainder of this book is an exposition of the non-reductionist human nature theory, of the reasons for accepting it and of the uses that can be made of it. One of the reasons for preferring it, a reason that should appeal to those with an interest in political philosophy, is the way it helps us to understand the principal writers in that field. In this chapter I will give some reasons for believing that before Burke all secular moral and political thinkers were human nature thinkers, and that before Hobbes all were non-reductionist human nature thinkers. Some explanation of the point of relating a present theory to some famous names from the past is necessary. Obviously it would make no sense to cite the older writers as authorities; no one now argues that something must be true because Aristotle said it. On the other hand, a theory that can argue that it both illuminates and is consistent with the thought of great thinkers of the past acquires thereby a claim to serious consideration and is more likely to be understood when associated with bodies of thought that have been intensively studied.

At about the time I began the study of political philosophy, it was being widely announced that "political theory is dead."[2] The dominant schools, reductionist human nature and culturalist, each had its own reasons for thinking so. We were then at a high tide of positivist thinking, when it was evident to many that both metaphysical and value thinking were essentially frivolous or meaningless. The thinkers in the older tradition were said to be victims and perpetrators of linguistic confusions that we had now transcended. They were also said to be "ideologists," in the sense that they took too large views of political reality and committed themselves to utopian visions of radically better worlds. The practical engineering approach of the late fifties and early sixties found them rendered obsolete by "the end of ideology." On the other hand, culturalists, Hegelians, and Marxists knew, often without the bother of reading them, that the traditionalists were mere historical curiosities, puppets of their time and place, spokespersons for the class interests of their day, at best to be praised for literary elegance or faint anticipations of contemporary ideas. By the late sixties, a rather extreme egalitarianism, coupled with a positive contempt for the past, made the study of the older writers seem irrelevant to our real concerns, indicative of a covert elitism.

The ethical literature of the past two centuries contains no statement of the moral theory of the traditional writers. It follows that they are no longer understood, that they are available to us only as literature, expressions of their times and places, or as curious eccentrics. The result has been the death, not of political philosophy, but of contemporary political philosophy. That study now consists largely of the study of the history of ideas, research in which discussion of the substantive merits or demerits of these ideas is considered out of bounds. Along with a few textual analysts and some who write in the style of literary criticism, the mainstream of political theory tolerates along its banks little sects of cabalistic interpreters, analytic philosophers, hard-core Marxists, and soft-core pop-sociologists with an interest in a synthesis of Marx and Freud. Few of these mean to connect us with our past or intend actually to create a contemporary political philosophy. Rarely do we see the explicit political analysis and policy recommendations of the classic political writers taken seriously. To take them seriously is not, of course, necessarily to agree with them; it is to treat what they say as discussable, as having a substantive basis.

We ought to be more careful of our reputation with posterity. Speaking of the British upper class during our Civil War, Henry Adams said of their vilification of Lincoln, "If Mr. Lincoln was not what they said he was—what were they?"[3] The intellectual barbarism and neurotic paralysis of the will to think responsibly about our problems that increasingly characterizes our age has some connection with our inability to find anything in our past to which we can relate our rapidly successive intellectual interests. The study of the traditional writers will never go completely out of fashion; we find an intrinsic attraction in philosophy, that highest form of playfulness. With no necessary regard for its practical uses or truth, some of us will always find a supreme delight in working through an argument by Aristotle or sharing such visions as that of Spinoza. The power of philosophy, however, is another matter from the pleasure of philosophy, and that power is largely lost upon us. The power that philosophy continually seeks and continually finds in one form or another is the power that all humans, just because they are human, seek. It is the power to conduct their personal and community lives in a way of which they can soberly approve. Philosophy, when not in the hands of academics and eagerly contentious youngsters, is the study of how we shall live, of how we shall live together and share in the administration of our common affairs. It is a response to the open and shameful secret that our ordinary lives, our ordinary words, actions, and assumptions, are absurd. This sense of absurdity is not new. What is new is our acceptance of it as necessary. This sense of absurdity is not of a rational incoherence; it is a value disorientation. Spinoza begins his philosophy with an examination of the ordinary life, even of persons reputed successful, and finds it absurd from the standpoint of human values.[4] Socrates begins with the argument that the unexamined life is not worth living.[5] From time to time we feel that our own lives are not worth living, and for reasons which we cannot always lay at the door of circumstance.

"How shall a man live?" is the question, and that question leads to another, "What is man?" This in turn leads to the directive "Know thyself," for the self we need to know is not our ephemeral, empirical unique self. That self is the problem. The self we need to know is our overall, long-term, substantial self, the self of which we ask, "What do I really want?" That self is the self we share with other humans. We see the empty quality of the unique self in our present obsession with personalities. Many readers are more interested in prying into the lives of famous writers than in reading what they wrote, while at the level of mass culture we are obsessed with a curiosity about the private lives of people whose fame is a product of the media. In the latter case we find, beneath the glamorous material tinsel, a pathetic psychic tinsel, ordinary people who have had thrust upon them expensive ways in which to achieve new lows in misery and inauthenticity. Such realizations of our dreams reveal to us the puerile nature of these dreams, the absurdity of our own inner life.

The practical study of politics, political philosophy, is the study of how we shall live in society. We cannot make that study without the assumption that we are sufficiently similar in important ways to make some societies more satisfactory than others and thus we are led to consider what model of society is best adapted to our common human nature. Political thinking requires that we know what people are like, what human nature is, how humans will be motivated in different kinds of circumstances. Political philosophy is necessarily normative and therefore must find a basis for its norms.

Whether a prescriptive ethic can be derived from a theory of human nature is a question that was not dealt with philosophically until Spinoza and Hume. That the major secular traditional political writers had all assumed the validity of what Hume attempted to show will now be argued. In so short a space, I certainly cannot hope to do more than suggest the possibility of the thesis. Very little has been written on the value bases of the major philosophers. The flip judgments that have been handed down through generations of textbooks are the despair of scholars, but those scholars have done very little to find better answers.

Plato

It is curious that academic commentators on Plato take his famous theory of Forms much more seriously than he himself does. In no single place does he give a complete account of them. In the late dialogue, *Parmenides,* he admits to serious difficulties with the theory, but makes little attempt to solve them. The common assumption that he deduced value judgments from the Forms is unfounded, nor does there exist, so far as I know, any serious study that attempts to show that he did.[6] Caution and modesty are the prime virtues in the interpretation of Plato. I do not pretend to know on what he himself thought he based his value theory. We can, however, easily see how he actually derives particular values.

Plato's arguments are principally against the Sophists, notably against their argument that "each man is the measure of all things." This is the theory of the individual relativism of fact and of value. One conclusion drawn by the Sophists is that nothing is intersubjectively true or of value, and so anyone may freely do whatever he or she pleases. Plato has two general replies to this argument. First, it is foolish to gratify immediate feelings at the expense of later feelings that we ourselves consider more important. The discovery of those more important feelings requires, not a search for Forms, but reflective self-examination. Because all, or most, humans have the same general pattern of underlying important feelings, those who practice self-examination have a common basis for the discussion of the humanly better and worse. The second reply arises out of Plato's distinction between the necessary and the unnecessary desires. The unnecessary desires are for those things that attract us but that yet do not satisfy our more important feelings. We are ill advised to invest heavily in their satisfaction. The necessary desires are the desires, not for the minimum requirements for survival, but for those things that are indispensable to the satisfaction of those important feelings we have as humans.

Although he wrote long before culturalism became a full-blown thesis, Plato is concerned in many places to point out the tension between nature and convention. Although he argues, in the *Laws,* that convention must be the law of society, he argues elsewhere that nature must be the law for philosophy. The philosophical exercises of the early dialogues are designed in good part to demonstrate the intellectual confusions and practical failings of a reliance on convention and to show the way to a steady reliance on general human feeling. The *Gorgias* is a particularly good example of how Socrates depends finally on the feelings that his antagonists share with him.[7] Each of them, Gorgias, Polus, and Callicles, is not logically refuted; rather he is shown to be ashamed to persist in the maintenance of humanly impossible values. Once we know our important feelings, we know that living for pleasure, for power, or merely for as long as possible does not produce happiness. "Happiness" for Plato is the satisfaction of our most general and enduring human feelings. Although he often, as in the *Republic,* says that justice is to be preferred for its own sake, he clearly means, as he says in other places, that justice is to be preferred for its own sake because it is coincident with happiness.[8] Plato's arguments are addressed, not to metaphysicians, but to the typical feelings of ordinary reflective people. A reflective person can see that the search for conventional or momentary pleasures results in a surplus of real pain; the struggle for conventional power results in maximum weakness; the idea that just any kind of life is worth living, no matter what its quality, does not withstand elementary human consideration.[9]

In every instance Plato's political and ethical analysis rests on his assumption of the central importance of an understanding of our species nature. For example, he defines courage as the knowledge of what is truly dangerous.[10] This knowledge cannot be knowledge of some abstract form of courage or of danger, for nothing is absolutely dangerous in any transcendent sense. Something is dangerous only with respect to some feeling and thinking organism. It is dangerous for me to stand up to a bully; I could be injured or humiliated. But it may be yet more dangerous for me not to resist if the life I lead thereafter is one of diminished self-respect and subjection to further bullying. Courage in this case consists not in standing up to the bully or not, but in knowing, and avoiding, what is really most dangerous to me. There is no single act, either fighting or fleeing, that is courageous in itself. Courage is always having the strength of character and the knowledge to do what is least truly dangerous to my most important feelings.

Justice is defined in the *Republic* as a harmony of the soul. All that Plato knew about the human soul he learned from the observation of humans. He observed that they contain competing appetitive, competitive, and intellectual passions. When we come to recognize these parts of our soul, when we learn the consequences of the dominance over us of each of these elementary passions, we see at once the importance of a harmony of them ruled over by the reflective or intelligent part. We see what justice is and also how to live. It is noteworthy in the case of justice, and in that of courage, temperance, piety, and the rest, how prominently empirical facts about the inner psychological world figure, how little a part, if any, is played by the theory of Forms. The political theory of the *Republic* depends upon empirical assumptions about the distribution of character types in a typical human population, on the empirical theory of justice just described, and on many beliefs about the feelings and propensities of ordinary people. The theory of Forms is brought in to legitimate the authority of the philosopher kings, but little explanation is given of how their knowledge of the Forms actually helps them to rule. In the more sober later work, the *Laws,* the philosopher kings and the theory of Forms drop out completely and morality appears what it has always been in Plato, activity in accordance with human nature to the end of producing the sort of happiness that is possible to humans.

Throughout Plato's writings, actual value judgments are supported by statements about the normal human feeling pattern. It is because the unreflective do not have sufficient understanding of their own feelings that the idyllic "city of pigs" in Book II of the *Republic* is necessarily short-lived, that in the ideal state the citizens must be protected from the wolflike qualities of the honor-seeking auxiliaries and the philosopher kings from their own latent passions for property and family interest, that the paired psychological and political typologies of Books VIII and IX inexorably devolve into the slavery and madness of the soul and of the society under a tyrant. It is our species psychology that, Plato argues in the *Gorgias,* determines that direct democracy in a large state must amount to the rule of orators.[11]

Some degree of truth in his psychological analysis and some degree of unity in political philosophy is suggested by the extent to which Plato's division of the human soul is continued by others. Modifications of this division are carried on in the thought of Machiavelli,[12] Aristotle, Hobbes,[13] Harrington,[14] and Locke,[15] not to mention Lenin[16] and Mannheim.[17] Machiavelli, Rousseau, and Spinoza support democratic polities, but only under conditions that take account of the truth of Plato's objections. Interestingly, some of these writers had no awareness of their relation to Plato and some of them had not even read him. Any such detectable convergence of thought among major thinkers of different cultures ought to be interesting to us.

Aristotle

The clearest formulation, before Hume, of the non-reductionist human nature theory is to be found in Aristotle. He sees us as a species among other species, differing principally from the others in intelligence. The main functions of intelligence are to understand the drift of the world, to assess our species-normal feelings, and to formulate value judgments based upon both. Morality is born out of the experience of the infinity of desire that afflicts thinking creatures, and of the conflict of feelings, and it consists in acting according to our broadest understanding of our nature, a nature that is the sum of those feelings.

Machiavelli

The initial reaction to the reading of Machiavelli is likely to be bewilderment. He was more interested in middle-range political theory than in the clarification of his overall value theory. He was particularly interested in the extent to which we are shaped by our society. He relied upon that shaping for his political programs. Religion—never mind whether true or false—produces good laws—never mind if they are "just" or not—whose object is to produce good humans who exhibit their virtue as citizens of a republic. It has been customary to emphasize the brutal realism of Machiavelli's thought in this fashion and it is not entirely wrong to do so. It ought also be realized that competent readers found in his thought much more than stark realism, reason of state, and the study of the means to power. Harrington, Spinoza, and Rousseau were among those competent readers, and they took him to favor a democratic republic and to be a follower of their own non-reductive human nature method. Machiavelli recognizes both good societies and good persons, but the goodness of the individuals is not defined in terms of their adherence to the mores of their society; rather the goodness of the society, or state, is defined in terms of the human virtues it promotes in its subjects. Virtue is a constant in all societies, and it is defined as that achieved balance of the passions most appropriate for members of our species. Machiavelli complains of his contemporaries, as we might of ours, because they think "as though heaven, the sun, the elements, and men had changed the order of their motions and power, and were different from what they were in ancient times."[18] Rather, "all men (as we have said in our Preface) are born and live and die in the same way and therefore resemble each other." "All cities and all peoples are and ever have been animated by the same desires and the same passions," and "human events ever resemble those of preceding times. This arises from the fact that they are produced by men who have been, and ever will be, animated by the same passions."[19]

Like the other traditional human nature thinkers, Machiavelli equates human nature with the species pattern of feelings and makes the necessary distinction between behavior and the feelings that motivate behavior but that do not determine it. Machiavelli justified his political thinking by claiming to understand human nature. His criticism of past and of existing societies is that they do not suit human nature, that they make our lives worse rather than better, and that there is a transcultural way of determining what is for humans the better and the worse.

Spinoza

In Spinoza we find the curious case of a writer who built a non-reductionist human nature political theory on the thought of the greatest of reductionists, Hobbes. Spinoza begins by telling us, almost in Hobbes's words, that nothing is good or bad except as the mind is affected by it, that is, except insofar as it arouses feeling in us. The feelings of which he speaks are species feelings; he never tires of telling us that humans are everywhere the same, that they are a part of nature, continuous with it and not a kingdom within it, that all of us have the same pattern of feelings.[20] It is therefore possible for all of us to share the same morality or ethic. It is the elaboration of that ethic that occupies Spinoza in his major writings. Nowhere in this "rationalist" philosopher do we find any attempt to arrive at a rationalistic ethic.

Rousseau

Because he barely survived Hume, Rousseau was the last of the great traditional moral thinkers. The opening pages of his *Discourse on the Origin of Inequality* are a manifesto of human nature theory:

> The most useful and least perfected of all human studies is that of man.
>
> How is it possible to know the source of the inequality among men without knowing men themselves?
>
> It is no such easy task to distinguish between what is natural and what is artificial in the present constitution of man, and to make oneself well acquainted with a state of which, notwithstanding, it is absolutely necessary to have just notions in order to judge properly of our present state.[21]

Rousseau is often ambiguous and sometimes seems to contradict himself—a common failure among those whose loyalty to the facts of life exceeds their ability to arrive at literal consistency—but he never wavers from his frequently and clearly stated belief that we discover political and moral truth through an understanding, not of society, nor of our unique individual selves, nor of rational necessity, but of our species being.

Hume

The political thought of Hume, and even his insights into human nature, are only moderately interesting compared with that of others mentioned here. His importance to us lies in the fact that he was the first to recognize that the traditional non-reductive human nature theory is not self-evidently true. He was the first, and the last, to provide the extensive philosophical support it now needs in the midst of alternative views. Perhaps some readers of Hume will notice, as my argument proceeds in the following chapters, that a fair part of what I have to say is a paraphrase of the Humean argument. Some will not, because they read Hume in one of the several other ways now current. Some commentators read Hume as a value skeptic, others as a believer in majority rule in moral questions, yet others as a proponent of the Ayer-Stevenson individually subjectivist emotivist theory. I hope to demonstrate in detail in a future work that Hume is indeed the principal non-reductionist human nature theorist.

In the Preface to his *Treatise of Human Nature*,[22] Hume says he intends to found a science of morality, a way not merely of knowing why people call things better and worse but of knowing what, for humans, is indeed better or worse. I have counted, so far, over thirty places where he refers to "the frame and structure of the species," or "the feelings common to all men," and so on, as a basis for making value judgments.[23] A good part of his *Enquiry Concerning the Principles of Morals* is devoted to showing that we are bound by the values that arise from our species nature, that morality is prescriptive for us, not only as cultural or emotive animals but also as philosophers. As if this is not enough, Hume goes on, in "The Standard of Taste," to argue that aesthetic judgments also can be humanly objective.[24] I fail to follow him in this last case, but only for lack of space and, perhaps, courage.[25] The whole matter of Hume's position is too complex to be argued in a few paragraphs. I appeal to the reader to go back to a consideration of Hume's moral writings and see if any interpretation other than the non-reductionist human nature theory can be placed upon them.

Unsystematic Writers

A great number of thinkers in the past millennia have expressed important and true insights into the nature of value, truth, humanity's place on earth and about the political process, but remarkably few have reached the level of coherence, comprehensiveness, and depth attained by the writers just mentioned. Cicero and Locke have had enormous influence on the way we talk and think, but neither seems to have had a coherent theory of the basis of value judgments. Both appeal to God, Nature, human nature, and reason as though they were the same thing. Locke compounds his intellectual felonies by dragging in, out of nowhere, a theory of natural rights, a theory that has no support in reason or in experience. "Natural Right" rings gloriously in the Declaration of Independence, in the rhetoric of the French Revolution, in the United Nations Charter, and in passionate appeals for political change or political stability, but not even its latest defender, Robert Nozick, has been able to find a sensible exposition or defense of this strange phrase.[26]

Many writers, from Solomon to Henry James, have contributed greatly to our understanding of ourselves. We cannot argue with them, for they do not argue with us. They do what is more important, expand our intuitive understanding of what it is to be human, but they do not improve our discursive understanding of it.

A Postscript on Hobbes[27]

A spectre is haunting modern civilizations: the spectre of Hobbes's *Leviathan*. Hobbes's reduction of human nature to that of a machine with many capacities and passions, all in the service of a single overriding directive, survival, reproduces in thought the actual reduction of our view of ourselves that accompanies the move into mass society. Hobbes has been thought to be an agent of Satan, of Cromwell, of the bourgeoisie, but he is most notably the advance agent of monopoly capitalism, the welfare state, state socialism, fascism, communism as we see it now—in short of modern society. Given his view of humanity, his advocacy of total obedience to an arbitrary, absolute sovereign follows flawlessly. As modern society demystifies and scrubs out of our minds the illusions of rights and duties, the loyalties, fellowships, and obscure sentiments and sympathies to which we are prone, we approximate ever more closely to his view of us. *Leviathan* was only a nightmare in the seventeenth century; we see it now in broad daylight. Our disenchanted intellectual elites and our realistic power elites agree that force and fraud are the bottom line in community affairs. The coming subelites will hope for the gratification of the dreams of the id, for power, random sex, revenge, self-display and fun, but will settle for survival. There are no logical flaws in Hobbes's thinking. When you say the "A" of his premises, you must say the "B" of his conclusions, and modern society is increasingly able to say only "A." Much of the political philosophy of the past three hundred years has been an attempt to avoid Hobbes's grim conclusions. As we drift toward a zero-sum society, toward the war of all against all, toward lives that promise to become increasingly nasty, brutish, and short, we would do well to find a different "A," to find a picture of human nature that does not justify those trends as necessary and inevitable. The return to ancient virtues and old-fashioned rectitude that some advocate, the attempt to escape from society in privatization, to wash one's hands of responsibility, to hide behind a mask of irony and disengagement, the extravagant exploitation of media resources to promote synthetic loyalties and feelings of community—all these strategies are in vain as long as the Hobbesian model of our nature prevails. The only present alternative model is the non-reductionist model. The only alternative, that is, compatible with our science, our common sense, and our deepest intuitions.

CHAPTER 11

Biological Human Nature

As it is commonly used, "human nature" is among the vaguest and most useless of explanatory phrases. If we are to make it clear and useful, we need to find a way to fit it into the ordered complex of our other clear and useful ideas and determine its relation to them. We must decide what we mean when we speak of human nature.

A metaphysical or complete definition of human nature is not necessary here, where we are interested in humans only as causal agents, as evaluating bundles of motivations. What we observe of them in this character is principally explicable in terms of genetic structure or cultural conditioning, or both. We need therefore to know what genetic structures are and how cultural conditioning works. Students of the social sciences, to whom this book is principally addressed, may be presumed to know about the culturalist insights but not about genetic structures. Even if I were qualified to instruct in the latter field, I could not do so in a short space. Nevertheless, something can be done to introduce non-biologists to the subject of our animal nature; I propose now to set forth a skeletal outline of how we may think about that nature usefully.

The clarification of the concept of human nature is one of the most difficult and important tasks to be attempted here. I have no interest in urging upon the reader any particular inventory of the characteristics that make up human nature; the examples I give from time to time are modest suggestions, illustrations. Partly this is to avoid more controversy than is necessary to make my major theoretical point; partly it is because I claim no special knowledge of humanity. Any mature, intelligent, sensitive, reflective, and experienced person who also has studied a fair amount of history and has immersed herself or himself in past and present literatures and arts already knows much more about human nature than any single book can express, much more than he or she can verbalize. My intent is not to instruct such people but to furnish a conceptual model useful for ordering and employing what they already know. The need for such structuring arises when our ordinary understandings result in paradoxes or when they do not extend to comprehend new or complex situations. Such occasions occur often when we talk about theories of politics, society, or value, in hard moral decisions, when values seem to conflict. Often when we argue about social and political ideals and practices, about human "rights" and "needs," we bring to the discussion random selections from our cultural heritages and human feelings and end up shouting at each other, angry and bewildered at the obtuseness of our opponents, at our incapacity to find a starting place or a guiding thread for our conversation. On such common occasions we badly need a knowledge of the general principles on which we are to understand human, indeed our own, motivation.

Political and moral philosophers of the seventeenth and eighteenth centuries commonly sought a beginning to the study of human nature in the postulation of an original state of nature. What we are, setting aside the particular institutions and cultures in which we find ourselves, was seen to determine what for us would constitute a satisfactory society. The pursuit of conventional goals sets us in conflict, and even attainment of these goals does not necessarily produce happiness. When we know what we are really like, we will know what kind of life suits us best. Most of these writers were well aware of their ignorance of the early life of humans and were careful not to make of their state of nature a historical condition. Most of them also knew that priority in time does not convey authority; it does not follow from the fact that we once lived in a certain way that we ought now to live in that way. The hypothetical states of nature set forth were deliberately ahistorical intellectual constructs, formed by imaginatively stripping from contemporary people all that seemed a product of socialization. This tactic requires highly developed critical and intuitive powers. Rousseau commented tartly on the absence of those powers among his predecessors, on their failure to get to the real state of nature, to the real nature of our species.[1] He thought that the state-of-nature thinkers before him had merely transplanted moderns, with all their neurotic passions and acquired tastes and needs, back into the woods. The people in Hobbes's state of nature are produced only in advanced societies, and Locke's natural state seems to be inhabited by staid village householders. Rousseau began his own exploration of the state of nature by going back too far, to a time when we were not quite human, when we had no language, no families or other associations. He pictured us as a generalized sort of animal with scarcely any species traits. He later corrects this oversimplification with an account of humans as tribal animals, with specifically human passions, with language and families. It is of this later state of nature that he speaks as being our truly natural condition, the condition to which we are best suited. As a political philosopher, therefore, Rousseau argues that the best life for humans is to be had, not in a return to our pre-human state, nor even in a return to the elemental village, but in the making or finding of a society that structures human interaction according to the human scale of that ancient village or tribe that we evolved to inhabit.

All other beginnings to our study of human nature fail. If we take ourselves to be complex machines that we understand, we are obviously mistaken. If we take ourselves to be machines that we happen not to understand very well, we have no beginning. If we begin with intellectual assumptions, as that humans are Reason incarnate, Spirit, or Freedom, or Will, we not only talk nonsense on stilts but fall into a reductionism more absurd than that of Bentham and close off, with a wall of words, all attempts to find a usable knowledge of ourselves. The safest and surest way to make the concept of human nature intelligible is to begin with the acknowledgment that we are, in most interesting ways, an animal species.[2] At worst we may find that the knowledge is not useful, does not lead on to an understanding of the humanity we each encounter and embody. We cannot know whether it is useful or not until we have understood the full scope of the argument that it is.

We have been learning about ourselves as animals for a very long time. Medical researchers do not keep animals in their laboratories for pets; they expect to learn something about human physical functioning from them. Their assumption is that we are continuous with the rest of the animal world, more like some animals than others, but no more different from all of them than they are from each other. From the study of animals we learn about human hearts and lungs, cells and reflexes, antibodies and healing processes. Psychologists also keep menageries, and from them they learn about human learning processes, conditioning, perception, memory, socialization, feeling structures, and even psychopathology.

The educated public is not likely to be much enlightened by the news that we are to be understood as animals. That public knows even less about animals than it does about humans, and much of the little information it does have is false or misleading. In view of this, it may seem that the study of ourselves as an animal species may merely add unnecessary complications in an already confused area, and it has sometimes done so. Such study is justified, however, if we can thereby achieve more objectivity in our view of ourselves and acquire a theoretical basis for thought about our own species. That objectivity is not easily had; it must be achieved. One of our oldest tricks is the attribution of human thought and feeling to animals, traits that we then read back to humans. A tiger attacking a deer seems to us to behave aggressively—she is *not* aggressive, either in intent or in feeling tone, only hungry and doing something about it—and we then speak of the tigerlike qualities of a human aggressor, or of all humans. One of our newer tricks is the mechanization of the animal world. We breed white rats selectively for tameness and for who knows what else, put them in specially contrived situations for which they have neither evolved nor been especially bred, and draw conclusions about rats that we then apply to humans. Such experiments are not necessarily without value, but in many instances laboratory animals are tested not so much for their species capacities as for their limitations, and in what is for them an unstructured situation. Even an experienced wild rat would in some experiments fare no better than would an Einstein, suddenly transported into membership of a tribe of Australian aborigines and told to go out to hunt for food.

Midway between the notion of animals as crypto-humans, or subhumans in strange bodies, and the idea of them as stimulus-response machines, is the idea gained by studying them in captivity. Blake may push criticism of this procedure too far when he says that "A robin red breast in a cage / Puts all Heaven in a rage," but we now know that the study of caged robins tells us remarkably little about them, not much more than does a dissection. There has been an explosion of knowledge in the past quarter of a century or so about animals in their natural environment, in the conditions for which they evolved. The relevance of this knowledge to an understanding of humans was immediately evident. Yet despite the accumulation of masses of data and much good low-level theory, that relevance has not yet been adequately thought out. Popularizers and speculators rushed into this theoretical vacuum and began pouring the new data into the old conceptual bottles. On balance, such writers as Robert Ardrey, Konrad Lorenz, and Desmond Morris did well in spreading knowledge of the new field and in beginning the undermining of establishment culturalism, but their writings are compromised by their tendency to use human language to describe animal feeling, to confuse behavior with motivation or feeling, to analogize too directly from animal feeling and behavior, and to interject personal political and social preconceptions and agenda. It may be too soon to characterize the recent school of sociobiologists, but at present they seem to be launching a new scientism, a new single-factor reductionist human nature theory. *The Selfish Gene*[3] is a replay of Bentham's "utility," and subject to the same criticisms. In fact, the actual scientific findings of the sociobiologists support neither their assumption that behavior is genetic in the higher animals nor their reduction of motivation from its real basis in a plurality of genetic feelings to the single selective process that called those feelings into being.

Our discussion here of humans as an animal species is not intended to add to the body of any of the established sciences, or to take sides in any controversy going on within them. In the attempt to find a paradigm for the study of human nature, it seems useful to consider humans as completely a part of the natural world, first of the world of organisms in general, then of the world of the "higher" animals. Paradigms are not supposed to be true, but useful. The present one is claimed to be more useful than any other, more in accord with our general scientific picture of reality, less in conflict with all levels of knowledge we have about ourselves.

We do not know much about something when we learn that it is an animal. The important thing about an animal is its species. When Jimmy reports an animal in his tent, we want to know whether it is a mosquito or a bear. No classification conveys more definite information, more completely describes an animal, than does its species membership. There is very good reason for this species distinctiveness. A species is like a vast inbred family; all its members are related to each other by blood; it is defined as a group that can interbreed and produce fertile offspring. Because such interbreeding can take place only among animals with matching genes, genes that account for hundreds of thousands of characteristics, members of any one species are very much more like each other than they are like any other animal. Except for the relatively minor individual differences, we might think of the members of one species as one animal, self-replicating, leading many simultaneous lives in different places and times. It is useful at times to invert our usual habit, to think of the genes as real, the perceived animals as the genes' method of replicating themselves. "A chicken is an egg's way of producing another egg" is the usual way of expressing this view. The genes are the building plans and operating manual, the essence, of a species; contained in their submicroscopic arrangement are not only the physical appearance of a species, but also the way a dog circles in place before lying down, the human and the simian smile, the courtship ritual of the herring gull, and an indefinite number of other psychological characteristics.

The genetic blueprint is not vague. The bits of information, the directives, contained in a set of genes, if wolf genes, specify not merely teeth, but teeth of a certain number, size, shape, order, thickness of enamel, mode of anchorage and replacement, nerve connections—and that, as dentists know, is only the beginning. Genes not only contain the instructions for the assembly and operation of the physical body of the animal, but may also specify instincts, behavioral propensities, feelings arousable by certain stimuli. It is in the genes of the wolf that it will hunt in packs, that it will behave in certain social, sexual, and parental ways.

We ask, sometimes with emotion, "what is the meaning of life?" Life has, of course, no meaning at all, or any of a number of meanings, depending on what the question itself means. Recently the question has received an interesting answer from the field of biology, in what is called "selection theory." Selection theory, valid or not, does not answer the question to the satisfaction of many people and is hardly even a theory. It is a definition, a potentially useful way of looking at things. It applies to all species, including ours, and it answers the question of what organisms are up to. How are we to account for all this energetic devouring, mating, photosynthesis, endless struggle?

We know from the theory of evolution that practically every characteristic of a species is the result of a selection process, a cross-examination of genes by the environment. Generation after generation, for over two billion years, this unremitting selection process has been exerted on every living thing. No detail of an organism is too trivial to be selected for: note the way the hair on your upper arm slopes differently from that on your forearm and think of this in terms of the ability to shed rain in the common bent-arm position. Presumably humans whose hair sloped differently were ever so slightly more likely to die of a chill. Given a long enough period of selection, only a tiny fraction of each generation would have to be harmed or benefited in order for a species to shed or acquire a trait.

We should be interested to know for what animals have been selected, for we could then understand the function of their physical and psychological traits, the "meaning" of their existence. The easy answer, survival, is insufficient. No animal survives; death comes to all. Genes have not been selected to favor enhanced longevity for individual species members. Humans could have evolved to live ten thousand years rather than eighty. They did not, and the reason is that individual survival is not what evolution, or any species, is about. Neither can survival of the species itself be thought of as the implicit goal either of genes or of individuals. As Darwin noted, not only does no species exist for the sake of another species; no individual acts for the preservation of its own species. The most deadly struggle in nature is not between species, or of a species against its environment, but among conspecifics. The answer—and once we have seen it, we see it also as a tautology—is that each organism has evolved to be and to behave in such a way as to maximize the advantage of its own genes, even to the drastic curtailment of its own individual existence. Each bisexual organism possesses in itself 100 percent of its own unique genes; its siblings each have about 50 percent of those same genes, as do its parents and offspring. It follows that each organism has been selected for so as to favor its own survival over that of any other member of its species, but to favor over itself the survival of, say, three siblings or offspring, nine first cousins, nieces, or nephews, or any combination that represents a greater probable gene survival potential. Parents and children are symmetrically related, of course, but children represent greater future reproduction potential, and so parents show greater concern for children than children do for parents—and this is precisely to the gene advantage of parents. It is important to know that no conscious intent is implied in all this, nor even any mysterious "drive" to favor gene advantage. Simply put, animals that are physically and psychologically put together in such a way as to favor the survival of their genes in direct or collateral descendants are most likely to have such descendants, and those descendants will inherit the favoring characteristics. Because no other selection process intervenes, and because of the severity of this selection process itself, we may say confidently, if tautologously, that the explanation of the present existence and character of genes and of their animal representatives is inclusive gene fitness, gene survival.

Those members of a species are selected for which make the greatest contribution to the perpetuation, not of their own lives or that of the species, but of their own genes, as represented also in their offspring and close relatives. Members of a species are selected not only for their ability to reproduce but even for their ability to die at the right time to make way for their offspring's attempts at reproduction.

All this makes way for the introduction of the idea of genetic altruism. Salmon have been selected for swimming up rivers to spawn and die. The sterile female worker ant labors all her life to forward the interests of the queen ant's larvae: such are the peculiarities of reproduction among ants that those larvae are more closely related to the worker ant than her own offspring would be. Matured Florida scrub jays sometimes remain at the nest to assist in the raising of the next batch of siblings. In this way they maximize the advantage of their own genes, for the siblings that survive as a direct result of their help outnumber the offspring they might have had if they had formed a new family unit. On the basis of kin selection theory we can see why individuals favor their offspring over their parents, why siblings engage in fierce competition with each other but join against an outsider. Most animals defend their offspring, and the inbred group to which they belong, at some risk to their own lives. The African deer that stops to warn the herd before it flees from a predator increases the danger of being eaten itself, but the sum of the fractions of its genes in the herd exceeds those that it personally carries and so its action makes genetic sense. Herds containing such "altruistic" members have a competitive advantage over herds of the same species that do not.

Caution is necessary when we apply kin selection theory to animal behavior. An animal does not consciously intend to favor its own genes; rather it has been selected to feel or behave as though it does. As for humans, they too are equally the product of a selection process that has shaped their bodies, minds, and feelings to favor their own genes, but our knowledge of this fact is too general to be of immediate use for the interpretation of most human action. Neither we nor the other animals have an urge, drive, or command from nature to "maximize inclusive gene fitness." Neither we nor they could begin to carry out such a directive in a trustworthy manner. Rather, we and they have built into our being those characteristics, physical and psychological, that in general bring about the effect of such fitness. The ascent of humans to consciousness and the ability to carry on abstract thought has not changed this situation; no new elements have been added to our motivational system: whence could they have come? But our motives have been complicated considerably. Our genetic feeling structure evolved to favor our genes, but our ability to think in metaphors has extended the application of our feelings from their obvious objects to less obvious objects. We still say that "blood is thicker than water," and parents usually incur heavy costs for their children, but we are capable of taking a nation to be our parent and a specially marked collection of strangers to be our group. The offspring of our mind and cultivated feeling can be substituted in our regard for our biological children. Such complications do nothing to reduce the force of kin selection theory, but they do render its use as an explanation of human action very uncertain. We display propensities that are illuminated by kin selection theory, but we usually cannot predict in particular instances just how the genetic feelings common to us all will attach themselves to the complex of symbols produced by culture and our own individual imaginations. Nevertheless, you are much more likely to send your own children to an expensive college than the children of an acquaintance, and the very word "stepchild" implies for us a position of relative insecurity.

The reductionist human nature theory sees each of us as a value island or independent sovereign nation, one that may trade, ally itself, and cooperate with other islands but whose relations with others must be understood as dominated by short- and long-range calculations of its own interest. The ahistoricist culturalist simply substitutes "culture" for "individual." Each culture is understood to act and to change in ways that are functional for the culture as a whole rather than for the individuals that comprise it.

Kin selection theory is between these two. It sees the individual rather than the culture as the sole generator or holder of values, but it sees the individual differently. The difference may seem slight, as slight as Hobbes's negligent exception of "the bonds of natural lust" from his view of us as universally and necessarily complete egoists. "The bonds of natural lust" are with those who are closely related to us and with a few bonded friends; they are a line crack in the hard nut of Hobbes's philosophy of egocentrism. The self that all our feelings serve includes those who share our genes and a few to whom we have bonded emotionally. (The genetic explanations of bonding are various, but the fact of bonding is well established in all our experience.) The crack widens as we see that the "bonds of natural lust" expand, in humans, through our proclivity for analogy and symbolization, to include anything whatsoever, but notably other persons, groups of persons, even inanimate objects of sentiment. This proclivity of ours makes the culturalist functionalist view of society understandable, but only operationally true to the extent to which the myths that persuade us to pursue a social interest at the expense of an individual interest are powerful within large numbers of us. It is easy to exaggerate both the extent to which this actually happens even in the most culturally homogeneous societies and the pureness of the "social interest" pursued; we've known for some millennia that persons and groups often see their interest as the social interest. Whatever interesting further complications we may see in this, the reality, for the study of culture, is that it is essentially composed of transient individuals who *use* it for their own purposes. Insofar as they find it of use, they will resist change, but they will try to make changes that they themselves find of use.

The use of kin selection theory in social analysis is to structure our approach to that study rather than lead us directly to conclusions. That structuring excludes both radical individualism and the social organism view but allows many of the conclusions often derived from either of them. We ought not expect scientific theories to settle large questions about society and value. On the other hand, kin selection theory provides a common language for those whose commitment to rival metaphysical views has made communication impossible.

Parenthetically, it might be important to note that cracking the hard nut of the belief in universal egoism is not necessarily a step toward a more optimistic view of human nature. We have seen only half of "altruism" when we think of charity, of dedication to humane causes. The other half consists of patriotic dedication in imperialistic wars, in the nepotism and cronyism that makes a mockery of many systems of justice. Even racism can be seen as a kind of group solidarity. The genetic feelings we have that favor the interests of others are themselves, in the value theory here propounded, value neutral.

Tropism, Instinct, Feeling-Thought[4]

If we had a clearer notion of what impels animal behavior, we should have a clearer understanding of human action. I suggest the following.

1. The behavior of many organisms, notably plants, can be understood in terms of such concepts as reflex and tropism, by what may ultimately be reducible to our knowledge of organic chemistry. Indeed, all animals are partly classifiable as "vegetables"; their autonomic behavior—perspiration, cell division, and so forth—seems in principle reducible to known physical processes.

2. Some animals have evolved a more complex kind of behavior called instinct. If only in principle, this too may be reducible to very complex chemical interchanges. Thousands of species go through their lives behaving in extraordinarily complex ways, ways that are far beyond the capacity of their tiny brains to intend, but that are, in ordinary circumstances, almost ideally adaptive for them. We call this behavior instinctive, a term defined here as relatively invariant, goal-oriented, not consciously intended, long sequences of motion. There is a kind of beetle that bores a hole in a tree, makes a chamber inside much larger than it needs, then bores another hole, again much larger than it needs, almost through the outer bark. It then returns to the chamber and spins itself into a cocoon. Later it emerges from the cocoon as a large butterfly that cannot bore through wood. The butterfly goes through the enlarged exit, pokes its way through the remaining bark to freedom. The whole process is instinctual. We cannot believe that the animal knew what it was doing at any point, or why, or even had the notion that it was doing anything at all. Instinct permits animals of extremely limited intellectual ability to occupy ecological niches that require relatively invariant complex movements in a certain order. The limitations of instinct are evident. A nineteenth-century French biologist found a species of caterpillar whose members attach themselves to each other to form a chain for the purpose of making their way each evening out of a fruit tree and back to the ground, where they spend the night. He induced such a chain to form a closed circle around the top of a large urn. They circled for days, until most of them died, unable to cope with a circumstance that did not arise in their ordinary life. When the environment changes, instinctual animals either become extinct, or if the change is gradual enough, they may evolve new instincts.

3. The "higher" animals, particularly the mammals, are defined as such because they have few and relatively flexible in-

stincts. Humans, and perhaps the other primates, may have none at all. Such behavioral uniformities as we exhibit are reflexes, as in the nursing reflex of infants and their cry of fear in free fall or when exposed to a loud noise. Instinct is relatively invariant behavior composed of a long chain of specific physical motions; we find no traces of such behavior among humans. The use of the word "instinct" in connection with human behavior and action—as though the goal-oriented but highly variable activities of courtship or mothering were comparable to the beetle's behavior—only serves to confuse our thinking about our nature.

The animals we usually refer to as "higher" have more or less completely discarded instinctual behavior in favor of a more complicated and finer-tuned method of coping with their environment. That method is a combination of learning ability and feeling capacity. There is an evident incompatibility between this learning-feeling method and that of instinct. They interfere with each other, and so any particular species is found to be dominated by one or the other. The more interesting (non-reflexive, non-random) motions of a member of a higher species are motivated by the emotive pattern of its species and guided by its past experience and grasp of a present situation.

If we are to understand how the higher animals operate, we must have a clear idea of intelligence and of feeling and of how they relate to each other. We must get rid of many cliches that are commonly found in this area, notably the "reason versus passion" opposition that has had such a long career.

Intelligence is the ability to receive and to process sense data so that the environment is structured in a way helpful to the organism. Intelligence is a means of acquiring information; information is all it can provide. It identifies, remembers, connects, induces and deduces, assesses probabilities. As Donald Campbell has pointed out in his "Evolutionary Epistemology,"[5] the ability to gather information is the result of an evolutionary process.

Information is vital, to the ivy seeking a foothold for a tendril, to a hungry lion, to the deciduous tree and the unemployed carpenter, but the need is selective, is not for all information but only for information relevant to the needs or feelings of the organism. The need is not for ideally true information, but for information that is pragmatically true for this creature at this time. The passion for information, curiosity, varies from species to species, depending upon the need and the capacity the species has for knowing more or fewer details of its environment. The higher animals actively seek information and their perceptual organs have achieved a very high degree of precision in those matters important to them. Sense data are relayed to the brain and are there selected, criticized, collated and summarized, compared and interpreted; the procedure results in the awareness of a structured external reality. Similar such realities from the past, and the relative success of various actions taken in response to them, are recalled and the strategy for coping with the digested present is formed. In most animals the process, here simplified, takes place at the unconscious level.

It is helpful to think of this conversion of sense data into information as a distinct process in the higher animals, and one that is much the same in all of them. Allowing for differences in interest, sense organs, and intellectual ability, these animals, including humans, all live in much the same world. As Aristotle put it, for men and for fishes "what is white or straight is always the same." The result of the perceiving-remembering-structuring technique is much the same for us and for a mouse. Verbally for us, non-verbally for it, the cat is equally on the mat, or not.

Our superior intelligence distinguishes us from other animals, but the function of our intelligence, as of theirs, is to enhance life success. It cannot determine what success is. "Success" is a member of the class of good things, whereas the function of intelligence is to provide information that is itself value-free. From the fact that something is, it cannot follow that it is good or bad or that something ought to be done about it. Information has no logical implications for action; from no experience, and from no deduction from value-free concepts, can we reason to a value.

The full quotation from Aristotle is: "What is healthy or good is different for men and for fishes, but what is white and straight is always the same."[6] With relatively minor differences, the cat that I and the mouse see on the mat is much the same, but the feelings it arouses in each of us varies according to our feelings about past experiences and probably as well according to some degree of unmediated genetic feeling propensity. To me the cat is a virtuous pest destroyer, a symbol of happy domesticity, a playful furry toy; I feel all this and stoop to pet it, remember to feed it. The mouse feels quite differently. Its blood pressure rises; adrenalin floods its blood stream; it trembles and silently departs.

Success and failure, the better and the worse, the desirable and the undesirable, are discovered not by the intelligence but by the feelings. Feelings come first in the higher animals and their intelligence is there to facilitate the satisfaction of the feelings. As Hobbes put it, "Reason is the scout of the passions,"[7] which Hume amended to read, "Reason is, and ought to be, the slave of the passions."[8] At least since Freud we have assumed that the passionate elements in us, what we have confusedly called the irrational, prevail over the intellect. We tend to bemoan this fact, as though it were somehow shameful and ought to be reversed. It is not shameful; nothing so inevitable and necessary can be shameful. The passions, although they dominate, are not in some value sense superior to the intellect. The passions and the intellect do not compete; we do not understand either if we think they do. Without intelligence we act unintelligently and the passions are frustrated; without the passions the intellect does nothing, it sits there like an unplugged computer, like a car out of gas, inoperative. Mice and men are curious animals, but although we may idealize this curiosity into a disinterested passion for pure knowledge, curiosity is yet for both species a passion and one that has been selected for in order to serve inclusive gene fitness.

Feelings, passions, emotions, affect—I need not distinguish among them here—have their physical basis in the old brain, in the hypothalamic-limbic region and some of the glands. When we are having them, our bodies are in an altered state, but yet, as red is not a light wave, feelings are not that altered state but irreducibly what we experience them to be. We ought not make things of them. The passions are not Envy, Sloth, Lust, Greed, and so on. They are emotional states that arise in response to certain situational perceptions, situations to which it has proven adaptive that the animal respond with particular kinds of feelings. There is, for instance, no single feeling of "maternal love." Mothers respond to their offspring with feelings that vary according to the actual perceived situation. Those feelings inspire fondling, protection, nursing, and also rejection and punishment. The feelings, not the specific behavior, are genetically present in the mothers, are triggered to occur in stereotypical situations rather than in response to a single stimulus. Mothers who have species-typical feelings, with the average intensity and at the usual times, tend to do the things that favor the survival of their genes in the infant; mothers who do not, generally fail to represent their genes in the future of the species.

The species of the higher animals are sometimes closely related to each other and so often display homologous feelings. Very different species sometimes share similar histories and so display analogous feelings. Nevertheless, although we can learn a great deal about human feeling patterns from the study of animals, especially of such closely related animals as the primates, what we learn is suggestive rather than conclusive. Humans and chimpanzees are said to have an astonishing 99 percent of common genes, and certainly the similarity between the apparent feelings of chimpanzees and of humans is found striking by all observers. Yet we cannot confidently reason directly from the feelings of animals to our own; we *can* reason from the overall relation of intellect and feeling in them to the same relation in us. Species are really different from each other. Each of the higher species, however similar some of its feelings may be to those of another species, yet has its own distinct and characteristic feeling profile. Other species may teach us of the existence and function of our own feeling profile, may suggest to us what sort of things to look for in it, but only a study of our own species can tell us what it is in us.

It is important that we realize that each of the component feelings of a species feeling profile has evolved independently of the others, to fit different circumstances at different times. This means that each of the feelings has, so to speak, its own power base, its own separate genetic basis. This is why attempts, so common in the seventeenth and eighteenth centuries, to produce a deduction of the passions have so consistently failed. The feelings of a female monkey when fondling its infant and when facing a high-status male are not reducible either to each other or to some more fundamental feeling. Each evolved to serve a distinct function, just as did the flat tail and strong teeth of a beaver. In some situations an animal may experience conflicting feelings, simultaneously or in rapid alternation, and be urged in contrary directions. This fact introduces an element of unpredictability into the behavior of the higher animals. We cannot tell precisely just how strongly each of several emotions will be aroused in a particular situation. We do not know quite how the animal perceives the situation or against the background of what kind of experience. A mother bird may attack the cat who approaches the nest. As the cat turns to fight, the bird is frightened and flies off, only to regain its nerve with distance and return to the attack. The bird certainly is not aware of its movements as meant to maximize gene advantage, nor even as a conflict of mothering feelings and personal survival feelings. It simply has this feeling and then that and acts on each feeling as it predominates. If the alternation is very rapid, its feelings may simply cancel out and it will remain motionless. The mother bird is neither courageous nor prudent; she does what at any moment she feels like doing and must do or she does nothing.

We should be able to construct a feeling profile for each of the higher animals[9] and thus prepare ourselves to construct one for ourselves. We already have a good part of such a profile for cognate species of primates. From controlled laboratory experiments and from detailed studies of their life in the wild, we know a great deal about the genetic, although not instinctive, character of their affective styles of interactions of dominance and subordination, threat and appeasement, sibling relationships, mother-infant behavior, shifting coalitions of elite members, and even techniques used in playing on each other's emotions. We think we see in them the germs of what in ourselves we would call moral outrage, and the sense of personal affront, whereas their feelings of envy, sorrow, sympathy, rage, depression, and elation seem beyond question very much like ours.

Just as it proves useful to invert our ordinary thinking about animals, to see species as dispersed packages of almost identical submicroscopic genes, assembling and using large bodies for their own survival, equally content in time to evolve into a mosquito or an elephant, just so the genes go on, so it is useful to consider the extent to which members of the higher species can be thought to have a nature that consists most importantly of a feeling pattern. Bodies are relatively plastic to the evolutionary pressures of feelings, notably in sexual selection. Human males are hairy faced, human females are "baby-faced," in response to the selective pressures exerted by feelings in the opposite sex. The startling case of the male peacock is in point. Its magnificent tail is a handicap in every race but in the race for peahen approval. The sensible peacocks who once scorned fashion may have lived prosperously for decades, but they attracted no females and left no descendants to carry on the tradition of their prudence.

Feelings are generally more stable and more ancient in a species than intellect or physical form; their satisfaction is the goal of the intellectual capacities; they are the sole motivators to action. What a higher animal wants to do, however concretely specified as a result of learning, is a product of its species feelings. There is no basis for resisting this conclusion. To act freely is to do what you want to do, what you feel like doing, what your feelings direct you to do. Feelings are not an external force to which we are subject; they are in the deepest sense our true selves; they are what we are. The nature of a higher species is its feeling profile. When we look for human nature, we are looking for the human pattern of species-specific feelings.

CHAPTER 12

The Human Animal

The respect that researchers acquire for the species they study in the wild is in sharp contrast to the contempt that many people implicitly have for "beasts" or the blurring sentimentality of those who try to love indiscriminately all that lives. Animals are not simple. The infinitely intricate orderliness that physicists find in matter, that biologists find overlaid upon this in organisms, is rediscovered at the levels of animal behavior and human action. That orderliness is determined, and although the determinism we insist on finding in nature becomes ever more complex and obscure as we go from atoms to cells and from apes to humans it nevertheless remains true that, when we say that we are a part of nature, we mean that we are committed to finding ourselves exhibiting lawlike characteristics.

When we know that we are an animal among animals, we know only that we are a product of evolution, that we evolved to meet the circumstances in which we lived, that those circumstances were very complex and demanding, and that our present being as an animal is accordingly complexly specified in ways about which it would be interesting to learn. We are not fluidly amorphous protoplasm; we are in innumerable ways clearly adapted to live a certain kind of life, just as are all the other species.

When we understand that we have evolved as one of the higher animals, we know that what we do and want to do is the result of the mix of learning ability or intelligence with specific genetic feelings that evolved to adapt us to particular situations. Once we have an adequate idea of what it is to be a species, a member of a higher species, we want to know what kind of species we are. In this investigation, physical characteristics are relatively uninteresting. It is not significant that we are a featherless biped, and if our upright posture and opposable thumb are thought to have been necessary to our present achievements, they are merely necessary conditions, do not constitute our essence. The interesting constitutive elements of our human motivation are our high intelligence and our feeling profile.

Human feelings are not more different from those of the other higher animals than these are among themselves. We have a few propensities, as for sharing food, that resemble those of predators, but otherwise our species-typical feelings are surprisingly similar to those of the other primates. There may be no feelings at all that are distinctively peculiar to us although the mix of feelings is as unique in us as it is in other species. Species feeling patterns are very stable as compared with physical attributes and intelligence. The notable characteristics of our feeling pattern probably go back millions of years, whereas our present level of intelligence may be no more than a hundred thousand years old.

Our information gathering and processing system is both ordinary and extraordinary. It is ordinary at the level of data collection: our senses are unremarkable in the animal world. We are special in what we do with the information we gather. The enormous development of our data-processing equipment, of our intelligence, makes us truly outstanding. No other animal approaches our ability to remember, to imagine alternatives to the present, to create and manipulate abstractions. The power that this has given us has been sufficiently celebrated.

The contrast between our ancient and relatively unchanging passions and our new intelligence, especially that intelligence as sharpened and developed through education and technology, has struck many observers. Some have even suggested that the passions are dangerous or a hindrance to us in modern civilization, that we ought to have no feelings, or that we ought to have different and better feelings. Yet our feelings cannot be intrinsically dangerous to us. Our genetic feeling pattern is our essence as a species. If our feeling pattern is changed, we are destroyed as a species. If we are to be destroyed in some other way, it is because our environment has changed drastically in ways beyond our control or because our intelligence fails to perform its task of assessing reality. Our liking for the taste of sugar is genetic and apparently evolved in us because those who ate fruit at its most sugary phase of ripeness also ate what was most nutritious for them. Now most of us eat more sugar than is good for us, but this is not the fault of our feeling for the taste of sugar, but the failure of our intelligence to use the fruits of technology sensibly, that is to say to use them in the interest of all of our passions taken together, rather than of this one and then that one disjunctively. There is no basis on which we can criticize our total feeling pattern, for criticism involves a value judgment, and value judgments can have their basis only in feelings. Neither is it practicable to select particular disfavored passions for excision, for although each passion operates in us independently, the passions are genetically intertwined. Our capacity to feel anger, for instance, seems inextricably connected to our capacity to feel affection. It is true that we can wish we were less influenced by some particular passion, but only on the basis of some other competing passion or passions that are similarly open to disapproval. What we cannot do is lift ourselves by our bootstraps, wish that our wishes overall were different from what they are, feel otherwise than in fact as a species we do. Our genetic feelings as they presently exist are our only basis for value judgments.

Human nature theory is concerned with humans as a species and depends for its interest on the degree of similarity obtaining among all humans. If different races were emotionally different, there could be no general theory of human nature. Further, because that theory takes the genetic feeling pattern as the essential, most interesting, element of human nature, and because that pattern is much older, more deeply rooted, and therefore presumably more uniform throughout the species than many other of our genetic traits, it follows that human nature thinkers will see us as more united by our common nature than will any other theorists. There are some geneticists who have argued that one race is more intelligent than another, and that this somehow justifies discrimination against the less intelligent race. The reasoning is poor. For one thing, there is no persuasive evidence that races differ in intelligence as presently measured. We may hope that no such evidence ever turns up. Suppose it does, what are we to do about it? It will not do to say that it is impossible. It is quite possible. The racist conclusion, however, does not follow. Some members of dumber race A would still be smarter than some members of race B and so ill treatment of a whole race would, on the very basis that was supposed to justify it, be unjustified. A consistent racist would have to discriminate against his or her own children if they were of less than average intelligence. Intelligence is a good, as are beauty, muscular strength, health, humor, wisdom, and tact, but we would be intolerably busy if we were to discriminate against everyone who is deficient in some one asset. Those (principally the culturalists) who are opposed to the idea of a determinate common human nature have made every possible charge against it, including racism and political and social conservatism. The charges are demonstrably false. It is culturalism, with its assumption that humans of different cultures are like different species of animals, that justifies any conceivable treatment of members of alien societies or ideologies. The fact that most culturalists are thoroughly humane persons does not help the fact that their beliefs allow, and even support in principle and sometimes in practice, the utmost inhumanity. The followers of the theory of unique individualism need have no sympathy for those whom they label inauthentic or indeed, on their principles, for anyone at all. There is nothing in the nature of a belief that our values come from God, Reason, or Nature to suggest that we ought to be merciful to those who are unreasonable, "unnatural," or heretical. Human nature theory, in its non-reductionist version, has always emphasized that we are a singularly social animal, that we have a genetic sympathy for others of our species. General theories of value do not dictate particular value judgments, but of all the sects, human nature thinkers seem most compelled by their own principles to maintain the importance of our common humanity as represented in our common feeling pattern. As far as I know, no geneticist has argued seriously for important racial difference in that pattern.

In view of the utopian character of so much secular human nature theory, it is difficult to see how some can think that it is politically or socially conservative. Human nature would, in that case, have to justify equally each of the very many and very different institutions that have existed, merely because they have existed. Is it not culturalism and historicism that notoriously do just this? Human nature theory is a basis, the only available basis, on which criticism of institutions and cultural practices is possible, the only basis on which the need for such criticism is self-evident. It is the only theory that provides an unsentimental, transcultural basis for human solidarity and interpersonal sympathy.

The means we have for the study of human nature are many. We can know it by shedding our cultural blinders and simply hearing and observing each other—rare and fleeting as that capacity may be. We can study the human species as it came into being over evolutionary time and note the constraints and opportunities of that ancient environment to which we are even now an adaptation. We can look at existing cognate species, study comparative anthropology, even consider predator species to which we are not closely related but that lead somewhat similar lives in similar circumstances. On the basis of all this and of some archeological evidence, it is reasonable to conclude that our ancestors, no more genetically different from us than we are from each other, evolved the complex psychological profile that we share with them. No more than any of the other higher animals could they have survived without it. They, we, lived in bands of from about fifteen to eighty persons, were hunter-gatherers, had a social organization modeled mostly on that of our primate ancestors but modified by the fact that we were largely predators. In those pre-agricultural days, men hunted and fought and woman foraged and tended children and the home site. Males competed with other males for status but also bonded with each other for communal hunting and fighting. In the resulting tension between the struggle for individual dominance and the need for cooperation, we can assume that intragroup politics was much what it is today in villages and small groups. Incest barriers were strong. Mating was probably not strictly monogamous but fairly permanent arrangements were the rule. Supernatural forces were everywhere; dealing with them was time-consuming and expensive. The product of the hunt, but not of the foraging, was generally shared. Other groups, at least those beyond the exogamous mating circle, were feared and hated, and those feelings worked to strengthen the internal cohesion of the group. Language involving symbolization of reality was in ordinary use, and the long childhood of the young was used to socialize them into the ways of the group and to sort them into their places within it. People killed other people, but even if those others were depersonalized enemies, the killer experienced shock, fear, guilt. The feeling pattern, the emotional profile of our species, was then what it is now.[1] It had evolved to suit the general environmental and social conditions of that time. Young women adorned themselves to attract high-status males. Young men competed for the status that would earn them attractive females. Mothers babied babies in ways we would find familiar; older women looked forward to grandchildren; older high-status males strutted and pontificated; low-status males grumbled and muttered of revolution but went along when necessary. There is no reason to think life then was either idyllic or miserable. No doubt some tribes were luckier or better organized and so better to live in than were some others. Political philosophy began in the thoughtful consideration of such differences. Further research will correct and refine this "likely story."

There we were then, and we now are those people. We are, genetically, the product of their environment. If one of them were transplanted to our society in infancy, we could not, at maturity, tell him or her from the rest of us. If a group of our infants were somehow transplanted into and could survive in that early physical environment, they would in the course of many generations learn about fire and stone axes and move on to reproduce the general form of our present societies. The feelings of ancient peoples, however different their objects, are the feelings we experience; the cultures we build are the product of the same feelings they had. If we find a conflict between our feelings and the demands of our society, so did they. Societies vary in the degree to which they satisfy the broadest range of human feelings, but none can satisfy, for all, all the feelings. The reason for this is that human feelings are necessarily in conflict, not only the feelings of one person with those of another, but those of each individual with themselves. This takes us to the special problems of human animals.

Special Problems of Humans

We noted above the behavior of the bird as it sometimes defended its nest and sometimes fled the cat. The ordinary life of one of the higher animals is full of such events. In appropriate circumstances it experiences some one feeling. This feeling, had in the context of the experience and intelligence of the animal, usually results in some kind of behavior or action. Either the feeling is then satisfied or it is not. If not, and depending upon what the feeling is, and how strong, and what else is going on in the environment, the animal will persist in the behavior, improvise new behavior, or accept defeat and await a new motivating feeling. Compared to ours the options of even the most intelligent other animals are very limited. Their feelings evolved to adapt them to a relatively narrow range of immediate circumstances; they do indeed adapt. Animals are normally quite comfortable. Walt Whitman dramatized the difference between them and us:

> I think I could turn and live with animals,
>   they are so placid and self-contain'd,
> I stand and look at them long and long.
> They do not sweat and whine about their condition,
> They do not lie awake in the dark and weep for
>   their sins,
> They do not make me sick discussing their duty to
>   God,
> Not one is dissatisfied, not one is demented with
>   the mania for owning things,
> Not one kneels to another, nor to his kind that
>   lived thousands of years ago,
> Not one is respectable or unhappy over the
>   whole earth.[2]

When they are not stimulated, they sleep, or lie quietly, waiting for day, or night, or for something to engage their interest.

Humans are different. Their new large brain produced the possibility of a technology that can be enormously helpful in dealing with the external world; more importantly it made possible a complex social organization that in turn made it possible for us to live in intense cooperation and to pass on the culture that includes and fosters technology. All this is to the good, but intelligence brought with it a side effect that raises a great problem for all of us. Humans experience what is about them and react with feeling. They also experience what they are thinking, which may not be about what is present, and they must react with feeling to that as well. There is no easy solution to the problems raised by this vast production of feeling that is not always immediately relevant to the present. We have all sorts of tricks to distinguish between dreaming and real life, between what we are presently imagining and our actual situation, but there is no clean-cut technique that enables us to do it instantly. Through our fertile brains rush many vivid sequences—alternative presents, pasts, and futures. The very success of historical humans depended upon their ability to take those imaginations seriously.[3] To each of them we must react as though it were real, with feeling. The consequence is that a human lying awake unable to sleep, or daydreaming, can in rapid sequence feel concern about a parent or child, be tense in an imagined fight, bristle at an insult, languish in sexual fantasy, yearn for social success, contemplate beautiful scenes, be ashamed at a social lapse. Humans think and imagine much more than do other animals.[4] They experience a corresponding multiplication of the occurrence of feelings. In man, said Aristotle, desire is infinite.[5]

Because feelings are our sole motivation to action, and can be aroused in us by our imagination, we are continually prone to act on the basis of what is not there, to our peril. Hamlet and other disturbed people who talk to ghosts are momentarily and dangerously open to attack from whatever is actually there. They are likely to act inappropriately, as by rushing over precipices or hurting people who happen to be near them. If our species had acquired its imaginative powers suddenly, rather than gradually, we might have perished from sheer inability to cope with the flood of images and the powerful passions they arouse.

Our imaginative capacities keep us in a continual state of incipient action. We suffer from this in many ways. We can become ill when those calls for action that follow upon our imaginations flood our bloodstream with adrenalin but our reality assessments keep us immobile. All the higher animals exhibit psychic pathologies with organic causes, and we are able to reproduce in animals, under laboratory conditions, many non-organic neuroses and psychoses formerly thought reserved to humans.

But only we experience serious functional psychic disorders in our ordinary social life. These disorders, which arise from our feeling conflicts, are the principal cause of human unhappiness, outranking disease, death, and physical deprivation. Freud only scratched the surface of this problem when he spoke of the unhappiness necessarily resulting from the permanent conflict between individual passionate needs and the needs of society for orderliness. Schopenhauer's more inclusive pessimism (we are doomed to oscillate between pain and boredom) came closer to describing our real situation. From the beginning, the central task of secular ethical theory has been to come to terms with this species problem. Actually it is not uniquely a human problem, but one that would afflict any feeling-learning species of high intelligence. Science fiction writers have correctly observed that an intelligent and adequately motivated (programmed) robot would necessarily produce morality and moral theory.[6]

Each species, highly intelligent or not, that acts on the feeling-learning basis has an implicit value system based on, expressive of, its species feeling pattern. Humans are no exception. Before the evolution of our high intelligence, we had a species value system, whether we knew it or not, and nothing about the addition of intelligence does anything to change either our feeling pattern or the species value system that rests upon it. The only possible basis for a moral or ethical system is a precedent implicit species value system which expresses a species feeling profile.

We begin the study of the human value system by an observation of our own feelings, being careful to maintain the distinction between the actual feelings and their specific objects. We know rivalry, spite, revenge, solidarity, the desire for esteem and success, panic and anxiety, the feelings toward infants and small children, the sense of horror at bloodshed and the killing of humans, and so on. Because our feelings in actual life experiences come to us confusingly blended with each other and rapidly shifting in response to each blink of consciousness, it can be all but impossible to disentangle them for analysis. Yet we can, for instance, distinguish many of the more obvious transcultural feelings that go to make up the general pattern of the universal human courting ritual. The complex feelings of each member of a couple, shifting from moment to moment, may be the evolutionary product of their biological strategies, but we gain at best a poetic, at worst a uselessly abstract and elementary, knowledge of ourselves if we concentrate on such strategies. It is the actual feelings as integrated further into endlessly ramifying cultural conditioning with which we must deal. Either or both of the parties may be intent on some culturally defined end, as money or security. In order to understand what is going on, we have to understand the way in which these things in their society serve to facilitate the satisfaction of genetic feelings that have little or nothing to do with the feelings specific to the courting ritual.

Astute students of human feelings are found in all fields, as in law, medicine, teaching, and bartending, but the literary artists are best at communicating their knowledge. Homer deals with the elementary social passions that we find in all male groups. We can apply his insights to a high-school basketball team, a hunting band of Indians, or the United States Senate, and we can apply them respectfully or in the spirit of mockery we find in Shakespeare's *Troilus and Cressida*. Such writers as Henry James deal with those same feelings as exquisitely refined and delicately distinguished among elites in a "high culture" such as prevailed in his time, or in similar cultures in Japan, medieval Europe, India, and elsewhere.

In our search for an understanding of our feeling structure we cannot overlook the professional psychologists. Of all the human sciences, psychology is the one most committed to the study of human nature as a transcultural phenomenon. Although they can make a few distinctions between the thought processes and objects of feelings of different cultures, psychologists can do so only on the supposition of an explanatory framework that includes the species psyche as a constant. The newness of the formal study of psychology, and the wide divergence and rapid succession of schools of thought within it, should warn us against the attempt to achieve a quick and easy grasp of human feelings. In psychology itself, it is a commonplace that those who do best at understanding us rely on an individually achieved intuitive wisdom rather than on a teachable theoretical system.[7]

The important questions remain: How do we solve the problems created by our emotional response to imagined situations? How do we get from the species value system based on our feeling profile to actual value judgments? How do we arrive at value judgments? How can we cross the is-ought gulf to a prescriptive ethic?

CHAPTER 13

Value Judgments

It is impossible to reason, deductively or inductively, from facts or concepts to a value judgment. That is, we cannot reason from an is to an ought, from description to prescription, from knowing to doing. This is why, in general, contemporary philosophers fail to produce positive moral theory. They assume they must base their thinking on public facts and concepts. Intentionality, sentiments, attitudes, feelings, action as opposed to behavior, in short, value, fall through their intellectual nets. As for the culturalists, unless they absurdly attribute immanent goals to society or history, they cannot discuss a value judgment on its merits but only as a reflection of social or historical conditions. Those who write on ethics are almost evenly divided into these two groups, and that is why there is at present no ethical theory that tells us plainly how we can distinguish the better from the worse, what we ought to do from what we ought not. Students of contemporary ethical theory often feel like a hungry person in a restaurant who is asked to choose between one menu that consists of a chemical analysis of all the common foods and another that gives him a history of their production and use. Yet although descriptive ethics, the study of value judgments as external phenomena, as behavior, is usually an exercise in futility, it seems to me, following Solomon's notion that "a fool who persists in his folly becomes wise," that anyone who follows the descriptive route persistently enough will finally arrive at prescriptive conclusions. The transition, impossible in theory, takes place easily and commonly in practice.

High in the tree, the cat stalks the nestlings. A parent bird attacks the cat; the cat hisses and claws at the bird; the bird flies away; the cat inches forward; the bird returns to the attack and is again frightened off. Let me stipulate that the bird is neither cowardly nor courageous, that moral language will not appropriately be used in describing its behavior, that what we observe in it is the rapid alternation of strong and simple motivations: fear and nest-protectiveness.

A shabbily dressed young man steps to the head of the line at the teller's window. There, behind the counter, are stacks of bills, the answer to all his problems and desires. The guard is old and drowsy; the way out is clear. Tell the clerk that the bagged lunch is a bomb; grab the money; run. But the guard has a gun and the teller will be able to describe him. Our young man sees himself on the marble floor in a pool of blood or, unhurt, facing his distraught mother through bars. The money, yes, but the terrible reverberation of the gun. The money, but the defeat and the shame.

The similarities between these two vacillating creatures will suggest to some observers that we cannot ascribe a moral character to the actions of the young man, or to anyone, any more than we can to the behavior of the bird. The bird must do, at each moment, what at that moment it most strongly wants to do. It has no alternative to doing what it wants to do, no means of changing what it wants to do. What it wants to do is dictated by its species motivational system as it is triggered by its understanding of the particular circumstances in which it is located.

The bird engages your services as a consultant. You say: "If you wish to save the young ones, you must attack the cat much more vigorously and continuously. If you wish to guarantee your own survival, you must stay far away from the cat. I cannot advise you further until I know your priorities." The bird responds:

"I seem to care equally about my survival and that of the young ones." You investigate, calculate, and advise: "Attack the cat as frequently as possible, but go no closer than three inches from its extended claws and for no longer than three-quarters of a second. If you follow this procedure, there is a 50 percent chance that the cat will retreat and a 50 percent chance that you will be killed." Some studies suggest that this is about what the bird will do in any case, not as a result of calculation, but because its species-normal motivations have been selected for to produce just this adaptive behavior. But whether the bird calculates or does what comes naturally to it, morality plays no part. The bird does what it wants to do.

The situation of the young man seems similar. He too must do whatever he is strongly motivated to do and has no control over what he wants to do. His basic motivational system, like that of the bird, is a product of the evolution of his species. We admit some complications. What the man perceives, and how he perceives it, what he values and disvalues, are powerfully influenced by his past personal experience and by the language, history, and present culture of his society. But are not these complications merely additional layers of determination? Where is the morality or immorality of the actions he contemplates? If he attempts to rob the bank and fails, we can accuse him of making poor reality assessments, but stupidity and ignorance are not moral terms. We might think he is not sufficiently socialized into the aspirations and inhibitions we consider desirable in members of complex societies, but that cannot be his fault, any more than is his failure to have all the feelings and information we consider appropriate to the situation. The general conclusion is that we do not see how we can hold him morally responsible, no matter what he does. He does what he must, given his feelings and perceptions, as must we. If, as seems quite clear, praise and blame are ultimately out of place, how can we employ it, even provisionally?

The practical answer to this question is rather obvious. Humans are emotional, verbal and social. We frequently experience strong feelings about the activities and character of our fellows. We too are parts of the universal chain of determination, and if we are internally compelled to judge others, then there can be no argument against our doing it, if only silently. We need not stop with judgments. We may go on to create systems of inducements and penalties aimed at modifying the circumstances under which others act and so modify the ways in which they do act. We cannot confer a metaphysical moral responsibility on others, but we have no difficulty in justifying public morals and the penal law. They work. They work for us in diminishing what we consider the evil and forwarding what we consider the good in our lives. Ultimately, praising and blaming are senseless. Provisionally they are sensible procedures.

This skeptical moral conclusion is, however, far removed from the position of those who believe that because our actions are determined it is a mistake to be concerned about or to discuss what we ought to do. This is not so, and we see how it is not by pushing further our study of the young man in the bank.

Birds and humans are parts of nature, nor does our intelligence or other presumed superiorities avail to take us one millimeter out of nature as a whole or out of our own nature. It is important to note that the man in the bank did not act at once on his various feelings. Humans, along with all other possible intelligent-imaginative creatures, must have a built-in inhibition against immediate action on the basis of feelings aroused by their imagination.[1] We need time to distinguish between what is imagined and what is there, time to integrate and react with feeling to the various futures we envisage, time to work out empirical probabilities and the force of future feelings. The delay may be very brief, as when a skilled basketball player makes physical, historical, and psychological calculations before he passes the ball to one player rather than to another. It may take a British Prime Minister years to decide whether to intervene in the American Civil War. Delay we must, for our strength as a species lies in our ability to imagine and compare alternative future realities rather than in our speed of reaction. We imagine different ways of satisfying a desire, produce scenarios that include the difficulties and pains attending each of these ways, react with feeling to the difficulties and pains as well as to the satisfactions hoped for. The strongest feeling or feelings present after these calculations determine which scenario shall be implemented. This seems much like a utilitarian calculation, except that the diverse and independently based feelings cannot be reduced to the desire for utility or pleasure. Each feeling demands an unqualified satisfaction for itself and will not be content with the pleasure afforded by the satisfaction of some other feeling. Pleasure often accompanies the satisfaction of feelings, but what is sought is not the pleasure but the satisfaction of specific desires.

We gave the bird the benefit of a (not very valuable) consultant. Let us offer one to the young man. He turns to you and asks what he should do. You interrogate him, calculate, and say: "If you try to rob the bank now, there is a 20 percent chance that you will be shot, a 10 percent chance that you will be killed, a 70 percent chance that you will be caught and jailed, a 12 percent chance that you will escape with upwards of $5,000." The young man is disappointed. "Too bad," he says, and turns toward the exit. Your interest has been aroused: "Wait. The money will still be there tomorrow. By then you could rig a disguise, set up a getaway car, figure out a way to distract or immobilize the guard. The odds would then be strongly in your favor." The man is pleased: "Great! I'll go now and get the disguise." Lost in a new train of thought, you scarcely notice he has left, but suddenly you dash off and catch up with him half way down the street: "Wait. I was thinking. If you succeed tomorrow, you'll quit your job, have a good time with the money. When the money is gone you'll have to rob more banks and the odds will shift against you. Even if you never get caught, you'll find the satisfactions of having the money are somewhat less than you anticipate. You'll be caught in a kind of life that can never offer you the kind of long-term satisfactions that are so much more important than momentary pleasures. I can't give you the exact percentages, but it seems clear to me that you would do better not to rob the bank, tomorrow or ever." The young man stares at you in exasperation: "Are you mad? You tell me to reconsider my whole scale of values, think about the range of possible lives I might lead, study my primary motivations and the world about me to discover what I really want to do, what sort of creature I am and might be! By God, I think you're right! Every moment I spend not thinking about this and acting on it is wasted." He abruptly leaves. You stand there numbly. Had you said that? Was it not true, and true for yourself as well?

Description, honestly pursued, leads to prescription. It is not necessary to abandon skepticism and the deterministic postulate in order to think constructively about morality and about what is to be done. The bird cannot be moral because it must act on the basis of motivations sparked by what is physically present before it. Morality begins for us with our ability to delay, to imagine futures, to react with feeling to those futures, to allow our feelings to get themselves in order, then to act on the strongest feeling. Moral philosophy does not free us from the determinism implicit even in this complex formulation. It is itself a part of that chain. Practical morality differs from bridge architecture only in the number and character of the independent variables involved and the relative imprecision of our knowledge of them. On the other hand, our motivation to make our lives worth living is much stronger than is our motivation to build bridges, and so true value judgments are more important to us than are true engineering judgments.

It is easy to see how we make value judgments in simple cases. The unequal strength of my various feelings accounts for why I cease to watch my favorite television serial when my house catches fire. When I tell you of my decision, you find it obvious. Your feeling hierarchy is all but identical to mine in this case. The problem for action posed by the independence of the different feelings, and the independent status of the values to which they give rise is settled by the feelings themselves. Stronger ones simply overmaster weaker ones. Might makes right. Would you have it otherwise? Which would you rather get, what you want less or what you want more?

The question of how we handle the conflict between passions aroused by immediate circumstances and those aroused by imagined distant or future events is more complicated. How does a future desire acquire authority over us? In a certain context, an object arouses desire, the desire produces a value judgment, the value judgment is followed by a plan for acquiring the object. There is then a delay. During the delay, the costs and consequences of having or getting the object in the way envisaged are imagined and the feelings that would accompany those costs and that having or getting are actually experienced. Prudence urges us to extend our imaginations. Some people are not very prudent. They are impulsive, hasty; we say they live for the moment or have a low threshold for frustration. We evaluate this characteristic in them as troublesome to us and dangerous to themselves. Prudence, delaying, acquires a positive value. We feel prudentially obliged to allow the feelings aroused by imagined future contingencies to be represented. We are able to save for "a rainy day" because we can so vividly imagine that rain and so can actually feel, now, the dismal quality of its cold wetness upon us.

Our life and the quality of that life depend upon our ability to delay, to imagine realistically, to experience and take account of the feelings aroused by our imaginings. We know this very well, and condemn not only the foolishness of those who habitually do not delay, or who are not sufficiently swayed by images of the future, but also our own frequent failure to do this as much as we feel we ought. Of course even those who are usually reflective and farsighted often overlook some practical probability or fail to realize sufficiently what a future feeling will be. The world of the future is not completely knowable any more than is our future self; many a Holy Grail has turned out to be a Dead Sea apple. Because of these painful uncertainties in our lives we anxiously consult with ourselves and with others, and not merely on practical affairs and the specific moral judgments that accompany them, but even on the principles involved in making such judgments. We urge ourselves and others to be patient, brave, cautious, to be ourselves but also not to be too much our immediate selves. Our experience and imagination tell us that some ways of living are better, will be experienced by us as better, than others. We observe that the lives of others are sufficiently similar to ours to make the interchange of value advice helpful.

So far the discussion has been about relatively simple decisions, where the sentiments are few and clearly identifiable. A single anticipatory experience of the feelings that would be aroused by a fire in my house induces me to forego a new gadget and buy fire insurance. Many of our decisions are more complex, involve a great many shifting and vague feelings and empirical uncertainties. If the case is trivial we toss a coin or act at random. If it is important to us, we worry; our life can come to a standstill while we consider. What we want is that state of mind and feeling wherein we can say "after all..." or "on mature consideration...." Mature considerations can be about empirical probabilities but at most of our important points of decision they are about overall or net feelings. We understand this most clearly when we advise someone to "sleep on it." We do not consider facts while we sleep; we interrupt a tide of feelings to awaken in a mood more typical of our enduring selves. Urgent feelings grow less urgent, tire themselves out, and as they loosen their grip on us, other feelings come forward to assert their claim. We arrive at what we consider in ourselves an average or normal state of feeling. We start anew to consider yesterday's question.

Hume described the average or normal state of the feelings that we seek in making an important value judgment as "the state of calm passion."[2] It is an adequate phrase, although it needs some explanation and expansion. The state of calm passion is a condition marked not by the absence of feeling, but by the presence of every principal passion we are likely to experience in our future life. Each such passion is represented in the strength, not that we think it ought to have, but that it actually has or will have. This assemblage of feelings is that state of calm passion, calm because each feeling is muted to allow for all the others. We summon these feelings by imagining the circumstances that evoke them, and as they appear we encourage each to stand by, quietly, as additional ones are discovered. The resources we marshall for our expansion into the state of calm passion include the events and understandings of our past life along with the feelings that accompanied them and the reflective commentary we have since scribbled along the margins of that history. Our scattered selves are blended into one self.[3] In the state of calm passion we find ourselves, find what life has made of us and we of it. This is the best we can do. Thus prepared, we cross our Rubicons and create, as responsibly as we can, our future.

Everyone has recollections of things done and undone under the influence of particular passions and has regretted some of those things. It is on the basis of this universal experience that we can say that humans prefer to make their decisions by the method of the parliament of feelings, in the state of calm passion. We call those who rarely or never reach this state shallow, and those who, like Hamlet, reach it and are immobilized, mad. To have all our feelings at once is to experience each one as a feeling, not as a concept or an idea. The power to do this is not the power of "reason"; it is the power of the feelings themselves, each one hurrying to the meeting. Some, like the littlest in a group of children, run up crying "wait for me!" Others, like non-combatants caught between intent hostile armies, wail in terror, reminding the fighters that, when the present passionate war is over, other elements of us, some perhaps the most important, must live on.

In the state of calm passion we say that we are "thinking about it," but the process is only marginally ratiocinative. We stand there, like the man in the bank, with images and feelings surging through us. Gradually the tumult subsides, the outline of what our whole self wants to do or be emerges from the confusion. Out of a fair fight, the strongest feeling or coalition of feelings emerges as the victor and urges us to a conclusion. What deals have been made in the smoke-filled rooms of our subconscious we may never know, but we do know that the outcome is accompanied by both relief and sadness. The relief is that we are going to be able to act, to move onward, with some sense of doing what is best for ourselves or for those for whom we care. The sadness that always accompanies moral decision is regret for those feelings that were defeated or that achieved only a slight gratification. Some of the little children are sent home to grieve; some of the non-combatants are sacrificed. Morality, for very young people, sometimes seems to be a rule that you must restrain yourself from doing anything that you very much want to do. Hume spoke truly of a moral decision as a kind of violence to oneself.[4]

The difference between the bird attacking and then fleeing the cat and human moral decision is slight but very significant. We often act as the bird does, on the urging of a single feeling, but we are capable also of acting as a collected whole. When we do so we are most truly human, most effectively responding to complex situations of danger and opportunity that our intellect and imagination make possible to us.

The bird is not courageous, even if it dies in the attempt to save the nestlings, for it can do no other than it does. Hector[5] was not courageous when he went out to fight Achilles under the illusion that supporters accompanied him, nor when he fought mechanically, like the trained killer that he was, nor when he fought desperately, like a cornered rat. He was courageous when he realized what was truly dangerous to him as a complete human being, when he fought knowing that there could be no life worth desiring, for himself or for his family and city, if Achilles won. He knew that Achilles would almost certainly win, and that he himself represented Troy's only chance for survival. Three millennia later we are still moved by the account of this mythical barbarian. We reproduce his going forth endlessly in stories about cowboys, fighter pilots, honest sheriffs. Courage is indeed the knowledge of what is truly dangerous, and that knowledge is not of an abstract concept but of ourselves, and of our total human feeling pattern.

We are not merely an advanced data processor attached to a bundle of successive and conflicting passions. We are the animal that can discover the natural order in our feelings and so in ourselves and then harness our biological informational and computing systems to the service of long-range goals. A merely intelligent primate without the ability to achieve a state of calm passion could imagine many wonderful things, but it could never make a stone axe. To do that it must work at it for a long time and, for much of that time, it will not feel like doing it. The ability to act under the influence of one's collected self, to override importunate present feelings in the interest of feelings relating to future states, is an acquired talent. Very young people commonly have less of this talent, which is why farmers used to say, "One boy is worth half a man, two boys are worth half a boy, three boys aren't worth a damn." It is the impulsiveness, more than the ignorance, of teenagers that the law has in mind when it does not allow them to make legal contracts. We wisely protect, and tacitly insult, many of our legally adult fellow citizens when we pass a law that allows them to cancel, within a short period, a contract made with a door-to-door salesperson. The ability to delay, to reflect, to summon our larger selves, we call wisdom, self-control; we wish we had more of it. We wish it not because wisdom is a conventional good but because it is the major human instrumental good.

We can think across cultural barriers to recognize the wisdom of a tribal chieftain, of an Oriental sage, of an illiterate toiler in our own society. Instances of this ability humble us. For all our prodigious technology, power, and learning, we often seem to ourselves to behave with the dignity and coherence of a troop of excited baboons. Which of us feels adequately summed by the part we play at cocktail parties, political meetings, academic conferences? It is no wonder that we envy the casual grace that other animals seem to have. But we have gone too far ever to return to their simple decisiveness and coherence. We cannot blot out our intelligence, imagination, and the infinity of desire that follows from it. What other animals achieve effortlessly, we must strive for along the hard route of delay, reflection, self-control, and the recognition of harrowing ambiguity.

CHAPTER 14

Moral Communication

The non-reductionist human nature theory is accurately described as "emotivist." Value judgments begin with, derive their force and direction from, are eventually about, feelings. People with similar feelings can be expected to understand a value judgment made by one of them, and if they have a similar reality orientation, they can be expected not only to understand it but to agree upon it. We all live in much the same world; we have similar senses, intellectual processes, and interests; our culture binds us into a common symbolic system. Value agreement is the norm for our species; later I will discuss why it is not always achieved.

Because "emotivism" has been so closely associated with reductionist, positivist, and behaviorist writers, I need to point out how the traditional emotivism differs from theirs. They find that when someone says "Brown is hateful," what he or she is really saying is "I experience feelings of hatred for Brown and I urge you to hate him also." No doubt some value expressions are of this sort. Most are not. When someone says "Brown is hateful," what is usually meant is "I hate Brown, and if you knew certain facts about Brown you too would experience feelings about him that would lead you to say that you hate him also."

On the emotivist theory, the possibility of discussing value questions or of arriving at value agreement depends upon the existence of a group with a common set of potential feeling responses. This becomes evident when we imagine attempts at moral communication with alien intelligent creatures, with typical humans, and with members of other cultures.

A very intelligent alien creature from outer space, with a feeling profile radically different from ours, suggests that we solve two of our problems—undernourishment of children and overpopulation—by grinding up half of our stock of children to make baby food for the other half. "Babies make the best baby food," it remarks; "try to overcome your squeamish scruples." If we call the creature inhuman, it thanks us for the compliment. If we call it unfeeling, it says that it has a great many strong feelings and that it finds us revoltingly lacking in many of them. It defies us to find the flaw in its solution. We respond that our scruples are based, not on empirical or logical reasoning but on our feelings, and that those feelings are not culturally induced but genetic in all or most of us. It admits that if this is the case, then we have a good, possibly a sufficient, reason for rejecting its proposal.

It continues: "Is it indeed the case that all or most members of your species have the same feelings? I admit that between intelligent species the possibility of value discussion is limited to the extent to which they share the same pattern of feelings. But even within one of your cultures I notice that not everyone has the same feelings. Today's paper reports a wave of child abuse. Don't some of you want to save the whale, while others are indifferent to that? Doesn't the same person who agitates against hunting also eat meat? There is a great diversity of expressions of feeling within your culture, and a greater diversity between cultures. How can you speak of a human feeling pattern? And if there is no human pattern, how can you have moral communication among yourselves any more than with me, except by chance and among a very few people?"

We must answer these points one by one, but we can answer all of them at once by pointing to the fact that the amount of moral communication is very large, and that this in itself points to a very high degree of feeling uniformity. Child abuse is reported in the press with the clear understanding that the general public will condemn it. All cultures condemn child abuse, although they vary somewhat in how they define it. The fashionable accentuation of cultural value differences focuses on special cases and ignores the actual mass of agreement. We may not understand a single word when we watch a Japanese or Indian television soap opera. We can yet follow and empathize with the play of feeling, the receipt of good news, weeping or mourning, the jealous glances, the uneasiness in the face of potential violence, the shamefaced looks, the anger at insult, and so on.[1] Through the *Iliad* and the *Bagavadgita* we follow the surges of passion as they are evoked in the common human way. Because of the differences in culture, differences in symbolization, we are sometimes puzzled that a certain feeling should be aroused or that it should motivate toward a certain end, but we understand that if we shared the symbolic world of that society we would join in its mode of feeling response, its values. The difference of value expressions in different cultures poses no problem for moral theory.

As for the differences in the manifestation of feelings among members of the same society, the situation is much the same. Leonidas dies for his polis; Timon prays for its destruction. The difference in their actions is accounted for on the basis not of a different set of feelings but of different experiences. Given different life experiences and perceptions of reality, their attitudes would have been reversed. Many apparent feeling divergencies are simply different applications of imagination. The woman who eats meat but will not trap a mouse in her house has failed to make a connection between two actions that others see as similar. The mouse is vibrantly alive before her eyes; the hamburger is shapeless and inert nourishment. If she should connect the two realms, the woman may well stop eating meat or start trapping mice. Moral discussion commonly consists in the attempt to apply already shared feelings to a world that is imagined in various ways. We move toward cultural value consensus with others when we agree to exercise our imaginations according to the same conventions. We move toward transcultural value consensus when we learn to transcend our culturally directed imagination and speak with others on the basis of a common perception of fact and of our common species-universal feelings. Saturation bombing is after all nothing but the extermination of termites once we believe that enemy populations are not human. I am not moralizing here, only illustrating the way culture and the pressure of necessity work through manipulated imaginations to produce incompatible and sometimes false value judgments out of the common stock of shared human feelings.

There are variations in the human feeling pattern. Young and old people, males and females, have slightly different feelings and these differences are stable throughout different cultures. Even among people of the same age and sex there are differences of the sort we associate with hormonal and body type variations. Such differences are the stuff of subtle literatures and the expressive arts. Our intuitive awareness of them makes it possible for us to make conscious allowance for them in moral communication. There are two other kinds of feeling difference among us, however, for which we can make allowance either not at all or only with difficulty. One is genetic, the other environmental. Since the species feeling pattern is genetic, and since what is genetic is subject to mutation and normal variation, we should expect to find, as surely as albinism or six-fingeredness, persons who do not experience quite the same feelings as we do. To the extent of their variation from the species norm, we find them moral strangers; they cannot be a part of our universe of moral discourse. Such mutations are probably very rare and difficult or impossible to distinguish from the second type of feeling deviants. These latter are those who have lived through extraordinary circumstances; some of their feelings are non-functioning or altered.

One understanding of environmentally induced feeling deviation is had from experiments on rhesus monkeys.[2] Studies have traced sequentially their changing modes of interaction with a mother, with members of their juvenile peer group, and finally with mature members of the group. The development of species-typical and functional feelings in young rhesus monkeys is clearly not culturally induced, for although the species does have some rudimentary culture, it has little to do with the raising of their young. Neither is that development an automatic biological change, as in the growth of body hair, for the progression of the young monkey through the ordinary stages of emotional development depends upon the presence and species-normal behavior of other members of its species. We would not have come to understand how delicate a balance is involved between emotional development and interaction with others, had we not "tortured nature," and some young monkeys, under laboratory conditions. There we found that no matter how ideal all other support systems, an infant rhesus monkey deprived of interaction with a mother or mother surrogate, or later with other young ones, fails to go through the normal stages of emotional development. It becomes incapable of maturing into a functioning adult. It cannot become a member of a rhesus monkey band, cannot mate, cannot nurture infants of its own. Such studies throw light on the complexity of the rhesus monkey feeling structure. Psychiatry does the same for our species.

We are made uneasy by the detection of atypical feelings in others. We do not know what they will do under given circumstances; we call them insane or inhuman. Often we cannot tell whether it is their perception of reality or their feelings that are non-standard, but when they kill or hurt one of us we lock them up in a hospital, rather than in a prison, and so reveal that we do not consider them members of our moral universe. We can restrain or afflict such persons, but we do not feel we can punish them.

Our common feeling pattern can be altered at any age. Every Saturday morning at a rear-echelon army base a firing squad is assembled. One man is on the squad every Saturday. His wife and children are in great need; he has volunteered for the extra pay. At first his tent mates joke with him, call him The Butcher, Killer Jim; then they drift away, do not go into town with him for drinks. They know his circumstances, sympathize with his plight, yet feel uncomfortable with him. The men shot are presumed to deserve it—traitors, saboteurs, spies—that is not the point; his friends feel that somehow he has become different from them. They are right. Humans who outrage the human feeling pattern in themselves are dehumanized. Not all at once, not in every respect, but steadily, inexorably, and often even blamelessly some of their ordinary human feelings are desensitized. Morticians, public executioners, collectors of excrement, butchers of animals, those who trade in sexual flesh, double agents, perhaps even advertising executives and actors, are commonly in many cultures viewed with awe, contempt, or fear. They tend to be pariahs, because we are not certain how much of our feelings they share, or which of their own expressed feelings are actually felt by them. Humans drift out of the universe of human moral discourse to the extent that their feelings vary from those of others or are perceived by others to do so. It might seem unlikely, when we consider how so many habitual activities tend to estrange us from the common feeling pool, that anyone at all can survive to join with others in it. In fact, ordinarily, we are quite resistant to feeling isolation; we reach out to bridge the gaps between us. The firing squad volunteer vigorously insists upon his normalcy. In later life he may indeed regain, almost, the normal range of feelings. The urge to remain within the circle of humanity, within the universe of feelings that unites us, is very strong. It is one of the more powerful incentives to morality, although not necessarily to the best morality. As members of the moral universe of a culture, we strenuously compartmentalize our consciousness, keep our emotional left hand from knowing what our practical right hand is doing. We see the glory and not the gore, censor our table talk so as not to spoil our appetites, praise the good ends and pack the ugly means into the skeleton closet. Some of this repression is necessary; some disharmony between the world and our feelings, and among our feelings, seems built into our nature and situation. But some societies, perhaps all historical societies, have gone too far in the direction of repression and the sponsorship of false consciousness. From a human nature perspective we can indict them for the production of unnecessary unhappiness, of dysfunctional values.

The communication of feelings, and so of values, is further complicated by the great variety of the feelings and yet greater variety of the circumstances that arouse them, as well as by the expectable conflict of feelings. We feel unhappy at the sight of a dead or badly injured animal, especially if we see it as resembling us in some way. The feeling is stronger for a human being in that situation, stronger yet for a human child, strongest for our own child. Yet a Yanamamo woman will sometimes kill her newborn child.[3] She does it without suggestion from anyone, with every appearance of deliberation. Is she not a monster of callousness? Put yourself in her place. The inescapable facts of her situation are that Yanamamo children must be nursed for about two years or they die. She has another child a little over a year old and a limited supply of milk. If she tries to nurse both children, both will die. She kills the newborn child and weeps for it. Not only is she not a moral monster, she is one of us, and one with more moral courage than some of us.

Many people have noticed that what is moral varies with the circumstances and have concluded that morality is relative, not absolute. They are right in this, but wrong when they conclude further that morality is amorphously relative, so fluid that no moral judgment can have any status as knowledge. It is important to see that moral judgments are composed of two variables, circumstances and feelings, and that both are independent variables. Circumstances are real, objective, not a matter of the point of view; feelings are real, objective, not a matter of the point of view. It follows that morality, statements about the better and the worse, about "what is to be done," is ultimately knowable, ultimately not a matter of the point of view. For a given set of known feelings embodied in an individual or a group, in a given set of known circumstances, there are humanly objective and in principle knowable better and worse moral decisions.

Perfect moral communication would be possible only if we knew all the circumstances and feelings involved in a situation. Human nature value theory has no hard and fast absolutes, therefore no unqualified commands or prohibitions. It would be a mistake to confuse this fact with the mushy thought that "to know all is to forgive all." Taking all the circumstances into account, there is nothing to forgive in the action of the Yanamamo mother. She did the right thing. If she had killed both children, or saved both now only to lose both later, she would have done the wrong thing.

Under unattainable ideal circumstances, in a utopia, the normal human feeling pattern would exemplify itself plainly in each maturing human and the public morality of groups and cultures would express that pattern without distortion or repression—although some inherent conflicts between individuals and within individuals would continue. In the real world of history, all societies inflict some degree of what has been called "normal madness" upon its members. Hume noted that the Greeks, surrounded by enemies and rent by internal wars, emphasized the martial virtues. Martial virtues are unquestionably virtues, but Hume questioned whether such a degree of emphasis on them, necessarily at the expense of other human virtues, is ideally appropriate for humans.[4] He concluded that it is not, but that the situation of the Greeks was such that they had no reasonable alternative. The minimum goal for individuals is satisfaction of their major feelings, but for societies that minimum goal is survival—the safety of the people is the supreme law. Ideally, societies exist for the production of ideally good, that is happy, human beings, but they are always in the position of the Yanamamo woman, forced to choose the second best.

"Death before dishonor," "women and children first," and similar sentiments that tend to embarrass us now are translatable into "an individual may have some interests that are more important than the prolongation of his or her own life." We can name those interests. But a society can have no altruistic interests stronger than the survival of its members. For the great mass of those members it exists as the only available structured framework within which they can achieve a good or at least a passable human life. The "reason of state" thesis of Aristotle,[5] Machiavelli,[6] Augustine,[7] Spinoza,[8] and Hume[9] finds its justification here. The truth of this thesis is obscured by the general abuse of it. The "reason of state" principle is most commonly used not in the interest of society but in the interest of particular rulers and regimes. We must admit that there are some societies that, in the light of possible alternative modes of organization, are so inefficient in the production of good for their members that their diplomats, defined as people sent abroad to lie for their country, do well to defect from it.

Moral communication is possible among us to the extent to which we share common genetic feelings and a common view of facts. With the rare exception of mutants, and the common and partial exception of those who have been traumatized by special experiences or styles of living, all of us do have much the same general feeling profile, the same possible state of calm passion. There may be practical limits to the extent to which we can discount personal and cultural idiosyncracies and arrive at a common view of circumstances, but whatever these limitations may be, they are expandable, and within them we are capable of moral communication.

CHAPTER 15

Obligation

There is a world of difference between the questions of how we make value judgments and what value judgments we ought to make. How can value judgments be binding upon us? That we do and even must make evaluations is just one more fact about us. Between that fact and the prescriptivity claimed for moral statements there is a significant gap. If values are neither "out there" to be perceived, nor implicit in the rational process with which we attempt to structure and to understand what is out there, then it would appear that the intelligence can know nothing of them. Even the feelings that are the source of evaluation are to our coolly observant eye just another set of factual events. No microscope or telescope, no sensory or intellectual capacity we have, can detect the slightest merit or wrong in the external world—an external world that includes, for the scientific mind, our physical and psychological internal worlds as objects of enquiry. All the attempts to deduce the better and the worse from a study of the meaning of words have failed. All the various attempts to posit a special intuitive capacity to detect values have foundered. The is-ought gap is indeed unbridgeable for discursive thought and there is no other kind of thought. No matter how hard we think, we cannot seem to get beyond knowledge of the existence and causes of value judgments to the question of their truth.

The impenetrability of the world of value to rational or empirical enquiry is mirrored in the indifference of our original feelings to factual truth.[1] Except with reference to human feelings, the whole scientific enterprise, the attempt to understand the objective workings of the world, is unutterably boring and pointless. As pointed out in Chapter 2, the world interests us only to the extent to which we eroticize it and make it an instrument of our passions. If we cannot do that at all, we cease even to believe in its existence. The difficulty of bringing together the two parts of our psyche is illustrated by the traditional hostility between romantics and utilitarians, poets and scientists, between sense and sensibility, the Sancho Panza and the Don Quixote each of us embodies.

Current models of training in the physical and social sciences encourage disregard and even contempt for the world of feeling and of the product of the right hemisphere of the brain. Those who angrily react to this contempt point out that our knowledge of fact is itself a conceptual muddle. Existence does not follow from concepts; factual judgments do not entail other factual judgments. The postulations of necessary causality and of the uniformity of nature are logically arbitrary. It is not rationally or empirically demonstrable that anything exists at all. If scientists retreat to the position that their conclusions are merely probable, we press them to state the probability of the truth of their probability statements—in an infinite regress. Adherents of sensibility have even tried to use Gödel's Theorem, Heisenberg's Principle of Indeterminacy, Einstein's Theory of Relativity, and the comic nomenclature of subatomic physics to undermine science itself. All this represents an attack on science understood, as it sometimes is, as a religion, a metaphysics, an attempt at total explanation. If we understand science as an earnest attempt to understand the world about us, an attempt that is the product of our species curiosity and of our desire to satisfy our other species feelings through orientation within and power over our environment, then all these attacks are beside the point. People who have suffered distorted developments of their reality-processing or feeling capacities may be in conflict, but there can be no conflict between knowing and feeling. We must expect tension, of course, as we expect it between men and women, young and old, but not warfare.

We would do well to accept Hume's suggestion that we consider humans as though they had two distinct and parallel structures for dealing with the world.[2] One is the train of capacities for data collection and processing. The other is the genetic pattern of feelings. In the life activity of successful humans, the two spheres are well integrated, but for philosophical analysis the division is helpful in understanding the fact-value gap. Thought, motivated by feelings, searches the world in vain for a value; feeling, as in the dream of the id, constructs a world to suit its desires, restrained only by a part of itself, the ego, the reality principle, fear.

Hume's further suggestion[3] is that we analogize our experience of feelings to our experience of what are called the secondary qualities of the external world—color, sound, odor, and so on—that exist only when perceived and only for the perceiver. Color and sound do not exist in the external world, any more than do affection and pride, but humans experience all of these, and experience each of them in ways which are sufficiently common to us all so that we can talk about them and act on the basis of our common experience. The physical and behavioral sciences cannot recognize colors and sounds, only light waves and sound waves, but humans and some other animals live in a world full of both, and also in a busy world of feeling states. Redness and envy are objectively encountered in human experience. The way in which we understand secondary qualities in intersubjective communication may be a clue to how we may understand feelings. We are genetically constituted to perceive a certain light wave as a color and to experience a certain feeling upon the stimulus of a certain configuration or event.

It may be of interest to note in passing that, although the value theory set forth here is a naturalistic theory, it does not commit the "naturalistic fallacy." According to the usual interpretation of G. E. Moore's argument (against the utilitarians), the good is irreducible to anything else, as pleasure; a thing, a good, is what it is, and not some other thing. Moore is quite right here. Red is not a light wave frequency, nor an excitation of the eye or the brain; it is what it is. It is not said here that fear is a quantity of adrenalin or that the goodness of the relief of escape from a danger is to be found in the analysis of the event itself or even in the pleasure that accompanies it. We have evolved to experience some sorts of things as good and some as bad, although past experience and our mode of symbolizing may direct how we will interpret and act on that perception. Moore argues that ethical naturalists equate a fact with a value. Perhaps some do, but to avoid the fallacy in doing that they need only limit themselves to the assertion that for a particular intelligent species certain feelings are predictably aroused by certain facts and that the experience of such feelings is the only basis on which we can make evaluative judgments.

Another parenthetical thought on the notion of value-free science: it is historically the case that much of the downgrading of value judgments arose out of a desire to clear a space for empirical science to operate free from the interference of prevailing cultural values and mores. The consequent appearance of a conflict between fact and value is merely an historical accident. It is worth repeating that without the feelings there would be no incentive to know, no way of deciding what to know; it is our curiosities and other feelings that guide the direction of our studies and keep us at them. On the other hand, a feeling person needs all the information available if his or her feelings are to be satisfied. Reasoning, both logical and empirical, is indeed the slave or scout of the passions, but in our state of calm passion, when our feelings have settled down to a steady regard for our long-term good, we desire that our sciences be conducted in as value-free a way as possible. This is so because we know that it is only in this way that they can serve our passions best. No sensible person would want a slave who spends all his or her time playing the flatterer and sycophant. She or he wants a coolly competent assistant, one who works away with maximum skill and freedom to produce things of use. The ideal of value-free science is supported by our calm feelings and is a major value of reflective people. Technology is not science, of course; the animus of many people today against science and scientists would more appropriately be directed against people and societies that deploy technology to antisocial or inhuman ends.

One more parenthetical remark: values follow upon feelings, and value discussion is possible because all or almost all of us share a common world and common species feelings. This commonality of species feelings has no normative authority over those who do not share it. If 99 percent of all humans condemn child abuse, you are not wrong if you feel that it is enjoyable. If you do not share this part of the normal feeling pattern, you are not bound by the morality that depends on it. But you would be wise to suppress a display of your species-idiosyncratic feelings. The species-human feeling for children is very strong, and if you are not wrong in not sharing it, we are not wrong in taking whatever action against you is appropriate to safeguard the children. The ideals of civil liberty and of human right, including the right to be different, arose out of the interplay of human feelings with a sophisticated awareness of certain probabilities in human social life. The appeal to the right to be different is an appeal to the calm passions against the immediate passions; no abstract human right can stand up against the verdict of the calm passions themselves. The case is quite different with contingent channeling of species values, with cultural or artificial values. If you fail to rise when the national anthem is played, the angry crowd will reasonably be appeased if they learn that you have no legs or that your rising might cause a heart attack. Given time and the rhetorical skills to play upon the leverage points in their symbolic system, you might even persuade them that the anthem stands for an oppressive power that ought to be resisted.

Value Judgments Are Predictions[4]

The beginning of the way out of the prescriptivity problem may be found in the understanding that value judgments are factual predictions. When I say "Lulu is hateful," I mean that if you knew Lulu as I know Lulu, you would experience certain feelings that would lead you to pronounce her hateful. My value judgment is an empirical prediction that is falsifiable. All value judgments, including aesthetic judgments, judgments of right and wrong, of better or worse, and of ought and ought not, can be understood in this way.

Some value judgments, as "it is better to have loved and lost, than never to have loved at all," may seem so vague and general that the idea of their being falsifiable seems absurd. Yet, upon examination, we find that what is being said is that "if you consider two possible lives you might lead, one involving an unrequited love and the other no love at all, you will find that, on balance, you feel impelled to choose the life in which you experience the unrequited love. You will choose it because, in your imagined future retrospection upon both possible lives, you see, feel, that the latter produced for you a wider, more intensive, more generally satisfactory self, one upon which you look back with more sense of completion." Other points of view are, of course, quite possible, and I do not claim that the truth of this empirical prediction can actually be firmly established or falsified. This is also the case with many falsifiable empirical propositions.

There is a common and peculiarly twentieth-century superstition to the effect that whatever cannot be explained in a reasonably short time to a normally intelligent person cannot be called knowledge. John Dewey insisted that knowledge that is not "public" in this way ought not be called knowledge at all. It is this demand, a demand that appeals to our egalitarian sentiments and plays upon an obliviousness to the stubborn recalcitrance of things and of thoughts to easy intellectual mastery, that leads so many to assume that splendidly difficult achievements are the result of luck or are merely the artifact of the media. In fact, some scientific-mathematical theories cannot be explained to all normal people, no matter how long they are trained. Some of us do not have the interest, span of attention, or intellectual capacity to grasp them. The kind of knowledge required to see or read a great work of art, much less to paint or write one, may be possible to many more than actually have it, but is is not universal among all of us equally. Just as you cannot explain sex to a four-year-old or the Declaration of Independence to a child of eight—because they do not have the experience, the concepts, the developed feelings to understand your explanation—so, many adults are incapable of understanding some scientific ideas, some artistic productions, some value judgments. Some predictions of future feelings require special knowledge of subtle facts about the world; others require a more than usual tactful or "intuitive" sensitivity to and acquaintance with the deep structure of the human feeling pattern; some require both. Fortunately, understanding of an ethical theory— such as the one now being explained—does not depend upon any more than ordinary intelligence, experience, and openness of mind, but the application of an ethical theory to particular cases may require special knowledge or an unusual grasp of subtleties of feeling. The discussion of a value question may not be equally and usefully open to all would-be participants.

Even where no special prior reflection or experience is required, the making of value predictions can, as in the parallel case of factual predictions in the sciences, be very difficult and sometimes impossible. In both cases the data may be incomplete or simply too confusedly tangled or there may be complicating external influences that we cannot fence out as we may in a laboratory. Folk wisdom, for instance, consists of many partial and usually trivial insights into value, but its real wisdom is in the fact that for every offered slice of wisdom it offers a contradictory slice. It is true both that you should "look before you leap" and that "he who hesitates is lost," that "a penny saved is a penny earned" and that some people are "penny wise and pound foolish." The world is full of uncertainties, as physicists discover when they apply their talents to a game of dice. Physics does best in the grand overriding uniformities of nature as displayed in the solar system and in controlled laboratory experiments. Value wisdom does best in understanding the overall uniformities of the human feeling pattern as it unfolds in the ordinary conditions of life. That all systems of knowledge falter somewhat in the face of the uniqueness of each practical reality is an argument not against trying to know, but in favor of caution and modesty.

Each scientific discipline has its own peculiar standard for determining when a proposition within its field has accumulated sufficient support to warrant belief. Scientists can neither believe every hypothesis nor disbelieve every theory and the knowledge of and acceptance of the standard of proof appropriate to a field is what distinguishes real scientists from the credulous ignoramuses or logic-chopping philosophers who intrude into it. Belief, in the sciences, is equivalent to the acceptance of obligation, of prescriptivity, in value theory. If value judgments are predictions of future feeling, then when they seem true to us in a present state of calm feeling we are bound to accept them as guides to action. Scientists have no guide to belief, no protection from credulity or skepticism, but their standard of proof; moralists have no guide to action but their present knowledge of facts and their achieved, sophisticated, and earnest calm state of passion.

Identity

Most of us, most of the time, feel like clothes in the washing machine of life. We hustle and are hustled about in all directions; we have neither sensible direction nor inner static poise. There are some notable secular theories about this matter. One, associated both with Stoicism and with Epicureanism, holds that there is a particular equilibrium of feeling that, unaffected by circumstance, we ought to seek. The other, associated with such names as those of Hobbes, Schopenhauer, and the Callicles of Plato's *Gorgias*, sees humans as necessarily engaged in the lifelong attempt to satisfy a succession of more or less randomly occuring passions.[5] The difficulties of both theories are evident. The first underestimates the variety and conflicting character of the passions and the degree to which they necessarily draw us forth into the world of contingency and of involvement with others.[6] Even if ivory towers were invulnerable, they could not contain the means to a satisfactory human life. The second, or "leaky sieve," theory inevitably overstresses the satisfaction of the more obvious and immediate passions, sees us as spasmodic jumping jacks, disregards the extent to which we are imaginative and live in a very extended present in which feelings aroused by future and past events will moderate, divert, and overcome feelings aroused by what is near. Thinking about large parts even of the whole of our life comes naturally to us. Our imagination, spurred on by feelings and beset by the swarm of further feelings it evokes as it proceeds, guarantees that we will have to consider, very often, what it is that we really want to do. Inevitably we come to wonder if there is some mode of life, some condition of being, that would resolve the main problems and gain our deepest desires. For some people with little experience or with poorly developed critical faculties, that ideal goal is achieved, they hope, by a car, a marriage, more money, or by joining some sect of religious or ideological believers. A few philosophers have set forth some rather good overall understandings of how life can best be lived—it is not at all remarkable how much they say the same thing—but few of us have the conviction necessary to follow their advice. Most of us are too sensible to join either the saffron-clad group dancing barefoot on the street corner or the angry and bloody-minded partisans of universal brotherhood, yet too distraught to accept the lessons of an Epictetus or a Spinoza. We do well if we encourage in ourselves whatever tendencies we have to reflect on our feelings in important matters, to practice the art of delay and of self-control. In doing this we are creating ourselves, making for ourselves a character.

Each of us *is* a "character" in a colloquial sense that he or she is a unique configuration of neuroses. Each of us also *has* character, something quite different. Character is the learned capacity to delay and to consult the calm passions, to act with an awareness not limited to immediate circumstances. More than money, beauty, strength, it is our achieved character that fits us for life and for happiness. Character is related to prudence, but since prudence may be taken to imply a concern centered on humdrum matters, it should be said that a strong character enables us to take glorious risks as well as settle for ordinary satisfactions. The achievement of character enables us to know what we want and to get it. All the interesting things we do, as opposed to what happens to us, are the result of our character—and some luck.

Life can be very different, in different times and places; we do well to cultivate the sort of character which suits our present circumstances. But circumstances change unpredictably, and so we do even better to cultivate an all-purpose character. Even if all goes wrong, as it does for many people, we have the satisfaction that we did our best, that we arrived at a degree of autonomy, that whatever happened, happened to a real person and not to a puppet. Those who find conventional success without having found themselves either become megalomaniacs or find their happiness diminished by a sense of having been merely lucky.

The achievement of character is accompanied by an awareness of oneself as a power, as counting. We call this awareness, identity. The overlay on Freudian psychology, in the past half-century, of what is called ego psychology is a tribute to the recognition that the sense of oneself as real, as coherent and mattering, is central to psychic health. It is no accident, I suspect, that this recognition should occur just at the time when many people seem to be in a perpetual identity crisis and profound uncertainty about values seems to be the rule. When we believe that our values have little or no merit, then we believe that we have little worth or reality. We are ill.

The other higher animals seem to have a very slight self-consciousness. The importance of this sense among humans is a consequence of the necessities introduced among us by our possession of higher intelligence and imagination. Humans have to make complex decisions under the stress of strong and conflicting feelings, and in the making of those decisions they are continually drawn back into that central core of themselves that makes and must live with the results of those decisions. It is a hard road we must take, and many of us try not to take it. Some of us are passive, dependent upon others for guidance. Many of us narrow our thoughts to the immediate and the short run and live in comfortable ruts of routine, blocking out death (but although "death destroys a man, the idea of death saves him"), aspiration, ecstacy, life itself. Members of many primitive tribes and of fanatical sects have handed their ego over to their society or group and do not see themselves as autonomous or responsible persons. There are real advantages to this retreat from life. A strong consciousness of the self (not to be confused with egotism) as a distinct and vulnerable thing is so fearful that some religions promise their adherents the reward of the extinction of the self. Who has not yearned to share the unconscious deftness and confidence of the stalking leopard, the overidealized yet real contented rootedness of the traditional peasant? In writing of the death wish, Freud said that the ultimate human utopia is a return to the placental waters and, beyond that, to the serene invulnerability of a stone.[7]

Kant found the sense of self in the synthetic unity of apperception, in that place where one's myriad perceptions are fused into a consciousness of oneself as a perceiver. It is more interesting to see ourselves as the achieved synthetic unity of our autonomic species feelings.[8] We recognize our important self in the history of our feelings, a history that culminates in the state of calm passion we can now achieve. In the sense in which Burke and Hegel spoke of the meaning of being an Englishman as consisting in vicarious participation in the dramatic history of England, individuals know themselves as the product of their individual histories, not as passively experienced but as made by their emerging selves.

The "I" that I am is the "I" that must live with the consequences of the actions I now undertake on the basis of a present state of feeling. The present ego comments on the decisions that put it in its present situation and looks ahead anxiously into imagined futures. There, in the midst of conditions now being created, with capabilities of the body, mind, and character now in formation, in those futures, I find myself again, commenting on my present decisions. I read the expression on the face of the future me and turn back to achieve a more general, a calmer, state of present feeling.

The other higher animals float self-possessed and self-sufficient on the stream of their eternal presents, neither hopeful nor regretful. Our existential present includes a consciousness of our past and our possible futures; all three tenses co-exist in us. We grow angry at the thought of an insult endured twenty years ago and some of our efforts are directed now by the thought of feelings we may experience years in the future. We feel responsible for the future. We feel responsible for the future of our children, our neighborhood, our country, in the sense not that we are to blame for whatever becomes of them, but that we feel unhappy at the thought of evil befalling them, even after we are gone. We want to do, feel responsible for doing, feel obliged to do, whatever may avert that evil.

Values are prescriptive, imply obligation, because we feel that they do. The fact of obligation is nothing more nor less than the feeling of obligation. Some explanation of this conclusion is necessary. Some people say they have a feeling of obligation to do something when to our eye they have no such obligation. Others deny they are obliged to do something when we think they are. Assuming they have the species feelings normal to the rest of us, there are two possible ways of reconciling such different views; both are familiar to us by now. Either we and they have different views of the circumstances, in which case, since the circumstances are objective and knowable, we have a principled means of coming to agreement, or we or they have failed to arrive at similarly informed calm states of feeling, in which case, since the calm state of feeling is much the same in all normal humans, we have ways of reflection, discussion, even psychological treatment perhaps, that can help to bring us to the same state.

The intellectual critic may object that no matter how one feels, it is yet possible to deny having any obligation to anything, or one may claim that in any particular case one can always undermine even a calm state of feeling by philosophical considerations. Rousseau says:

> It is reason which turns man's mind back upon itself, and divides him from everything that could disturb or afflict him. It is philosophy that isolates him, and bids him say, at the sight of the misfortunes of others; "Perish if you will, I am secure." ... A murder may with impunity be committed under his window; he has only to put his hands to his ears and argue a little with himself, to prevent nature, which is shocked within him, from identifying with the unfortunate sufferer.[9]

Reason does not contradict the feelings, but we can reason ourselves into a state of alienation from our own feelings and pretend, from an unacknowledged cowardice or a desire to appear more intelligent, that we are what no organism can ever be, an unmotivated pure intellect.

A strong sense of identity enables us to take responsibility for our future, to feel more and deeper obligations. We increase the influence of our calm state of passion over our important decisions and then in time over the less important ones and acquire dignity, self-respect. We inquire more earnestly into the actual facts of our environment, but principally we try to understand ourselves as we are and as we might be. We construct an ideal model of ourselves, or adopt some other real or fictitious person as an exemplar. In that model our uniqueness, our idiosyncratic selves, are sifted out. Is it not shameful that we talk so weightily of our special childhood, of our clever investments, of our taste in French wines and narrow lapels? It would be better if some of us confined our conversation to such sandbox topics, and only with those who impatiently await a turn to display their own precious individuality. No one is qualified to talk about how we shall live, to talk politics, art, the problems of value, who has not come to terms with what is simply human in him or herself, who as a human dreads more than anything the emptiness of a life without a center, a life that no matter how filled with striving and aspiration makes no sense, is unreal because there is no integrated self to connect its parts. Out of such terrors emerges the prescriptivity of value judgments.

Against any particular feeling that expresses itself as a particular value, that externalizes itself as a possible plan of action, some other feeling or coalition of feelings can come forward. But when every passion has been fairly represented in its full strength, when every circumstance that can practically be considered has been considered, and when the calm passions, in the light of the best available understanding of the circumstances, have spoken, that decision is prescriptive to us. We can delay further, and go through the whole process again and again, but unless we refuse ever to move, then at some point reconsideration must end and we must act. At that point we are obliged to follow the directions of the calm passions. We feel obliged to do so; we want to do so; not to do so is to abandon all the resources we have and to act at random. To say that we are not obliged is to say that our wanting to do something, when there are no undesired consequences that follow from doing it, is somehow not a sufficient reason for doing it. Morality is not something out there that we can ignore if we choose. It derives its force from the only thing that can move us, our own feeling, and its direction from the resultant of all the independent passions, the sum of which is what we are. Policy decisions can be agonizing to make. It is fortunate that the similarity of our feeling pattern and bundle of factual information with that of others make it possible for our internal discussion to include contributions from other people.

Prescriptivity and Alternative Value Theories

Values can be said to be both prescriptive and truly discussable only on the presumption of the human nature theory.

Culturalist value judgments are indiscussable between members of different cultures. Within a culture, they are indiscussable because there is no method for choosing among the conflicting strands of the cultural value directives or of establishing priorities among them. Cultural values are prescriptive for all members of a society except for those who understand them to be merely conventional. If we find reasons for obeying cultural imperatives, such as convenience or advantage, we no longer speak as culturalists. Under the unique individual theory, value judgments seem to be prescriptive, but there is no intelligible way of arriving at them. When arrived at, both they and the personal authenticity that is said to validate them are equally indiscussable.

Reductionist human nature ethical theory supports value judgments that are both prescriptive and discussable. On the basis of the single factor of human motivation to which this theory is committed, however, the ultimate value is personal advantage, narrowly conceived, and the discussion is limited to those who are willing to accept an inacceptably limited view of human feeling.

Of those asserted value bases that transcend humanity, none solve the problem of discussability. There is no way in which we can arrive at agreement on what it is that God, Nature, or Reason bids us do, even if we assume that they do command us. As for prescriptivity, all these transcendent moral authorities are external to us and so there is an impossible gap between their command and our obligation to obey. If we are asked to obey an omnipotent God or Nature, we may yet defy mere force and take the consequences with an easy conscience—and, in any case, our motivation for obeying would be utilitarian. If we obey God or Nature through our affection for one of them, we have an adequate motive, but one found in so few of us that the point is moot. As for Reason, even if it could be shown—as it cannot—that a certain action somehow entails a logical contradiction, I can yet say that I contradict myself in this instance. The principle of non-contradiction applies to statements, not to actions or things, and in any case has no moral component.

A central problem in moral theory is the problem of moral obligation. That problem is met adequately only by the traditional non-reductionist human nature theory.

CHAPTER 16

Illustrations and Complications

A general theory of value neither implies nor rules out any particular value judgment. The function of such a theory is to show what bases value judgments can and cannot have and to set forth a method for the carrying on of value discussions that have agreement as their end.

Astute readers will easily have detected some value commitments or biases of mine, and some may have concluded that the theory must be false if it "tends" to such commitments or biases. But those who promulgate value theories have no special qualifications for making good value judgments. They are as likely as anyone else to be misinformed about the world or to be in a neurotic or less than calm state of feeling. As for the allegation that this value theory "tends" to favor certain value judgments, those who make the charge display some degree of intellectual desperation along with an ignorance both of the nature of value theory itself and of the long history of how particular theories have been associated with the most disparate bodies of practical morality.

When all is said, however, some readers would yet be helped by examples of the present theory in use. With the stipulation, therefore, that what illustrations are presented here are not meant to describe either the theory itself or its necessary consequences, I attempt some possible applications at various levels of complexity. The reader may be able to use the theory to come to practical conclusions quite the opposite of mine. The theory itself leads us to expect this to happen and furnishes the method whereby we may discuss and eventually reconcile our differences.

Elites

Incidentally to the process of the struggle to survive, grow, and reproduce, all living things assert themselves. Seedlings jostle each other, nestlings quarrel for food. The higher social animals are either territorial, and compete for a parcel of space the possession of which promises a better chance at representation in the next generation, or practice social stratification and compete for standing within their group, or both. A major characteristic of humans, not much taken into account by contemporary social thinkers, is their desire for such standing, for what is variously called fame, honor, social status, or power. Fortunately for the peace, the struggle for social position, in humans and the other higher social animals, is mitigated by a willingness under the right circumstances to give honor, to allow precedence, to follow the leader.

The self-respect so necessary to our happiness, sympathy for our fellow humans, and a sense of our own vulnerability impel us also to prefer to live in a society of equals, and that has been a political ideal from Aristotle to Rawls. It has not been an overriding ideal, either in Aristotle or Rawls, because of practical considerations and other competing ideals. No human society has ever been, or is ever likely to be, truly egalitarian. Our knowledge of our nature suggests that at any level of technology or culture, under any possible regime, and without regard to the size of the society, there will be leaders and led, elites and masses, and that within the ranks of the led and the leaders there will be further honorific or invidious distinctions. The consequence of the attempt to abolish hierarchy in human society, or to deny its existence, is to free unauthorized elites from the possibility of social or political control.[1]

Elites are said to have power, and power is commonly understood to be the capacity to influence the behavior of others to one's own advantage. The understanding is inaccurate. Power is an end in itself; the struggle for it is a struggle for social status, honor, for being noticed. The president of the United States has been said to be the most powerful person in the world, but really he or she commands little. The lure of the office is that the holder is the one person who will always be heard when he or she speaks. Ultimately, the principal advantage of power to its possessor is the recognition of the fact that one has it, rather than what one does with it. This is not to deny that elites seek power for more than social status; the blatancy of their simple greed can be scandalous and oppressive. It is for this reason that, because we cannot abolish them, the central practical problem of political philosophy is the production of institutional means for the taming of elites. A survey of the major traditional political thinkers shows that this is indeed the major purely political problem they addressed.

The study of history and political thought reveals only two basic means for the management of elites. One prevails in the society in which custom and internalized social norms rule. In this case, the arbitrary power of the elite is restrained and channeled by the power of the mores, by a uniform and united public opinion. Each member of such a society has ascribed status at some level and an accompanying social right that the whole society stands ready to protect. The elite itself is inhibited by its own socialization as well as by the understanding that its honorific status depends upon the maintenance of the mores. These mores are assumed to be part of the order of nature; the elite reigns rather than rules. The cost of this kind of social organization, of "Gemeinschaft," is stagnation of thought and of technology and consequent vulnerability to destruction from the power or mere example of more dynamic societies. The corresponding advantages, of psychic orientation, community, and individual security, have been well celebrated.

In the other model, similarly an ideal type, each member is a "rational actor," free of superstition, useless loyalties, and social inhibitions, busily engaged in maximizing personally defined interests. The status of elites in such a society is ambiguous. On the one hand, they are seen as persons whose position is justified in terms of luck or their (usually inadvertent) contribution to the general welfare; on the other hand, in the general equality they are seen as equals, in the sense that they gain no honor, only envy and notoriety. The second model offers maximum scientific and technological productivity and progress, freedom of thought and of movement. Of course, as remnants of old customary inhibitions and the moral influence of society are phased out, so also are residual sentiments of social unity, and Hobbes's rules of government come into play. The final appeal in such a society must be to brute force. A "Gesellschaft" society cannot give honor or legitimacy to its elites, only the power to compel attention and other people. That power will be as unlimited as its holder can make it in the general struggle of all against all.

These two pure forms of society cannot exist in real life; actual societies exist along the spectrum between them. We understand the political necessities of our time when we locate our own society along that spectrum and consider which way it is urged when we advocate this or that policy and also what problems a move in that direction will raise for us. Western post-industrial societies assume the basic Gesellschaft character of human relations. They superimpose upon it a perfunctory indoctrination in the old mores, add a system of rewards and punishments designed to channel the energies of individuals and of groups into the general service[2] (what Bentham called the artificial harmonization of interests), finish with a written or unwritten hallowed constitution supported by a secular civic morality. That civic morality assumes and exploits innate feelings of human solidarity that the underlying Gesellschaft philosophy itself denies. As we have learned from ill-fated attempts to export this method to countries not accustomed or ready for it, the system requires a delicate balance of just the right amount of "non-rational" civic virtue with a fairly large number of independent and competing elite members. This system of competition within a framework of rules seems, as Machiavelli pointed out, to afford the best protection for non-elites. Elites are mildly inhibited by internal restraints, checked a little by public opinion, and so divided against themselves that some elite element will always find it to its interest to defend the social contract and the interests of non-elites.

The sensible strategy for those who favor the cause of the non-elites would be to promote the pressure of constitutional restraints upon as large a number of independent and competing elites as possible and to support the cultural solidarity that is the only support of the constitution. Within this system there is room for many kinds of economic modes of production and distribution. Justice and mercy can be communal values to be defended and extended. The elites can be restrained from their savage proclivities while full use is made of their talents.

Inequality need not be economic or exploitative. If we are to pay off our elites in honor, which is what they really seek, we must have a society that is capable of giving honor, of according deference on a basis other than simple fear or sycophancy. The apparent solution to our present slide into ungovernability, an ungovernability that must eventually land us in a tyranny, is the evolution of a moral consensus based, as it must be in our times, on a reasonable and secular moral theory.

The twentieth century excels in furnishing proof that power corrupts, and that absolute power corrupts absolutely. It matters not at all whether that power be exercised by radicals or reactionaries, by generals, financiers, politicians, commissars of the people, bureaucrats, or clergy. Over a period of time, the unrestrained ability to render the lives of others happy or bitter dehumanizes everyone who has it. This is why we must institutionalize the exercise of power and why we must support the restraining institutions with what Bernard Shaw called the most powerful force on earth: moral indignation. The contemporary world is rapidly depleting its inherited fund of moral indignation and has no current bases for its renewal. The non-reductionist human nature theory is available as a basis for the powerful force of community indignation.

Abortion Policy

The current shouting match about the legalization of abortion is one of the better examples of the bankruptcy of most value talk. Both sides are strongly animated by feelings, some of which arise naturally out of the question itself and some of which have a basis in quite other matters. Both sides strive to arouse in the opposition and among the uncommitted the feelings that they think appropriate to the question. Both sides sense that the appeal to feelings is somehow insufficient, that some other grounds are necessary for respectability. The forces opposed to abortion appeal to a bible or a natural law that are not authorities for most of us. They appeal to the "sacredness of human life," a good working principle, but give us no clue as to how that principle is to be integrated into the whole body of principles that guide our actions. I take it as obvious that there is no good principle that will not be an evil principle if inappropriately applied. If human life is truly and absolutely sacred, then under no circumstances is it legitimate to contribute toward taking it, or even endangering it in the least. No one believes that. The pro-choice thinkers commonly appeal to our cultural tradition favoring the autonomy of individuals—but since they just as commonly oppose that tradition on utilitarian or culturalist grounds, it is difficult to take their argument seriously.

A conspicuous word in the controversy is "right," used in the sense of a natural or human right, not as merely legal or customary. Women are said to have a right to the control of their own bodies, and unborn children are said to have a right to live. We have no such rights. Since its development in the writings of Locke and to the present day, no sensible account has ever been given of natural right theory and no philosopher of any standing has defended it. When I assert a natural right, I enter a claim upon someone's feelings. If he or she does not have the feelings, or if he or she does but they are overridden by other feelings, there is nothing more to be said for my supposed right.

The question of whether the unborn child is, in some abstract sense, a human being is of no interest. What is of interest is how we feel about it and how that feeling fares in its conflict with other feelings. Everyone admits that an abortion is most unpleasant for all concerned, not merely because it is a surgical operation, but because of the similarity of a foetus to a child. Our innate emotional inhibitions against injuring or killing children are very strong. The claim a foetus has on us is a claim on our feelings, and those feelings are more or less intense according to how imaginatively and emotionally we see it as a child. The emotions originate in our genetic nature but our imagination is a mixed product of culture and intelligence. It seems probable that, if we abstract from special cultural conditioning, the image of a one-month-old foetus will arouse a very slight protective feeling, whereas that of an eight-month-old one will arouse a much stronger feeling. The 1973 Supreme Court ruling that abortion is a constitutional right if performed before the third trimester is based on a compromise between our feelings for the plight of a woman unwillingly pregnant and our feelings for a creature that gradually comes to resemble us. There is, and can be, no other sensible basis for such a decision.

We ought to sympathize with the feelings of those whose imaginative powers make abortion seem to them, under any circumstances, unacceptable, but not with those whose objections are merely a product of the accidental historical development of their politics, subculture, or religion. Such sympathy does not, of course, imply agreement. For a moral person, any specific imagining-feeling-action sequence must be subjected to the process of the summoning of yet further imaginings and further feelings. How else could we allow surgeons to cut into living flesh, how could we build and support prisons, discipline children, defend ourselves against bullies and aggressors, prefer long-range to short-range ends?

From the standpoint of normal human feelings, an abortion is always undesirable, although frequently it will be the lesser of two evils. As general laws are ill suited to combat such undesirable behaviors as vanity, ingratitude, and vulgarity, they are also not very effective in solving "lesser of two evils" questions. Laws regulating abortion ought not be different from those regulating other medical procedures. If we must have a law, then my conclusion, which I urge upon no one, is that the Supreme Court decision in *Roe v. Wade* achieves a rough adaptation to our feelings. Of course, a law or the absence of a law does not settle the question of whether some specific contemplated abortion is in accord with that morality that should rule individuals. Although it is practically impossible for outsiders to make this moral judgment,

because the circumstances in each case are so subtle and complex, it does not follow that the moral question is individually subjective. Although outsiders may rarely if ever know whether some specific decision about an abortion was well made, it remains a fact that it was well made, or not.

Political Obligation

A feeling of solidarity with some human aggregation larger than our immediate family is natural to us, as is its correlate, fear or hatred of strangers. We differ from other social animals in that our symbolic system makes it possible for us to feel attachment to a group so large that we can know little or nothing of most of its members. In such cases, our feeling is not directly for the unknown other members as persons, but for the symbolic system that we and they share. Since the beginnings of our species, this innate "tribalism," however beneficial or necessary, has delivered us into the most grisly slaughters, into the hands of the most unconscionable manipulators. In advanced societies, where these evils are most clearly seen, two opposite reactions to such miseries appear. One is a drive toward privatization, toward disregard for the larger social or political sphere. The other is universalism, the attempt to expand tribalism to include all humans. Privatization entails a stunting of human feeling. Private worlds tend toward impoverishment of thought and feeling, toward meanness and brutality toward others. As Machiavelli and Rousseau[3] pointed out, it is self-defeating, for it opens the political sphere to a tyranny that destroys all privacy. Universalism founders on the fact that, although we can sympathize with all other humans, we can identify only with those with whom we share an orienting symbolic system, a system that necessarily contains the notions of "the foreigner," "the unbeliever." "External conflict promotes internal unity" is the sociologist's rule; some tension among groups, although not necessarily armed conflict, may be the necessary price for the optimum level of social unity within a group. Anyone without a tribe, whether of this world or the next, whether a nation, a people, or a neighborhood, "clanless and heartless," is, by reason of his or her human feeling pattern, in psychological trouble.

We can mature to what autonomy is possible to humans only within the confines of a culture, a large historically enduring society, a network of concepts and eroticized symbols. As Socrates in prison said, our society is a parent to us, a parent to whom we feel we owe something of ourselves. Problems arise when that required loyalty conflicts with other feelings and loyalties. E. M. Forster said, "If I had to choose between betraying my country and betraying my friend, I hope I should have the courage to betray my country." But William Tell risked his son's life to strike a blow for the liberty of his country. Which was right? Without more information, we cannot tell. It is possible that either, neither, or both were right. What personal and political events led Forster to be angry with his country? What would we have thought of Tell if his arrow had killed his son? What did the child's mother think of this exploit? How does this story fit in with other stories about Nathan Hale, the Dutch boy at the dyke, the Spartan boy and the fox, Horatio at the bridge? Does not the worth of the community determine the rightness of sacrifices for it?

Children pledge allegiance to the flag of the United States. The flag stands for "the republic." "The republic" stands for "liberty and justice for all." If the children grow up to believe that the republic does not by their standards stand for liberty and justice, they wear the flag on the seat of their jeans. Possibly they will raise a new flag, which they believe stands for humanity; possibly they will drift back into a privatized youth culture. In either case they lead alienated, necessarily unsatisfactory, lives. Adults have a responsibility, in all cultures, to make sure that the link between cultural aspiration and practice is not severed.

When both general and particular loyalties are intact, and also in conflict, we decide as we do when we have to choose between claims of two of our own children. Emergencies are taken care of first, resources are divided, the circumstances and our feelings are consulted carefully. The case of the hard decision that must be made in the face of equal contrary motivations is fortunately rare, for no ethical theory can solve such problems. More common is the hard decision that is hard because we do not feel we have the character or the calmness of feeling to make it properly. Traditional moralists recommend in such cases the adoption of what Spinoza[4] called an "exemplar," a real or imagined person who serves as a model of the wisely balanced person we hope to be. One of our major modern deprivations is our learned inability to give honor, to adopt models for moral action. No prevailing moral theory is able to make sense of "exemplars" or of honor.

A cultural community has a tremendous claim on our sympathy and support. We ought to tolerate in it as many faults as we do in those near and dear to us. In both cases there is some breaking point, although long before that we have gradually withdrawn our affections. Impulsive people oscillate rapidly between love and hatred. Their support is not worth much. Someone with more stability of feeling moves slowly and reluctantly to a rupture. A country or a friend is a terrible thing to lose.

Personal Morality

Perhaps none of us gets through life without some lying, stealing, and brutality. Much of this is never punished either by the law or by public opinion. As for feelings of guilt or remorse, it seems to be a fact that many perpetrators of evil do not experience any such pangs. In view of all this, any coolly calculating person may ask her or himself why she or he should forego the advantages that often follow from inhumane and antisocial practices. The question is that addressed by Hume[5] in his discussion of "the sensible knave," and by Plato[6] in his story of the Ring of Gyges. Some modern moral writers have tried to answer the question in terms of rational calculations of damage to a social fabric upon which we are each dependent. It is clear enough that this tactic will not work, for a great advantage to ourselves may be had at the price of moderate damage to society as a whole.

The answer, in the traditional moral theories, is to be found in the consideration of damage done to ourselves. This damage is not to be found in the consciousness of evildoers—they are often cheerful, complacent, even self-congratulatory—but in their inner being. We must distinguish between two sorts of such damage. The first sort occurs when we violate our natural feelings of sympathy for other human beings—as in the case already discussed of the member of the firing squad—with the consequence that our capacity to enter into moral relations with other people is impaired. The second sort involves crimes committed against the moral community of which we are a part. To the extent to which we secretly and successfully violate the necessary conditions of that community, we emigrate internally from it, alienate ourselves from a sense of belonging that we urgently need. The rationalizations offered for lying, stealing, and brutality always involve the depersonalization of the victims and the consequent narrowing of the scope of our moral community to include only fellow criminals. The degree of cynicism about the values of the larger society that we must generate in order to justify our bad actions is enough to exclude us from that participation in it that is necessary if we are to become fully human. Those who terrorize, exploit, oppress, the liars, cheaters, and thieves often gleefully and contemptuously thumb their noses at the rest of the world, but they cannot enter with us into a discussion of how one should live. Either they know that their lives cannot stand examination or their lives have rendered them incapable of such examination.

Nature and Convention

As far back as we know it, the history of our species most of the time has been the history of the pursuit of conventional goals through conventional means. Presumably this will continue to be the pattern of human behavior. Conventional ends and means are not logical systems but a miscellaneous collection of value judgments and practices that embody the feelings and experiences of members of a society over a long period of time. Such collections have in general been functional for most people, meaning good for them in an overall way, considering the range of possibilities actually open to them and without taking too exalted a view of their real potentialities. Conventional morality saves most people from evils they would encounter if they lived on their own unassisted talent for value reflection. It is the best basis for ordinarily successful living.

Most people learn to do well without ever thinking much about what "well" is, except that it is what they are trained and expected to do. We cannot withhold admiration from those members of society who live up to and even exceed the moral demands of their culture. We do not know our present selves until we know what heroic humans, our other possible selves, have done to uphold conventional virtues under extreme circumstances. At the same time, it is evident that many excellences and dedications can just as well be directed toward ends that we must regard as evil. Hitler's armies contained as high a proportion of heroes as did any others. We need a way to distinguish between conventional and natural virtue or morality. It is "the Nuremberg problem."

Virtue, or excellence of character, is so commonly acquired and perfected through cultural habituation, that the two can be confused. Nevertheless, when society fails to perform for us its character-building function, or furnishes us with inhuman goals, our need for virtue can drive us to seek it through other means. Plato wrote at a time much like ours in that cultural values were widely questioned and had lost much of their peremptory quality. Most of the characters in his early moral dialogues are either young or old. The old are portrayed as conventionally virtuous; the young have been liberated to a sophistic amorality. In his defense of virtue, Plato had to distinguish between virtue as conventional and as natural. The oldsters in his dialogues are temperate, pious, courageous, and so forth, but they can give no account of why they are so, nor do they know how to implement their virtues except under precisely those circumstances for which they learned them. As conventionally religious people cannot distinguish between the trivial rituals of their religion and the core of its message, do not in fact have much awareness of that core, so conventionally virtuous people do not know virtue itself but only its temporary and local traditional appearance. When such people are placed in uncommon circumstances, for which their value formulations are inappropriate, they act confusedly, crazily. One of many contemporary examples of this would be that objectively immoral minority that calls itself the Moral Majority. In our time, as in Plato's, this kingdom of darkness is the predictable reaction to that value relativism that in turn is a consequence of rapid social change. There is a similar parallel in the case of the young. They are at sea, wavering between the remnants of their insufficient and in any case partly inappropriate conventional upbringing and a random collection of individual intuitions, faddish attitudes, and new political and religious salvations. Many of them drop eventually to the level of the satisfaction of the immediate itching desires and irritations, to a half-cynical pursuit of conventional goals.

What natural morality is has been the subject of this book. It can be achieved by those whose culture has failed them if they begin with a serious consideration of the relation between their strongest and most enduring feelings and the life they lead and move on to the production of themselves as integrated humans, always the first priority, and then to the attempt to find with others a common decent life. It is amazing how determinedly the most ordinary people generate modest islands of morality in and among themselves. The passion for survival, for identity, for a better way of living burns within all of us. The production of more inclusive and generously imaginative conventions, based on nature, on human nature, should be the task of those who rise above the ordinary.

Cultural Relativism

The cultural relativists are good at pointing out to us the wide variety of values held by different people today, not to mention the long record of such variety in the past. All this evidence of difference is true, and it militates as it is meant to do against the old idea that moral truth must be what all people, in all times and places, have held to be true. Yet this emphasis on difference serves to obscure the opposite evidence for sameness that strikes us in the study of comparative anthropology and of history. Once we get over our tourist's astonishment at the exotic values of other societies and settle down to study them in detail, we find them no longer marvelous, given the special circumstances, quite explicable in terms of our common feeling pattern. A resident anthropologist of long standing comes to feel at home in his or her adoptive tribe. This can only be done by those who share the moral community of that tribe. They can do this, and remain anthropologists, not by learning to accommodate two contrary value systems in their minds and feelings, but by finding the common human feeling pattern that underlies the two contrary value terminologies.

Society is a good, but not all societies are equally good. Some make better use of resources to produce better humans than do others; some are in such bad situations that they have little chance of producing many good people. We ought, of course, be very cautious in making value judgments about whole societies. The alien, even repellant, quality that many of us find in, say, Aztec or Babylonian cultures may well reflect the poor communications between them and us. When an alien culture finds a Thucydides to speak for it, the sense of oddness disappears and we learn of a people who are only circumstantially different from us.

The study of other societies is a way of understanding our own only because the same people inhabit all societies. What we learn is not that values are relative, but that local and temporary value languages are so. The full value of the study of other times and places is not had, however, if we confine ourselves to the prosaic and conventional expressions of value. We ought also to listen to Job, Proverbs, and Plato, to Tolstoi and Dickens, to Dante and Herrick and those others who move us out of our confined calculations and puddles of fussy worries into the wider oceans where the major human passions exhibit themselves with sails unfurled. We may consult with Aristotle, Epictetus, Spinoza, and others on the conduct of our life. It is not mere intellectual curiosity that impels us along this route of exploration. The internal dialectic of human thought and feelings urges us to the ordering of our existence in accordance with an understanding of the deep structure of that existence, of the magnificent human potentialities that we sometimes feel within us.

The study of the traditional human nature theory of value has more than intellectual interest. We cannot understand the theory without being transformed by it. As we examine human nature, and so ourselves, we see, not so much the solution to this or that particular knotty moral problem, as the very general mode of life we ought to live, the sort of human being we want to be. The rest of our task consists in dealing with circumstances, changing what we can, enduring what we must.

Complications and Objections

There are a number of reasons why the traditional human nature value theory might be considered inacceptable. Some critics will rap the table and demand proof, thereby demonstrating their inability to understand the problem. Some degree of proof is possible in many empirical and logical questions, but a value theory can only be persuasive. As Hobbes said of his own superbly logical theoretical structure:

> But let one man read another by his actions never so perfectly, it serves him only with his acquaintance, which are but few. He that is to govern a whole nation must read in himself, not this or that particular man, but mankind; which, though it be hard to do, harder than to learn any language or science, yet when I shall have set down my own reading orderly and perspicuously, the pains left another will be only to consider if he also find not the same in himself. For this kind of doctrine permits no other demonstration.[7]

When Polus cites "what everybody knows," Socrates responds:

> But for my part, if I fail to produce you yourself as my sole witness to testify to the truth of my statements, I shall think

I have accomplished nothing of importance toward solving the matter under discussion; nor, I imagine, will you believe in your own accomplishment if you don't procure me as your sole witness and leave all these others out of account.[8]

For those for whom the arguments of the traditional theory ring true, there is the further consideration that there is no coherent alternative view. Nevertheless, some readers will be disturbed by the "literary" character of the arguments, by the imprecision of the method of coming to value judgments, by the inconclusiveness of the judgments when made. Our education has not fitted us to distinguish between common sense and common report or between certainty and weakness of mind. The reductionist human nature writers promised simple and certain answers to value questions. They failed, but even in their failure they led us to expect that value theory ought to achieve simplicity and certainty. The traditional theory cannot match the precision of the reductionists. It begins with the postulation in us of many conflicting feelings of uncertain strength and endurance. From such a plurality of ambiguous premises only tentative conclusions are possible.

There are both honest and dishonest objections. It is dishonest, or at best naive, to define the problem of finding a value basis in a way that rules out any answer that does not have the crisp dogmatic quality of the views of Bentham or Sumner. I call this objection dishonest or naive because we know, as well as we know anything, that the most important of our concerns, how we shall live, is not to be met by a formula such as can be taught by rote to a group of unwilling school children or that supplies facile answers to momentous or tangled value questions.

The honest difficulties deserve a longer reply. One involves a puzzle about what the feelings themselves are; the other questions the procedure whereby value questions are to be resolved among two or more people.

The identification of the feelings is the more difficult conceptual problem. We have been talking about feelings for millennia and have not yet arrived at an adequate terminology. We are not likely to do better in the future. Many of the words we use as names for feelings are actually interpretations of behavior. When we call some action "spiteful" or "arrogant," we do not describe either the simple action or the feeling that prompted it. Is there a feeling of "arrogance" and can we distinguish it from proper pride or self-respect, from confidence, indignation, contempt, scorn, and aggression? We can distinguish interpreted behaviors; the question is whether we can also precisely distinguish feelings. It seems evident to me that we cannot. I have named many feelings in this account; I should say now that each such naming should have been in quotation marks. A feeling is not a material object, a physical event, or a thought. Feelings do not come in discrete labeled packages. "Love," for instance, is a word used to name many disparate feelings. If we specify what we think is one of them, "mother love," we still have not come to a definite meaning. A mother does not always "love" her child in the same way. She "loves" it differently when it is safe or in danger, asleep or awake, hungry or not, nursing or being weaned, one year old, four, or seventeen. The feeling she has about it at any particular moment is what it is, not a version of something else. We do not increase our understanding of feelings simply by naming or attempting to classify them. The number of feelings, if it is not a mistake even to speak of their being numerable, is extremely large, and each shades off into another with every slight shift in our perception or imagination.

The way to cope with this nomenclatural chaos is very simple. Let us abandon the attempt to deal with the feelings with words and deal with them as they come. Suppose I am the young man in the bank: there is the teller, the money, the armed guard, and there am I, agog with perceptions, passions, and plans. I am making a series of reality assessments at the same time as I assess the strength and probable endurance of my feelings. The reality assessments can and often will be thought of in cold propositional terms; the feelings need not and usually will not be named or described. Now if I later want to describe my experience in the bank to a friend, I will put names on the feelings but I will not merely name the feelings, I will describe the context in such a way that she can also experience those feelings. I describe my feelings not by saying, "I was afraid of the guard; he was armed," but by saying, "This guard, see, he had this big .45." My fear is not only of being hurt but of being almost blown apart by a thunderous small cannon. Literary artists are very good at such descriptions. They are not necessarily good value judges or good at accurate descriptions of real events. They know how to arouse chains of complex and interesting feelings in us by the skillful use of evocative language. Shakespeare's Claudio does not simply say that he is afraid of death. He imagines what it is "to lie in cold obstruction and to rot."[9] There is no language of feeling; there is only language that evokes feeling.[10] As value theorists, we do well not to attempt the impossible construction of a science of feelings.

A note about the common attempt to evaluate the feelings themselves: It is important to see that there are no good or bad feelings, none that are in any sense better or preferable to any others. Every simple and non-instrumental feeling we have has a claim to satisfaction. It does not have an equal claim, for not all feelings are of equal strength. The attempt to evaluate the feelings has its root in a confusion between feelings and the expression of feelings, or between instrumental and non-instrumental values. "We ought to tax the rich" is the expression of a feeling, but not of a "tax the rich" feeling. Perhaps I don't like the rich or I want my own taxes reduced or I think the money could be used for a good purpose I have in mind. Even these explications do not bring us to simple feelings. Now, if we find that my desire to reduce my own taxes is based on a desire to make sure that my children are fed, we have gotten down to a simple feeling, usually called something like parental feeling. There is nothing good about parental feeling in itself; we approve of it because it is a strong and enduring feeling in almost all of us. If I don't like the rich because I am experiencing a feeling called spitefulness, resentment, or status anxiety, others may say I have a bad feeling. There is nothing bad about it. Spitefulness seems to have "inclusive fitness" value for humans. We disapprove of it because it is a feeling that is weaker and less enduring and that we see as often interfering with the satisfaction of feelings we take more seriously. Further, language plays tricks on us; it furnishes different words to point to the same thing, one expressing approval, one disapproval. "Carnal lust" and "physical attraction," "usury" and "fair return," are Bentham's favorite examples of this trick we play upon ourselves.

Those who demand a science of the feelings, who want to make value distinctions among the feelings, or who want to go beyond the feelings to some other bases for values, cannot be satisfied. Yet the feelings are not mysterious. Everyone has them and has them in much the same way and in the same strength, in a way in which they do not have the same experiences of the extended world. As a roomful of tuning forks will each resonate when a tone to which all of them have been pre-set is sounded, so in a theater full of humans, each will respond in unison with the others to certain presentations with certain feelings. Together they sob, sigh, laugh, and shudder because they are one species, a species that evolved to have certain feelings in certain circumstances.

The other difficulty that must be confronted here is the question of how we can arrive at value agreement. The answer is, not easily and not always.

The first necessity is a willingness on the part of the discussants to follow the argument where it goes, without the bar of previous commitment. This does not mean that no one may have an opinion prior to discussion; it means that he or she must have a commitment to the truth, that is, to his or her real interest, stronger than to any original opinion. This necessity rules out those with overwhelming ties to religious or ideological formulations. Past a certain point, such people cannot be reached; they have decided beforehand that any view that differs from theirs must be false.

We must get our facts straight. Before we join to save the child from the river, we have to agree, however rapidly, that there *is* a child in the river and that something can be done to save it, that there is not some other danger, say to five children in a nearby burning building, that might have a higher priority. Decisions of social magnitude—shall we go to war, shall we socialize the means of production—require the assessment of many scenarios of the future. The traditionalists have, of course, no special insights into circumstantial facts; value theories are to help us deal with our environment, but the knowledge of that environment is the trained common sense called science.

Then, the parties to the discussion must have species-normal feelings. It is not possible to arrive at a consensus of feelings about agreed-upon facts among persons with different basic feelings. This prerequisite rules out not only those few with mutated feelings but also those whose life experience has desensitized them to normal human feelings or whose experience or lack of it has prevented them from ever maturing to those feelings. This exclusion is similar to the exclusion from the sciences of those with abnormal perceptual capacities, as well as those with short spans of attention, neurotic responses to stimuli, poor data processing equipment in the way of intelligence, for example.

Finally, all participants must arrive, at some point in the discussion, at a state of calm passion. This state, it will be recalled, is that condition wherein we transcend immediate passionate excitation, take the position of one whose whole life is before his or her eyes—present, past, and future—and who then summons simultaneously, or in quick succession, every passion he or she might have that bears on the present problem and on each of the possible solutions to it. Strong passions are represented strongly, weaker ones weakly. The final state of feeling with which we confront the facts represents our whole self in its most serious and reflective condition.

Because the elemental feelings and their relative strength are similar in all or most of us, and because we share common perceptual and data processing systems, there can be only contingent, accidental, reasons for a failure to come to value and action agreement. Such contingent reasons may be many and powerful. They include ignorance, prejudice, misunderstanding, present passion, and perceptual and imaginative inadequacies, but their existence represents merely a practical difficulty, however overwhelming, not a principled objection. With all due respect to the massiveness of the practical difficulties that lie between us and value agreement, it must yet be said that there is no alternative to the attempt to overcome them and good reason to believe that the attempt may sometimes be successful.

CHAPTER 17

Conclusions

The problems of value theory are difficult, but that difficulty lies, not so much in its inherent complexities, as in our failure to produce an adequate conceptual structuring of the subject. The exhaustive and analytic classification presented in Chapter 1 is not offered in any dogmatic spirit. The reader is invited to refine, revise, even to replace it with another ordering. The point is that without some such ordering, the study of value can only oscillate among idiosyncratic, passionately held moral intuitions, culturally derived conventional values, logical and linguistic puzzles, and ideological dogmatisms. Once we have attained a comprehensive view of the whole field of value theory, we can proceed to the examination of the claims of each of the possible positions within it. This was done in the first part of the book, with the conclusion that only the non-reductionist human nature view survives for further examination. Part II argues that it survives on the basis of the criteria of faithfulness to the facts of human life, internal coherence, explanatory power, the ability to incorporate without loss the insights of competing theories, and that prescriptivity without which value theory does nothing.

A few disclaimers are appropriate. This is a book about value theory, not about value theorists. It has been convenient to follow the conventional attribution to some writers of certain value notions, but for the purposes of this book it is of no interest whether they actually held those ideas. Similarly, the question of the truth of my belief that all the major secular value theorists prior to Burke were human nature thinkers, and before Hobbes were non-reductionists, is not essential to the main line of the argument. Further, no specific value judgments, no concrete value recommendations, are attacked or defended here. The traditional theory does not tend to favor conservative, liberal, or radical political views or causes. Those who hold one of these positions need not fear it, except that to the extent to which their position floats on a cushion of inflated rhetoric they ought to fear any sober analysis of the basis of their value judgments.

The conclusions reached are few but significant:

The imaginative capacities of humans make them the only animal that must consider the question of how it shall live. There is but one conceivable motivation to the desire to act, to live, in one way rather than in another. That motivation is feeling. Feelings are not in short supply. We humans are flooded with emotion at every moment, sometimes by strong passions that dominate our consciousness, sometimes by weaker feelings of the sort evoked by associations with the objects in our environment or which suffuse our symbolic vocabulary. Every human is faced with the problem of the management of those feelings. This management is motivated by the force of the feelings themselves; no other force is to be found. We experience a passionate desire to arrive at that state of calm passion that enables us to make decisions that accord with our long-term and deepest feelings. In that moment of calm passion we are able to rank our goals in terms of their real importance to our total feeling structure. That ranking is experienced by us as prescriptive for our future actions.

The feeling pattern of humans is genetic and uniform within the species. It follows from this that we can understand each other's feelings. When we come to a common understanding of the facts, of the circumstances in which our feelings and those of oth-

mathematical symbols and raw neologisms to produce the introduction to a prolegomena to a new value theory. All to no avail. Every turn taken by contemporary ethical theory is now known to lead to a dead end.

Beneath the formal expression of ideas there lies a seedbed of unverbalized intuitions. The traditional value theory is underlain by a vision of our species as a profoundly and intricately determinate kind of being. In our modern cultural and technological environment we have become unable to see ourselves for the species we are. We have forgotten what species membership implies. To recall that, we ought to familiarize ourselves with some other species, not necessarily because we are like them in any interesting way, but simply to learn how much freight is carried in the adequate idea of a species, what a tremendous amount of information, of determinateness, is implied by species membership. Our ability to do social and value theory may yet hang on our awareness of our species being. With that awareness, we will be cured of the passion for understanding humans as stimulus-response mechanisms, products of their time and place, as creatures dominated by a single passion. The maunderings of intoxicated metaphysicians and ideologists will appear in their true absurdity. We are what we are, and not some other thing. We are real, full of blood and held together by bones and sinew. We see color, feel heat, pain, terror, and regret. We feel, and think, and get by, and when we have time we consider how we could have gotten along better, and what "better" means.

When I was young I studied Pitman's shorthand, a system that takes consonants seriously and sets them down carefully in lines and curves, and that takes vowels lightly and sets them down in accompanying dots and dashes, usually omitted as unnecessary. Then I discovered an obscure alternative system, invented by a man called Dement, that inverted Pitman and took the vowels seriously and the consonants lightly. It worked. Many systems can be turned inside-out in this fashion. Modern analytical value thought has taken concepts, facts, and relations to be real and serious, whereas emotions are considered frivolous, a kind of background noise to decision making. In value theory we ought to begin by reversing these priorities. Value begins with the feelings. Value theory must begin with human feeling, with the study of the feelings, with the understanding of feelings not as words but as experiences had similarly by all, or almost all, of us.

Notes and Index

NOTES

Chapter 1

1. G. E. Moore, *Principia Ethica* (Cambridge, Eng.: Cambridge University Press, 1903), pp. vii, 79, 144, 148, 173.
2. Roderick F. Firth, "Ethical Absolutism and the Ideal Observer," *Philosophy and Phenomenological Research* 12 (1952): 317–45.

Chapter 2

1. David Hume, *Enquiry Concerning the Principles of Morals*, in *Hume's Enquiries*, ed. L. A. Selby-Bigge (2nd ed.; Oxford, Eng.: Oxford University Press, 1902), pp. 169–79.
2. W. T. Stace, *The Concept of Morals* (New York: Macmillan, 1937), pp. 38–47.
3. Daniel Bell, *The End of Ideology* (Glencoe, Ill.: Free Press, 1960).
4. J. J. Rousseau, *Discourse on the Origin and Foundation of Inequality Among Mankind*, in *The Social Contract and Discourse on the Origin of Inequality*, ed. L. G. Crocker (New York: Washington Square Press, 1967), pp. 182, 203.

Chapter 3

1. Aristotle, *Metaphysics* 1062b.
2. J. J. Rousseau, *Discourse on the Origin and Foundation of Inequality Among Mankind*, in *The Social Contract and Discourse on the*

Origin of Inequality, ed. L. G. Crocker (New York: Washington Square Press, 1967), p. 177.
3. Aristotle, *Politics* 1252b; Aristotle, *Nichomachean Ethics* 1145a.
4. A. J. Ayer, *Language, Truth, and Logic* (London: Gollancz, 1950). See also Charles L. Stevenson, *Ethics and Language* (New Haven, Conn.: Yale University Press, 1944).

Chapter 4

1. Martin Luther, quoted in Roland H. Bainton, "The Reformation," *Chapters in Western Civilization* (New York: Columbia University Press, 1961), p. 358.
2. John Calvin, *Institutes of the Christian Religion* (Grand Rapids, Mich.: Eerdmans, 1964), II, 281–95.
3. Thomas Hobbes, *Leviathan* (Oxford, Eng.: Blackwell, 1960), pp. 96, 279.
4. John Locke, *Second Treatise of Government* (New York: New American Library, 1965), par. 6, p. 311.
5. Hobbes, *Leviathan*, pp. 240–41.
6. David Hume, *A Treatise of Human Nature* (Oxford, Eng.: Oxford University Press, 1888), p. 469.
7. *Ibid.*, p. 416.
8. Hobbes, *Leviathan*, p. 86.
9. Immanuel Kant, *Lectures on Ethics* (New York: Harper & Row, 1963), pp. 227–28.
10. Max Black, "The Gap Between 'Is' and 'Should,' " *Philosophical Review* 73 (1964): 165–181.
11. John Searle, "How to Derive 'Ought' from 'Is,' " *Philosophical Review* 73 (1964): 43–58.
12. Peter Singer, *The Expanding Circle* (New York: Farrar, Straus, & Giroux, 1981), p. 111.
13. *Ibid.*, p. 37.

14. *Ibid.*, pp. 53, 77, 84.
15. Alasdair MacIntyre, *After Virtue* (South Bend, Ind.: University of Notre Dame Press, 1981), p. 55.
16. John Rawls, *A Theory of Justice* (Cambridge, Mass.: Belknap Press of Harvard University Press, 1971), pp. 494–95. See also pp. 260, 398, 414, 424–25, 432, 456, 472, 485–88, 494, 402–4, 516.

Chapter 5

1. Sigmund Freud, *Civilization and Its Discontents*, trans. James Strachey (New York: Norton, 1962), p. 44. See also Aristotle, *Politics* 1267b, and Niccolo Machiavelli, *Discourses*, in *The Prince and the Discourses* (New York: Modern Library, 1940), pp. 108, 208.
2. Stephen G. Salkever, "Aristotle's Social Science," *Political Theory* 9, no. 4 (1981): 481–82. For a closer look at the transition from traditional to reductionist human nature and rationalist theory, see L. A. Selby-Bigge, *The British Moralists* (Indianapolis: Bobbs-Merrill, 1964).
3. Jeremy Bentham, *Introduction to the Principles of Morals and Legislation* (Oxford, Eng.: Blackwell, 1948), p. 125.
4. Robert D. Cumming, *Human Nature and History* (Chicago: University of Chicago Press, 1969), I, 173.
5. John Stuart Mill, "Coleridge," in *The Philosophy of John Stuart Mill*, ed. Marshall Cohen (New York: Modern Library, 1961), pp. 60–86, and, in the same volume, "Bentham," p. 19.

Chapter 6

1. James Harrington, quoted in Charles Blitzer, *An Immortal Commonwealth* (New Haven, Conn.: Yale University Press, 1960), p. 91.

2. Thomas Hobbes, *Leviathan,* (Oxford, Eng.: Blackwell, 1960), p. 438.

3. *Ibid.,* p. 32.

4. Adam Smith, *The Wealth of Nations* (New York: Modern Library, 1937), pp. 13, 268.

5. James Mill, *An Essay on Government* (Indianapolis: Bobbs-Merrill, 1955), p. 48.

6. B. F. Skinner, *Walden II* (New York: Macmillan, 1948).

7. David Truman, *The Governmental Process* (New York: Knopf, 1949).

8. Richard Rorty, "The Contingency of Language," *London Review of Books* 8, no. 7 (1986): 3–6; "The Contingency of Selfhood," *London Review of Books* 8, no. 8 (1986): 11–15; and "The Contingency of Community," *London Review of Books* 8, no. 13 (1986): 10–14. See also my reply, "Making Truth," *London Review of Books* 8, no. 21 (1986): 4–5.

9. Harrington, in Blitzer, *Immortal Commonwealth,* pp. 49–50.

10. Thomas B. Macaulay, *The Miscellaneous Writings of Lord Macaulay,* I (London: Longman, Green, Longman, & Roberts, 1860), p. 292.

11. John Stuart Mill, "Utilitarianism," in *The Philosophy of John Stuart Mill,* ed. Marshall Cohen (New York: Modern Library, 1961), pp. 331–33.

12. Sigmund Freud, *Beyond the Pleasure Principle* (New York: Bantam, 1959).

13. John Stuart Mill, "Bentham," in *Philosophy of Mill,* ed. Cohen, p. 22.

Chapter 7

1. Talcott Parsons, *Structure of Social Action* (New York: McGraw-Hill, 1937), p. 391; *Toward a General Theory of Action*

(Cambridge, Mass.: Harvard University Press, 1951), p. 23; *The Social System* (Glencoe, Ill.: Free Press, 1951), pp. 542–43. See also Emile Durkheim, *The Division of Labor in Society* (New York: Free Press, 1964), p. 428 ("The positive science of morality is a branch of sociology"), and Melville J. Herskovits, *Cultural Relativism* (New York: Random House, 1972), p. 8 ("The recognition of the impossibility of evaluating different cultures is today firmly established and represents a great advance toward clarity of thought").

2. Niko Tinbergen, *The Herring Gull's World* (New York: Harper & Row, 1971), pp. 140–41, 234.

3. J. J. Rousseau, *The Social Contract*, in *The Social Contract and Discourse on the Origin of Inequality*, ed. L. G. Crocker (New York: Washington Square Press, 1967), p. 7. See also H. F. Harlow and M. K. Harlow, "Social Deprivation in Monkeys," *Scientific American* 207 (1962): 136–46.

4. Karl Mannheim, *Ideology and Utopia* (London: Routledge & Kegan Paul, 1954). Mannheim is now generally thought to have become a naive ideologist at that point where he implies that his intellectual class is above ideology.

Chapter 8

1. Edmund Burke, *Reflections on the Revolution in France* (Indianapolis: Bobbs-Merrill, 1955), p. 215.

2. *Ibid.*, p. 290.

3. Michael Oakeshott, *Rationalism in Politics* (London: Methuen, 1962), pp. 123–24.

4. Emile Durkheim, *Selected Writings*, ed. Anthony Giddens (Cambridge, Eng.: Cambridge University Press, 1972), p. 120.

5. Oakeshott, *Rationalism in Politics*, p. 124.

6. Niccolo Machiavelli, *Discourses*, in *The Prince and the Discourses* (New York: Modern Library, 1940), p. 117.

7. Burke, *Reflections*, p. 69.
8. William Graham Sumner, *Folkways* (New York: Dover, 1958), p. 2.
9. *Ibid.*, p. 26.
10. *Ibid.*, p. 27.
11. *Ibid.*, p. 33.
12. *Ibid.*, p. 33.
13. *Ibid.*, pp. 30–31.
14. Noam Chomsky, quoted in *New York Review of Books*, Nov. 11, 1976, p. 48: "The concept of the 'empty organism,' plastic and unstructured, ... serves naturally as the support for the most reactionary social doctrines."
15. Many of the articles are included in Leonard I. Krimerman, ed., *The Nature and Scope of Social Science* (New York: Appleton-Century-Crofts, 1969), pp. 585–688; May Brodbeck, ed., *Readings in the Philosophy of the Social Sciences* (New York: Macmillan, 1968), pp. 239–336; and Robert Borger and Frank Cioffi, eds., *Explanation in the Behavioural Sciences* (Cambridge, Eng.: Cambridge University Press, 1970).
16. A. James Gregor, "Political Science and the Uses of Functional Analysis," *American Political Science Review* 62, no. 2 (1968): 427: "It is a public secret that functionalism and systems analysis have their origins in some one or other form of organicism."
17. Aristotle, *Politics* 1253a.
18. F. H. Bradley, "My Station and Its Duties," *Ethical Studies* (Oxford, Eng.: Oxford University Press, 1962), pp. 166, 168, 173.
19. Alvin W. Gouldner, *The Coming Crisis of Western Sociology* (New York: Avon, 1971), p. 47: "a sociological tradition that tends to obscure and to cast doubt upon the importance and reality of persons, and to view them as the creature of grander social structures." See also pp. 51–52.
20. Emile Durkheim, *Suicide* (New York: Free Press, 1966).
21. Plato, *Crito* 54.

22. David Hume, "Of the Original Contract," *Essays, Literary and Political* (London: Ward, Lock, & Co., n.d.), p. 283.
23. Emile Durkheim, *The Rules of Sociological Method* (New York: Free Press, 1938), p. 75.
24. Kenneth E. Boulding, "Toward the Development of a Cultural Economics," in *The Idea of Culture in the Social Sciences*, ed. Louis Schneider and Charles H. Bonjean (Cambridge, Eng.: Cambridge University Press, 1973), p. 54.

Chapter 9

1. Benedict de Spinoza, *On the Improvement of the Understanding*, in *The Chief Works of Benedict de Spinoza*, II (New York: Dover, 1951), p. 7; Spinoza, *The Ethics*, in *Chief Works*, pp. 250–51; Robert J. McShea, *The Political Philosophy of Spinoza* (New York: Columbia University Press, 1968), p. 134.
2. Eugene Kamenka, *Marxism and Ethics* (New York: St. Martin's Press, 1969), p. 47. Kamenka discusses some humanist Marxists.
3. G. W. F. Hegel, *Reason in History* (Indianapolis: Bobbs-Merrill, 1953), p. 9.
4. Oswald Spengler, *The Decline of the West* (New York: Knopf, 1934).
5. Karl Marx, *The German Ideology*, in *Marx-Engels Reader*, ed. Robert Tucker, (2nd ed.; New York: Norton, 1978), pp. 151, 154–55, 157, 169.
6. Aristotle, *Politics* 1266a, 1268d.
7. Niccolo Machiavelli, *Discourses*, in *The Prince and the Discourses* (New York: Modern Library, 1940), p. 255.
8. James Harrington, quoted in Charles Blitzer, *An Immortal Commonwealth*, (New Haven, Conn.: Yale University Press, 1960), pp. 45–50.
9. Karl Marx, *The Eighteenth Brumaire of Louis Bonaparte* (New York: International Publishers, n.d.).

280 / Notes to Chapter 9

10. Vernon Bourke, *The History of Ethics* (New York: Doubleday, 1968), II, 88: "For Marx, good or bad is accordance, or not, with the historical process."

11. Leszek Kolakowski, *Toward a Marxist Humanism* (New York: Grove, 1969), p. 114.

12. Wolfgang W. Fuchs, "The Question of Marxist Ethics," *Philosophical Forum* 7, nos. 3–4 (1976): 245; David B. Myers, "Ethics and Political Economy in Marx," *Philosophical Forum* 7, nos. 3–4 (1976): 253.

13. Saul Bellow, *The Dean's December* (New York: Harper & Row, 1982), p. 199: "although it's true enough that a simple belief in progress goes with a deformed conception of human nature."

14. J. J. Rousseau, *Discourse on the Origin and Foundation of Inequality Among Mankind*, in *The Social Contract and Discourse on the Origin of Inequality*, ed. L. G. Crocker (New York: Washington Square Press, 1967), p. 210, and *The Social Contract*, pp. 7, 19, 43.

15. Kolakowski, *Marxist Humanism*, p. 142.

16. William Blake, "Augeries of Innocence," in *The Poetical Works of William Blake* (London: Oxford University Press, n.d.), p. 171.

17. Lynn White, *Medieval Technology and Social Change* (Oxford, Eng.: Oxford University Press, 1962).

Chapter 10

Acknowledgements: Early and partial versions of the argument in Part II have appeared in the following articles: Robert J. McShea, "Ethics and the World Order," *Philosophy Forum* 15 (1977): 207–23; "Biology and Ethics," *Ethics* 88, no. 2 (1977): 139–49; "Human Nature Theory and Political Philosophy," *American Journal of Political Science* 22, no. 3 (1978): 656–79; "How Power Corrupts," *Journal of Value Enquiry* 12 (1978): 37–48; "Human Nature Ethical Theory," *Journal of Philosophy and Phenomenological Reseach* 39, no. 3 (1979): 386–401; "Toward a Theory of Practical Morality," *Journal of Value Enquiry* 21 (1987): 269–89.

1. Kai Nielsen, "On Taking Human Nature as the Basis of Morality," *Social Research* 29, no. 2 (1962): 162: "What evidence have we for claims that all people accept these fundamental moral principles?" A well-known writer on value theory, Nielsen fairly represents the contemporary ignorance of human nature value theory.

2. Isaiah Berlin, "Does Political Theory Still Exist?," *Philosophy, Politics, and Society* (2nd ser.), ed. Peter Laslett and W. G. Runciman (Oxford, Eng.: Blackwell, 1962), pp. 1–33.

3. Henry Adams, *The Education of Henry Adams* (Boston: Houghton Mifflin, 1918), p. 131.

4. Benedict de Spinoza, *On the Improvement of the Understanding*, in *The Chief Works of Benedict de Spinoza*, II (New York: Dover, 1951), pp. 3–4.

5. Plato, *Gorgias* 500c.

6. Richard Taylor *Good and Evil* (London: MacMillan, 1976), p. 65: "The Socratic reduction of morals to psychology is not the part of Socratic ethics that has endured in philosophical literature."

7. Plato, *Gorgias* 481c.

8. Plato, *Symposium* 205a.

9. Plato, *Gorgias* 511–12.

10. Plato, *Protagoras* 360c.

11. Plato, *Gorgias* 457b.

12. Niccolo Machiavelli, *Discourses* and *The Prince*, in *The Prince and the Discourses* (New York: Modern Library, 1940), pp. 122, 163, 36.

13. Thomas Hobbes, *Leviathan* (Oxford, Eng.: Blackwell, 1960), pp. 92, 97.

14. James Harrington, quoted in Charles Blitzer, *An Immortal Commonwealth*, (New Haven, Conn.: Yale University Press, 1960), pp. 58–59.

15. John Locke, *Second Treatise of Government* (New York: New American Library, 1965), p. 333.

16. V. I. Lenin, "What Is to Be Done?" in *Selected Works*, (New York: International Publishers, 1967), pp. 122, 162–63.

17. Karl Mannheim, *Ideology and Utopia: An Introduction to the Sociology of Knowledge* (London: Routledge & Kegan Paul, 1954), pp. 9, 138–39, 232.

18. Machiavelli, *Discourses*, p. 105.

19. *Ibid.*, pp. 530, 261, 216, 108.

20. Spinoza, *Political Treatise*, in *Chief Works*, I, p. 313.

21. J. J. Rousseau, *Discourse on the Origin and Foundation of Inequality Among Mankind*, in *The Social Contract and Discourse on the Origin of Inequality*, ed. L. G. Crocker (New York: Washington Square Press, 1967), pp. 167, 168–69.

22. David Hume, *A Treatise of Human Nature*, (Oxford, Eng.: Oxford University Press, 1888), pref., p. xxiii.

23. David Hume, *Enquiry Concerning the Principles of Morals*, in *Hume's Enquiries*, ed. L. A. Selby-Bigge (2nd ed.; Oxford, Eng.: Oxford University Press, 1902), pp. 278–84.

24. Hume, "The Standard of Taste," in *Essays, Literary and Political* (London: Ward, Lock, & Co., n.d.), p. 144.

25. Robert J. McShea, "What Basis for Aesthetic Judgments?" in *Value and the Arts*, ed. Ervin Laszlo and James B. Wilbur (Geneseo: State University of New York at Geneseo, 1979), pp. 129–38.

26. Robert Nozick, *Anarchy, State, and Utopia* (New York: Basic Books, 1974), p. ix.

27. Hobbes, *Leviathan*, p. 5.

Chapter 11

1. J. J. Rousseau, *Discourse on the Origin and Foundation of Inequality Among Mankind,* in *The Social Contract and Discourse on the Origin of Inequality,* ed. L. G. Crocker (New York: Washington Square Press, 1967), p. 176.
2. David Hume, *A Treatise of Human Nature* (Oxford, Eng.: Oxford University Press, 1888), pp. 325–28.
3. Richard Dawkins, *The Selfish Gene* (New York: Oxford University Press, 1976); Richard D. Alexander, *Darwinism and Human Affairs* (Seattle: Washington University Press, 1979), p. 19.
4. Ronald Fletcher, *Instinct in Man* (New York: Schocken, 1966), pp. 60–70.
5. Donald T. Campbell, "Evolutionary Epistemology," in *The Philosophy of Karl Popper,* ed. P. A. Schilpp (LaSalle, Ill.: Open Court, 1974), pp. 414–63.
6. Aristotle, *Nichomachean Ethics* 1041a.
7. Thomas Hobbes, *Leviathan* (Oxford, Eng.: Blackwell, 1960), p. 46.
8. Hume, *Treatise of Human Nature,* p. 415.
9. Sherwood Washburn and David K. Hamburg, "The Study of Primate Behavior," in *Primate Behavior,* ed. Irven Devore (New York: Holt, Rinehart, & Winston, 1965), pp. 3, 83–85. See also Jane Van Lowick-Goodall, *In the Shadow of Man* (New York: Dell, 1971); Charles Southwick, ed., *Primate Social Behavior* (Princeton, N.J.: Van Nostrand, 1963).

Chapter 12

1. Colin M. Turnbull, *The Mountain People* (New York: Simon & Schuster, 1972), p. 31: "Hunters frequently display those characteristics that we find so admirable in man: kindness, generosity,

consideration, affection, honesty, hospitality, compassion, charity and others.... For the hunter in his tiny, close-knit society, these are necessities for survival; without them society would collapse."

2. Walt Whitman, "Walt Whitman," in *Leaves of Grass* (Philadelphia: McKay, 1900), pp. 62–63.

3. Susanne Langer, *Philosophical Sketches* (New York: New American Library, 1964), p. 125: "Imagination is probably the greatest force acting on our feelings."

4. David Hume, *A Treatise of Human Nature* (Oxford, Eng.: Oxford University Press, 1888), pp. 397, 231.

5. Aristotle, *Politics* 1258a; Niccolo Machiavelli, *Discourses*, in *The Prince and the Discourses* (New York: Modern Library, 1940), pp. 108, 208, 231, 274.

6. Isaac Asimov, *I Robot* (Greenwich, Conn.: Fawcett, 1950).

7. Henry A. Murray, quoted in a review of *Selections from the Personology of Henry A. Murray*, in *New Republic*, Aug. 22, 1981, p. 34: "Academic psychology has contributed practically nothing to the knowledge of human nature."

Chapter 13

1. Sigmund Freud, "Formulations Regarding the Two Principles in Mental Functioning," in *Collected Papers of Freud* (New York: Basic Books, 1959), IV, 16.

2. The concept of "calm passion" is central to Hume's ethical theory. For relevant passages see David Hume, *A Treatise of Human Nature* (Oxford, Eng.: Oxford University Press, 1888), index, p. 686, and *Enquiry Concerning the Principles of Morals*, in *Hume's Enquiries*, ed. L. A. Selby-Bigge (2nd ed.; Oxford, Eng.: Oxford University Press, 1902), p.239.

3. Mary Midgley, *Beast and Man: The Roots of Human Nature* (Ithaca, N.Y.: Cornell University Press, 1978), pp. 262, 266.

4. David Hume, "The Sceptic," in *Essays, Literary and Political*

(London: Ward, Lock, & Co., n.d.), p.101; *Treatise of Human Nature*, p. 488; "The Standard of Taste," in *Essays*, p. 143.
5. Homer, *Iliad* xxii.

Chapter 14

1. Charles Darwin, *The Expression of the Emotions in Man* (Chicago: University of Chicago Press, 1965), p. 350.
2. H. F. Harlow and M. K. Harlow, "Social Deprivation in Monkeys," *Scientific American* 207, 136–46.
3. Napoleon A. Chagnon, *Yanamamo: The Fierce People* (New York: Holt, Rinehart, & Winston, 1968), p. 74.
4. David Hume, *A Treatise of Human Nature* (Oxford, Eng.: Oxford University Press, 1888), pp. 256–59; *Enquiry Concerning the Principles of Morals*, in *Hume's Enquiries*, ed. L. A. Selby-Bigge (2nd ed.; Oxford, Eng.: Oxford University Press, 1902), sec. IV; *A Dialogue*, in Selby-Bigge, ed., *Enquiries;* "Of Commerce," in *Essays, Literary and Political* (London: Ward, Lock, & Co., n.d.), pp. 151–53.
5. Aristotle, *Politics* 1313a–1315a.
6. Niccolo Machiavelli, *The Prince* and *Discourses*, in *The Prince and the Discourses*, (New York: Modern Library, 1940), pp. 64, 139, 521, 528.
7. Augustine, *The City of God*, Book XXII, ch. 6.
8. Benedict de Spinoza, *Theological-Political Treatise*, in *The Chief Works of Benedict de Spinoza*, I (New York: Dover, 1955), p. 204; *Political Treatise*, in *Chief Works*, I, p. 288.
9. Hume, *Treatise of Human Nature*, p. 566, and *Enquiry Concerning the Principles of Morals*, p. 206; Plato, *Republic* 389.

Chapter 15

1. Robert Plutchik, *The Emotions: Facts, Theories, and a New Model* (New York: Random House, 1962), p. 50.

2. David Hume, *A Treatise of Human Nature* (Oxford, Eng.: Oxford University Press, 1888), p. 458.
3. *Ibid.*, p. 469; Hume, "The Standard of Taste," in *Essays, Literary and Political* (London: Ward, Lock, & Co., n.d.), pp. 138–39.
4. Alexander Sesonske, *Value and Obligation* (New York: Oxford University Press, 1964), pp. 45, 55.
5. Thomas Hobbes, *Body, Man, and Citizen* (New York: Collier, 1962), p. 224; Hobbes, *Leviathan* (Oxford, Eng.: Blackwell, 1960), p. 39.
6. David Hume, *Enquiry Concerning the Principles of Morals*, in *Hume's Enquiries*, ed. L. A. Selby-Bigge (2nd ed.; Oxford, Eng.: Oxford University Press, 1902), p. 256: "These pretensions ... are by far too magnificent for human nature."
7. Sigmund Freud, *Beyond the Pleasure Principle* (New York: Bantam, 1959).
8. Plutchik, *Emotions*, p. viii: "I began to recognize, too, that an intimate relationship exists between emotions and personality and that the latter in some sense represents emotions which have become mixed and 'frozen' in the course of an individual's lifetime."
9. J. J. Rousseau, *Discourse on the Origin and Foundation of Inequality Among Mankind*, in *The Social Contract and Discourse on the Origin of Inequality*, ed. L. G. Crocker (New York: Washington Square Press, 1967), p. 203.

Chapter 16

1. George Orwell, *1984* (New York: Harcourt-Brace-Jovanovich, 1949), p. 217.
2. Niccolo Machiavelli, *Discourses*, in *The Prince and the Discourses* (New York: Modern Library, 1940), p. 119.
3. *Ibid.*, pp. 161, 166, 252–54; J. J. Rousseau, *The Social Contract*, in *The Social Contract and Discourse on the Origin of Inequality*, ed. L. G. Crocker (New York: Washington Square Press, 1967), pp. 43, 99; Plato, *Crito* 50–51.

4. Benedict de Spinoza, *On the Improvement of the Understanding,* in *The Chief Works of Benedict de Spinoza,* II (New York: Dover, 1951), p. 6.

5. David Hume, *Enquiry Concerning the Principles of Morals,* in *Hume's Enquiries,* ed. L. A. Selby-Bigge (2nd ed.; Oxford, Eng.: Oxford University Press, 1902), pp. 282–83.

6. Plato, *Republic* 359–60.

7. Thomas Hobbes, *Leviathan* (Oxford, Eng.: Blackwell, 1960), p. 6.

8. Plato, *Gorgias* 472.

9. William Shakespeare, *Measure for Measure,* Act III, scene 1.

10. Susanne K. Langer, *Mind: An Essay on Feeling* (Baltimore: Johns Hopkins University Press, 1967), I, 64.

INDEX

Aesthetic judgments, 163
Altruism, 17, 176–79
Aquinas, 54
Ardrey, Robert, 172
Aristotle, 147, 159–60; agrarian laws, 135; organisms, 115; reason of state, 221; species morality, 182–83; unique persons, 47
Augustine, 221
Ayer, A. J., 48

Bellow, Saul, 280n.13
Bentham, Jeremy, 68–69, 80–81, 86–87, 106–7, 170, 172, 245, 258; on language, 261
Black, Max, 59
Blake, William, 145, 171
Bourke, Vernon, 280n.10
Bradley, F. H., 116
Burke, Edmund, 234; freedom, 122; human nature, 69–70; social change, 99–104

Calm passions. *See* Parliament of passions
Calvin, John, 51
Campbell, Donald, 181
Character, 232–33
Chomsky, Noam, 278n.14

Cicero, 164
Cumming, Robert D., 71

Darwin, Charles, 175
Descartes, 42
Determinism, 203, 206
Dewey, John, 229
Drives, 85
Durkheim, Emile, 70, 101, 277n.1; on social laws, 111–19

Emotivism, 213, 267
Epicureanism, 231
Erasmus, 50
Existentialism, 41

Feelings, 15–17, 48, 75–78, 84–85
Feeling variations, 216–17
Forster, E. M., 250
Freud, Sigmund, 45, 84, 183

Galileo, 79
Gemeinschaft, 244
Gesellschaft, 244
Gouldner, A. W., 278n.19
Gregor, A. James, 278n.16
Gresham, Thomas, 117, 132

Harrington, James, 73, 82, 135
Hegel, G. W. F., 54, 130–48, 234

289

Herskovits, M. J., 277n.2
Hobbes, Thomas, 10, 42, 52, 147, 161, 164–65, 183, 231; human nature, 68–69; promises, 58; proof, 257; reductionism, 78–81; state of nature, 169
Homer, 199
Hume, David, 31–32, 119, 134, 151, 162–64, 183, 220–21, 252; is-ought question, 57; secondary qualities, 225; skepticism, 31–32; social morality, 121

Ideal observer, 27–28
Instinct, 179–81
Intuition, 27
"Is-ought" gap, 151

Justice, 158

Kant, Immanuel, 58, 234
Kamenka, E., 279n.2
Kin selection, 178–79

Langer, Susanne K., 284n.3
Locke, John, 42, 164; natural right, 247; state of nature, 169
Lorenz, Konrad, 172
Luther, Martin, 46–47, 50

Machiavelli, Niccolo, 10, 135, 159, 160–61; reason of state, 221
MacIntyre, Alasdair, 61–62
Mannheim, Karl, 272n.4
Marx, Karl, 51, 132–48
Marxists, 129, 132

McShea, Robert J., 279n.1, 280–81, 282n.25
Mill, J. S., 71–72, 83–86
Mill, James, 71–72, 81, 83, 147
Moore, G. E., 226
Morris, Desmond, 172
Murray, H. A., 284n.7

Naturalistic fallacy, 151
Natural right, 164, 228, 247
Neilson, K., 281n.1
Nozick, Robert, 164

Oakeshott, Michael, 101–3

Parliament of passions (calm passions), 16, 209–12, 262–63, 266
Participatory democracy, 51
Parsons, Talcott, 70
Passions, 184–87
Personal morality, 121
Philosophy, 154
Plato, 10, 156–59, 231, 252, 254
Plutchik, R., 286n.8
Prescriptivity, 17
Protagoras, 44
Psychology, 170, 200

Race, 192
Rawls, John, 62, 242
Roe v. Wade, 248
Romanticism, 42
Rorty, Richard, 81
Rousseau, J. J., 10, 51, 151, 159–60, 162; freedom, 143; reason,

37, 236; rights, 95; state of nature, 169; uniqueness, 47
Russell, Bertrand, 144

Salkever, Stephen G., 275n.2
Schopenhauer, A., 198, 231
Searle, John, 59
Selfish Gene, 172
Shakespeare, William, 200, 260
Shaw, Bernard, 246
Singer, Peter, 60
Skinner, B. F., 28, 69, 81
Smith, Adam, 81
Social morality, 121
Social organism, 114–16
Sociobiology, 172
Socrates, 119, 154, 250, 257
Sophists, 120, 156
Spengler, Oswald, 130–32
Spinoza, Benedict de, 14–15, 154, 159–62; exemplars, 251; historicism, 128; reason of state, 221

Stoicism, 231
Sumner, W. G., 70, 104–10, 118, 258
Supreme Court, 248

Taylor, R., 281n.6
Tinbergen, Niko, 93
Tropism, 179
Truman, David, 81
Turnbull, C. M., 283n.1

Value: judgments as predictions, 228–31; relativism, 28; skepticism, 25–26; solipsism, 26, 41–48

White, Lynn, 146
Whitman, Walt, 196

Yanomamo, 219–21